A DICTIONARY OF FAMILY HISTORY

FAMILY HISTORY FROM PEN & SWORD BOOKS

Tracing Secret Service Ancestors

Tracing Your Air Force Ancestors

Tracing Your Ancestors

Tracing Your Ancestors from 1066 to 1837

Tracing Your Ancestors through Death Records

Tracing Your Ancestors through Family Photographs

Tracing Your Ancestors Using the Census

Tracing Your Ancestors' Childhood

Tracing Your Ancestors' Parish Records

Tracing Your Aristocratic Ancestors

Tracing Your Army Ancestors – 2nd Edition

Tracing Your Birmingham Ancestors

Tracing Your Black Country Ancestors

Tracing Your British Indian Ancestors

Tracing Your Canal Ancestors

Tracing Your Channel Islands Ancestors

Tracing Your Coalmining Ancestors

Tracing Your Criminal Ancestors

Tracing Your East Anglian Ancestors

Tracing Your East End Ancestors

Tracing Your Edinburgh Ancestors

Tracing Your First World War Ancestors

Tracing Your Great War Ancestors: The Gallipoli Campaign

Tracing Your Great War Ancestors: The Somme

Tracing Your Great War Ancestors: Ypres

Tracing Your Huguenot Ancestors

Tracing Your Jewish Ancestors

Tracing Your Labour Movement Ancestors

Tracing Your Lancashire Ancestors

Tracing Your Leeds Ancestors

Tracing Your Legal Ancestors

Tracing Your Liverpool Ancestors

Tracing Your London Ancestors

Tracing Your Medical Ancestors

Tracing Your Merchant Navy Ancestors

Tracing Your Naval Ancestors

Tracing Your Northern Ancestors

Tracing Your Pauper Ancestors

Tracing Your Police Ancestors

Tracing Your Prisoner of War Ancestors: The First World War

Tracing Your Railway Ancestors

Tracing Your Royal Marine Ancestors

Tracing Your Rural Ancestors

Tracing Your Scottish Ancestors

Tracing Your Second World War Ancestors

Tracing Your Servant Ancestors

Tracing Your Service Women Ancestors

Tracing Your Shipbuilding Ancestors

Tracing Your Tank Ancestors

Tracing Your Textile Ancestors

Tracing Your Trade and Craftsmen Ancestors

Tracing Your Welsh Ancestors

Tracing Your West Country Ancestors

For more details see www.pen-and-sword.co.uk.

A DICTIONARY OF FAMILY HISTORY

The Genealogists' ABC

JONATHAN SCOTT

Pen & Sword
FAMILY HISTORY

> *'Well, frankly children, this is beyond me.'*
> *For Genevieve*

First published in Great Britain in 2017 by
Pen & Sword Family History
an imprint of
Pen & Sword Books Ltd
47 Church Street
Barnsley
South Yorkshire
S70 2AS

ISBN 978 1 47389 252 1

A CIP catalogue record for this book is available from the British Library

Typeset in Ehrhardt by
Mac Style Ltd, Bridlington, East Yorkshire
Printed and bound in the UK by CPI Group (UK) Ltd, Croydon, CRO 4YY

Pen & Sword Books Ltd incorporates the imprints of Pen & Sword Archaeology, Atlas, Aviation, Battleground, Discovery, Family History, History, Maritime, Military, Naval, Politics, Railways, Select, Social History, Transport, True Crime, Claymore Press, Frontline Books, Leo Cooper, Praetorian Press, Remember When, Seaforth Publishing and Wharncliffe.

For a complete list of Pen & Sword titles please contact
PEN & SWORD BOOKS LIMITED
47 Church Street, Barnsley, South Yorkshire, S70 2AS, England
E-mail: enquiries@pen-and-sword.co.uk
Website: www.pen-and-sword.co.uk

ABBREVIATIONS

BL	British Library
BMD	Birth, marriage and death certificates
CWGC	Commonwealth War Graves Commission
FHS	Family History Society
GRO	General Record Office
IGI	International Genealogical Index
IWM	Imperial War Museums
LDS Church	Church of Jesus Christ of Latter-Day Saints
LMA	London Metropolitan Archives
MI	Monumental Inscription
MiD	Mentioned in Dispatches
MoD	Ministry of Defence
NAI	National Archives of Ireland
NAM	National Army Museum
NAS	National Archives of Scotland
NLI	National Library of Ireland
NLS	National Library of Scotland
NLW	National Library of Wales
NRS	National Records of Scotland
OPR	Old Parish Registers
PCC	Prerogative Court of Canterbury
PRONI	Public Record Office of Northern Ireland
RAF	Royal Air Force
RBS	Royal Bank of Scotland
RFC	Royal Flying Corps
RN	Royal Navy
RNAS	Royal Naval Air Service
SoG	Society of Genealogists
TNA	The National Archives
UCL	University College London
WRAF	Women's Royal Air Force

PREFACE

This book is part encyclopedia, part dictionary, part almanac, part directory.

The idea was to create a work of reference where definitions of obsolete terms rubbed shoulders with facts, dates, tips, advice, websites and little-known sources.

I set out to include useful guidance relating to the likes of the census, civil registration, parish registers, probate material and more, and to explain how such sources were created – how the systems functioned and changed over time, and draw attention to genealogical peculiarities that can trip up the unwary.

Websites have become the institutions of our hobby. Alongside archives, libraries and museums there are also hundreds of websites relating to different subjects. Sometimes these websites appear beneath a parent subject, others are important enough to warrant their own entry.

My approach may seem random at times. You will find, for example, some entries relating to specific army regiments, but not every army regiment. This is because some of the regiments and regimental museums in question have produced very useful websites, with catalogues and searchable databases aimed squarely at family historians. Similarly I have included lots of obscure and interesting-sounding occupations – but I can't claim to have included every occupation.

In general I adhered to the rule that if I found it interesting or useful, hopefully someone else would too. I've tried to cover as much ground as possible, but if you have any suggestions just let me know (@thejonoscott).

In short: this is 'A Dictionary of Family History'. I wouldn't presume to call it 'the' dictionary of family history.

A

ABERDEENSHIRE:

Aberdeen City and Aberdeenshire Archives (aberdeencity.gov.uk/archives) Holds Aberdeen Burgh records (the finest and most complete medieval and early modern burgh records in Scotland), burial registers and rent rolls dating from 1795. There's an online catalogue available for both city and county collections. One unique source is the 'return on prostitution' which records the names and declared ages of all persons engaged in prostitution known to the Police Commissioners in January 1855.

Aberdeen & NE Scotland FHS (anesfhs.org.uk)

Able Seaman: RN rank of sailor – above ordinary seaman, below leading seaman.

Abney Park Cemetery: One of the 'Magnificent Seven' cemeteries in London located within the London Borough of Hackney. It was opened in 1842. The others are: Brompton (1840), Highgate (1839), Kensal Green (1832), Nunhead (1840), Tower Hamlets (1841) and West Norwood (1836).

Abstract: A summary of the contents of a book, article, speech or document. You will often come across the term in probate material – 'abstracts' of wills and administrations recorded in consistory courts, for example. These summarised information and so make excellent working guides to the names, relationships and place names contained within the original documents. You can explore examples held at NLW, for example, via www.llgc.org.uk/discover/nlw-resources/wills/.

Accomptant: An obsolete name for an accountant. You may well come across this term in census records and trade directories.

Accoucheuse: A midwife.

Acre: An area of measurement equal to about 4,840 sq. yd – although acres were traditionally much larger in certain parts of the UK.

Addiscombe Military Seminary: The East India Company's Military Seminary, established in January 1809 at Addiscombe Place near Croydon to provide education for company cadets. It closed in 1861.

Addressing History (addressinghistory.edina.ac.uk): Project that combines data from Post Office directories from Edinburgh, Glasgow and Aberdeen with historical maps.

Administration: Before a will could take effect, a grant of probate had to be made by a court. However if someone died without a will, the court could grant 'Letters of Administration' to the next of kin or creditor who applied for them. They would then swear an oath, or sign a bond, to carry out the management and distribution of the estate. These Letters of Administrations, also called Admons, normally reside within diocesan collections. Within the legal documents the person who applied for the Letters of Administration would be identified as the administrator (male) or administratrix (female).

Administrative divisions: Country/State/Parliament > County/Shire > Borough/District > Hundred > Parish.

Admiralty, Court of: Held jurisdiction over cases of offences committed at sea, to begin with primarily concerned with piracy or disputes over salvage rights. TNA has records of both civil trials (wages, collisions, salvage, etc.) and criminal trials (piracy, treason, mutiny, etc.).

Adoption: A number of factors may lie behind cases of adoption – death, divorce, illegitimacy, abandonment. Often poverty-stricken parents would seek out adoptive parents in the hope that this would give their child a chance of a better life. Prior to the Adoption of Children Act 1926, adoptions were usually informal affairs conducted between the child's parents or guardians and the adoptive parents. Often a child would simply be taken in by other family members, friends or neighbours. Some adoptees would retain their original name, while others might take the family name of the adoptive parents.

From 1927 all adoptions had to be approved by magistrates meeting in a petty sessions court and each court maintained a register, which remained closed to public inspection for seventy-five years. Adoptions were also arranged by societies such as the Church of England Children's Society, which kept records of the adoptions it arranged. There's a chance that references to adoption cases will survive in Boards of Guardians and parish chest material.

In Scotland, following the Adoption of Children (Scotland) Act (1930), adoption was arranged by charitable bodies, local authority social work departments and then ratified by civil courts – mainly local sheriff courts.

The Registrar General for Scotland has maintained the Adopted Children Register since 1930.

www.gov.uk/adoption-records

nrscotland.gov.uk/research/guides/adoption-records

Age of Nelson (ageofnelson.org): Hosts two useful databases – RN officers in the French Revolutionary and Napoleonic wars (1793–1815), and the seamen and marines who fought at the Battle of Trafalgar (1805).

Agnate: Someone descended from the same male ancestor as another person.

Agricultural gangs: Groups of women and children organised by a gang-master who would carry out agricultural piecework for farmers.

Agricultural labourers: Agricultural labourers, or 'ag labs', are notoriously hard to research, but there are places where you can try your luck. The names of many rural workers appear in family and estate collections – perhaps in account books, documenting amounts paid for work on the land, or in the records of tenants and rent. An early nineteenth-century example from the Lilleshall Estate in Shropshire, for example, lists tenants in alphabetical order with type of property, occupation, size of family and even habits – from 'industrious' to 'indifferent'.

Archives of individual farms do also survive, but they are rare. Bedfordshire and Luton Archives has the farm account book for West End Farm, Stevington, showing each labourer's name, daily occupation and weekly sum paid.

Ague: A largely obsolete word for any acute fever.

AIM 25 (www.aim25.ac.uk): Electronic access to collection level descriptions of the archives of over 100 institutions, societies and livery companies within Greater London.

Air Historical Branch (www.raf.mod.uk/ahb/): Offers various research services and assistance to anyone tracing RAF records. There's information about records of service, POWs, burials and memorials.

Air Transport Auxiliary: Civilian organisation set up during the Second World War to ferry military aircraft between factories, workshops and front-line squadrons. Men and women flew the aircraft, including pioneering aviator Amy Johnson. She was flying an Airspeed Oxford for the ATA when the aircraft crashed into the Thames Estuary. As a member of ATA who has no known grave, she is commemorated by the CWGC on the Air Forces Memorial at Runnymede. The ATA Museum website is at www.atamuseum.org. The RAF Museum (rafmuseum.org.uk) has personnel files relating to members of the ATA.

Alderman: A senior councillor – just below mayor in rank.

Alehouses: Premises licensed to sell ale (as distinct from inns, which could accommodate travellers, and taverns, which sold wine). The term alehouse was gradually replaced by public house during the eighteenth century. The Alehouse Act 1552 meant that alehouse keepers had to be licensed by local Justices of the Peace – so what records survive should be at the local record office. Bonds from purveyors of victuals, including innkeepers, 1578–1672 are in TNA, E 180.

Aliens: Records of immigration often refer to individuals as 'aliens' – non-citizens of the parent country. In August 2016 Findmypast released over 139,000 records of Enemy Aliens and Internees, in association with TNA. These were foreign nationals who were investigated and interned in camps across the UK and the Commonwealth during the First and Second World Wars.

Aliens Acts: Researching migration to England becomes much simpler after 1793. This was the year of the Aliens Act, passed in response to mass migration caused by the upheaval and unrest of the French Revolution and the Napoleonic Wars. The Act meant that all arriving migrants had to register with the Justice of the Peace, providing personal information, which would then be passed to the Aliens Office.

Although original Aliens Office certificates have not survived (some indexes have), original Justice of the Peace records relating to arrivals sometimes survive locally at county record offices – usually among quarter sessions material. Hull History Centre, for example, has certificates of arrival of aliens issued at the port between 1793 and 1815.

A further Aliens Act was passed in 1836. Now newly arrived migrants had to sign a certificate of arrival, and these certificates, for arrivals to England and Scotland, are held at TNA (series HO 2). The certificates should record nationality, profession, date of arrival, last country visited and other details. Through Ancestry, thanks to its partnership with TNA, you can search Alien Arrivals (1810–11 and 1826–69), as well as Aliens' registration cards (1918–57) covering the London area only.

The new Aliens Act 1905 meant that aliens could only enter the UK at the discretion of the authorities. After 1919 they had to register with the local police. A few cards for aliens who registered with the Metropolitan Police are at TNA, and examples also sometimes survive at local record offices.

Allegation: A person applying for a marriage licence had to provide the church with a bond and an allegation. The bond was signed by witnesses, one of whom pledged to cover any expense in the event of any wrongdoing. The allegation, on the other hand, was a formal statement with ages, marital status, places of residence and an oath that there was no formal impediment to marriage.

Almshouses: Charitable foundations offering accommodation for poor elderly people.

Useful websites

Almshouse Project (fachrs.com/content/alms.html)

A Family and Community Historical Research Society project researching almshouse provision from 1500 to 1914.

Buildings History (buildinghistory.org/buildings/charities.shtml)

Guide to records of almshouses, workhouses and hospitals.

Museum of the Order of St John (museumstjohn.org.uk)

St John's Hospital, Bath (stjohnsbath.org.uk/about-st-johns/our-history/)

St Pancras Almshouses (stpancrasalmshouses.org)

Has samples that include reports, images and residents recorded in the 1861 census.

Amanuensis: A taker of dictation – or a copier of manuscripts.

American Jewish Historical Society: ajhs.org/family-history

Amherst Flag: One of the unique artefacts preserved at the museum of the Prince of Wales's Own Regiment of Yorkshire – now the York Army Museum (www.yorkarmymuseum.co.uk). The flag was flown above the Citadel at Quebec after the Victory of the British Army led by Lord Amherst. Other more practical sources held here include enlistment registers and war diaries – including that of the 15th Leeds Pals Battalion covering the first day of the Somme.

Anabaptists: Christian sect that believes in delaying baptism until adulthood.

Ancestry: Ancestry.com LLC is a privately held company based in Utah, and is the largest for-profit genealogy company in the world. Its origins lie in a 1990 company called Infobases which started life selling LDS Church publications on floppy disks. Ancestry itself was officially launched online in 1996 (you can explore the October 1996 version of the website via web.archive.org). Today it offers users access to billions of historical records alongside vast amounts of user-generated content. Ancestry products, brands and websites include AncestryDNA, Family Tree Maker, Find a Grave and Rootsweb. To dip into what's here for UK researchers you could start with the parish registers landing page (ancestry.co.uk/parish), which leads to background information about parish sources and latest additions to Ancestry's roster through partner organisations such as LMA. Remember that much of Ancestry's holdings are likely to be accessible free of charge through your local library.

Anchorsmith: A maker of anchors.

ANGLESEY:
Anglesey Records & Archives (www.anglesey.gov.uk/leisure/records-and-archives/)
Gwynedd FHS (gwyneddfhs.org)

Anglo-Afghan War: The Second Anglo-Afghan War was fought between 1878 and 1880, culminating in British victory at the Battle of Kandahar, 1 September 1880. There's an exhaustive history of the conflict at garenewing.co.uk/angloafghanwar/, put together by illustrator Garen Ewing. It includes the Second Afghan War database project – a collection of names, family histories and stories concerning those who participated in the campaign.

Anglo-Boer War (angloboerwar.com): Encyclopedic online resource dedicated to the Anglo-Boer War (1899–1902). Material includes technical details of honours and awards, such as the Queen's South Africa Medal (with an index), biographical information of notable individuals and details of the units that participated. At the time of writing it had just gone over 435,000 soldiers' records, along with a forum that boasted 45,000 posts, as well as 94 free-to-view books, 18,000-plus images and 3,000 articles.

Anglo-Boer War Memorials Project (casus-belli.co.uk): Hosts the Register of the Anglo-Boer War 1899–1902 and the allied Memorials

Project, recording memorials across the world and currently with almost 300,000 names.

Anglo-German Family History Society: agfhs.org.uk

Anglo-Jewish Miscellanies (jeffreymaynard.com): A collection of genealogical information about the Jewish community, including the London Jews Database (*c.* 1790–*c.* 1860), and indexes to birth, marriage and death announcements printed in the *Jewish Chronicle*.

Anglo-Jewry Database: The 1851 Anglo-Jewry Database is one of a number of databases and finding aids produced by Jewish Communities and Records (www.jewishgen.org/JCR-uk/), a joint Jewish Genealogical Society of Great Britain/JewishGen project. The 1851 Anglo Jewry Database covers mainly England, Wales and Scotland, but also Ireland, the Channel Islands and Isle of Man. Most of the 29,000-plus entries appear in the 1851 census and it is estimated this represents 90-plus per cent of the Jewish population in the British Isles.

Anglo-Saxon England, Prosopography of (pase.ac.uk): An attempt to record the names of all inhabitants of England from the late sixth to the end of the eleventh centuries, drawing on all kinds of sources.

Anglo Zulu War Historical Society (anglozuluwar.com): Society dedicated to the study of the conflict fought between the British Empire and the Zulu Kingdom between January and July 1879.

Anguline Research Archives (anguline.co.uk): Republishes rare books on CD/PDF download, including many volumes of UK parish transcriptions from around the turn of the century.

ANGUS:
Angus Archives (www.angus.gov.uk/history/archives/)
Dundee City Archives (dundeecity.gov.uk/archive)
Tay Valley FHS (tayvalleyfhs.org.uk)
Aberdeen & NE Scotland FHS (anesfhs.org.uk)
Friends of Dundee City Archives (fdca.org.uk)

Angus Library and Archive (theangus.rpc.ox.ac.uk/): The 'leading collection of Baptist history and heritage worldwide'. The family history page has information of over 5,000 Baptist missionaries. The Angus is located at Regent's Park College in Oxford.

Anilepman: A smallholder or sub-tenant of a manor.

Ankle beater: Someone who helps drive cattle to market.

Annuity: An annual amount of money paid to an individual, usually for life.

Antiquaries of London, Society of: sal.org.uk/library/

ANZAC: The Australian and New Zealand Army Corps. Formed in 1915, it comprised troops from the First Australian Imperial Force and 1st New Zealand Expeditionary Force. Its first major action was the Battle of Gallipoli. To find out more the Australian War Memorial website (awm. gov.au) includes all kinds of material relating to the Australian experience of war, including centenary digitisation project ANZAC Connections. There's a useful guide for researching NZ soldiers at www.nzhistory. net.nz/war/researching-first-world-war-soldiers.

Apiarist: Beekeeper.

Apothecary: A pharmacist or druggist who prepares and sells medicine. The Worshipful Society of Apothecaries (apothecaries.org) was incorporated as a City Livery Company in 1617. Microfilm copies of many of the major series of the Society's pre twentieth-century records are accessible at the Guildhall Library, Aldermanbury, London EC2P 7HH.

Apprentice: To become an apprentice, parents/guardians negotiated with a guild's master craftsman to agree conditions and price, which would then be recorded in an indenture. There were also pauper apprenticeships, arranged specifically by parish-level Overseers of the Poor to remove the child from being a financial burden on the parish. And unlike traditional trade apprenticeships, the pauper apprentice indentures were not subject to any duty.

Records normally give name, addresses and trades of the masters, and the names of the apprentices, along with the sum the master received for the apprenticeship.

Apprenticeship records often survive in papers of guilds, businesses, charities, families, individuals and parish collections.

The Statute of Apprentices passed in 1563 made it a formal requirement that to enter a trade a person had to serve an apprenticeship. But there was no centralised record of apprentices kept in England and Wales until 1710, when stamp duty was payable on indentures of apprenticeship. The resulting registers of the duty paid are at TNA and you can search these apprenticeships via ancestry.co.uk or browse them on digital microfilm. There are also eighteenth-century indexes of apprentices on findmypast. co.uk, which also has London Apprenticeship Abstracts (1442–1850), drawn from records of London livery companies. There are 'articles of clerkship' (1756–1874) available via Ancestry – contracts between an apprentice clerk and the attorney or solicitor – and TheGenealogist.co.uk also has a large collection of apprenticeship records.

Finally the Workhouses website (workhouses.org) has information about the workings of the pauper apprenticeship system, and there's a TNA guide to researching apprentices and masters.

Archdeaconry: An ecclesiastical administrative unit. This is a subdivision within a diocese, literally the area for which an archdeacon is responsible.

Archive: Historical documents/records relating to a subject. Also the place where archives are stored.

archive.org: Hosts a vast and free digital library of digitised periodicals, newspapers, journals and books. Also home to the 'Wayback Machine' Internet Archive, useful for tracking down defunct websites.

Archives New Zealand: archives.govt.nz

Archives Portal Europe (www.archivesportaleurope.net): Provides information on archival material from different European countries.

Archives Wales (archiveswales.org.uk): Allows cross-searching within archive collections across Wales.

Argosy: An English term for a flotilla.

ARGYLL:
Argyll & Bute Archives (argyll-bute.gov.uk/community-life-and-leisure/archives)

Glasgow & West of Scotland FHS (gwsfhs.org.uk)

Highland FHS (highlandfamilyhistorysociety.org)

Lochaber & North Argyll Family History Group (lochaberandnorthargyll familyhistorygroup.org.uk)

Arkwright: A skilled maker of chests or coffers.

Arkwright, Sir Richard: Preston-born pioneer of the Industrial Revolution, whose many innovations include the spinning frame/water frame – using water to power the mass-production of yarn. He is also seen as the father of the modern factory system and his mill at Cromford is now part of the Derwent Valley Mills heritage site.

Arley Hall Archives 1750–90 (arleyhallarchives.co.uk): Illuminates life and work in a country house in Cheshire in the late eighteenth century.

Armiger: Someone entitled to heraldic arms.

Army Children Archive: archhistory.co.uk

Army Lists: Published Army Lists stretch back to the mid-eighteenth century and can be used to trace officers' careers. In general these were published monthly, quarterly and half-yearly and they list active officers and contain details of promotions. Remember if your ancestor was not on active duty at the time, the name will not appear.

Army Medical Services Museum: www.ams-museum.org.uk

Army Museums (armymuseums.org.uk): The website of the Ogilby Trust is the best place to find out more about 139 military museums across the UK. There's a homepage map, or you can search by name, collection, regiment or region. There's also a Research Advice section, full of guidance for tracing officers and other ranks.

Army Ranks
Other ranks:
Private
Lance Corporal
Corporal
Sergeant
Staff/Colour Sergeant
Warrant Officer

Officer ranks:
Officer Cadet
Second Lieutenant
Lieutenant
Captain
Major

Lieutenant Colonel
Colonel
Brigadier
Major General
Lieutenant General
General

Army sources: There are different collections of records for Army soldiers and officers. And although lots of material has been made available online, always remember that some First World War files were lost or damaged by bombing in 1940.

Army sources include service, casualty and medal records, or unit/ operational histories. Most service records for soldiers discharged before 1919 are with TNA. Service records thereafter are with the MoD – although TNA does have other sources relating to the Second World War such as Army casualty lists (WO 417) which cover officers (currently available on thegenealogist.co.uk), other ranks and nurses.

Ancestry's Army collections, in partnership with TNA, include First World War service records, pension records and medal rolls. There's also the Military Campaign Medal and Award Rolls (1793–1949) database, which contains lists of more than 2.3 million officers, enlisted personnel and other individuals entitled to medals and awards – although this particular dataset does not include First World War or Second World War medal and award rolls.

British Army Service Records (1760–1915) is an important collection available via Findmypast, and also through partnership with TNA. It contains records of more than 2 million soldiers – ordinary soldiers and officers, drawn from militia service records, Chelsea Pensioners service and discharge records, and Boer War soldiers documents from the Imperial Yeomanry. The site also has the 1914–20 Service Records collection, drawn from WO 363 service records and WO 364 pension records.

You can search for officers' service records (*c.* 1760–1919) through TNA's catalogue. In addition, for a fee, you can search campaign medal index cards (1914–20).

Arriage: An office or duty carried out by a tenant.

Arthur Lloyd (arthurlloyd.co.uk): Music-hall and theatre-history site inspired by performer Arthur Lloyd (1839–1904).

Artisan: A skilled craft worker.

Ashman: A dustman.

Assizes: Until 1871 the assize courts, or assizes, dealt with criminal cases too serious to be tried at the quarter sessions. They were arranged in six circuits in England (Home, Midland, Oxford, Norfolk, Northern, Western) and four in Wales (Brecon, Carmarthen, Chester, North Wales). This TNA guide (nationalarchives.gov.uk/records/research-guides/assizes-criminal-1559-1971.htm) details what records are held where – generally TNA has records of the assizes, while records of quarter sessions/petty sessions held at magistrates' courts will be at local archives. In 1971 the assize and quarter session courts merged to form Crown Courts.

Association of Genealogists and Researchers: www.agra.org.uk

Association of Professional Genealogists in Ireland: www.apgi.ie

Association of Scottish Genealogists and Researchers in Archives: www.asgra.co.uk

Asylums Act: The County Asylums Act 1808 began a process that would lead to an established network of county level institutions to care for people with mental health problems. The Lunacy Act and County Asylums Act of 1845 established the Lunacy Commission and a system for monitoring asylums.

Attainder: The forfeiture of an estate because of a sentence of death for treason or felony.

Atte: The prefix 'atte' meant 'at the' and frequently appears in shortened form within locative surnames such as Atwood. Other common archaic words for valleys, hills, woods, streams, farms and towns, which form parts of place names and surnames include: 'adder', 'beck', 'den', 'don', 'bury', 'ham', 'ley', 'more', 'stead', 'stow', 'ton', 'wick'.

Aulnage: The official 'rubber stamp' over the shape/quality of manufactured cloth.

Austen, Jane: You can download Jane Austen's last will and testament, dated 1817, via nationalarchives.gov.uk/documents/records/will-j-austen. pdf. 'I Jane Austen of the Parish of Chawton do by this my last Will & Testament give and bequeath to my dearest Sister Cassandra Elizth every thing of which I may die possessed, or which may be hereafter due to me, subject to the payment of my Funeral Expences, & to a Legacy of £50 to my Brother Henry, & £50 to Mde Bigeon – which I request may be paid as soon as convenient.' Madame Bigeon was her brother's cook. There's a Jane Austen Trail you can explore via Southampton's Tudor House and Garden which takes in eight plaques relating to the author (tudorhouseandgarden.com).

AUSTRALIA:

Australasian Federation of Family History Organisations (www.affho.org)

Genealogical Society of Victoria (www.gsv.org.au)

National Archives of Australia (www.naa.gov.au)

National Library of Australia (trove.nla.gov.au)

Queensland State Archives (www.archives.qld.gov.au)

Society of Australian Genealogists (www.sag.org.au)

State Records of South Australia (www.archives.sa.gov.au)

State Records Office of Western Australia (www.sro.wa.gov.au)

Australia, migration to: There are many resources for researching individuals who migrated (or were transported) to Australia. After the American Revolution in 1776 convicts had to be sent elsewhere and the first convict ships, known as the First Fleet, arrived in Australia in January 1788. The flow of convicted transportees finally slowed during the 1850s and ceased altogether when the system was abolished in 1868. While the records for this period of transportation are fractured, there are lots of websites with data and information about the history of transportation and how to research individuals.

The New South Wales Archives has original correspondence, entry books and registers of arrivals from between 1784 and 1900. These contain lists of names of emigrants, settlers and convicts. There are also Convict Indexes to Certificates of Freedom (1823–69).

The website of the National Archives of Australia has more information about emigration to Australia. In addition, details of some 8.9 million free settlers to New South Wales (1826–1922) can be searched and downloaded online at ancestry.com.au, for a fee. Other Antipodean sources include registers of cabin passengers emigrating to New Zealand (1839–50).

Amateur site Convicts to Australia (members.iinet.net.au/~perthdps/convicts/) has lots of advice, as well as transcribed lists of the First, Second and Third Fleets.

NAI (nationalarchives.ie) has an online database of Irish convicts transported to Australia, compiled from transportation registers and petitions to government for pardon or commutation of sentence. There is also Migration Heritage Australia (migrationheritage.nsw.gov.au).

Australian Medical Pioneers (medicalpioneers.com): Free database of over 4,500 colonial doctors from the 1700s to 1875.

Australian War Memorial (awm.gov.au): Includes all kinds of material relating to the Australian experience of war, including centenary digitisation project ANZAC Connections and details of personnel serving in conflicts from before the First World War up to the end of the Second World War.

Auxiliary Territorial Service: When conscription for women began in 1941 they could choose between working in an industry or joining one of the auxiliary services – including the ATS. One useful website where you can find out more is ATS Remembered (www.atsremembered.org.uk) which has personal stories and photographs contributed by women who served in the ATS in jobs ranging from cooks and drivers to searchlight operators and police. The ATS was formed on 9 September 1938 and in 1949 it became the Women's Royal Army Corps.

AYRSHIRE:
Ayrshire Archives (ayrshirearchives.org.uk)
Runs archive centres in Ayr, Saltcoats and Kilmarnock.
Alloway & Southern Ayrshire FHS (asafhs.co.uk)
Glasgow & West of Scotland FHS (gwsfhs.org.uk)
Troon & Ayrshire FHS (troonayrshirefhs.org.uk)

B

Badging the poor: The Poor Act 1697 required all recipients of parish-level poor relief (including family members) to wear prominent red or blue badges with the first letter of the parish and the letter P sewn to their right shoulder or sleeve.

Bagnio keeper: A lesser known term for a brothel keeper.

Bailie: A local government civic officer – the Scottish equivalent to an alderman or magistrate.

Bailiff: An agent or official with authority to carry out certain tasks on behalf of estates or courts. A 'bailiwick' is the area over which the bailiff had jurisdiction.

Bal maiden: A female mine worker. Derives from the Cornish language word 'bal' (mine). There's an interesting website on bal maidens and mining women at www.balmaiden.co.uk.

BANFFSHIRE:
Aberdeen City and Aberdeenshire Archives (aberdeencity.gov.uk/archives)
Aberdeen & North-East Scotland FHS (anesfhs.org.uk)

Bank of England (bankofengland.co.uk): The history section of the Bank of England website explains the origins of the institution, alongside details of archives, lists of Chief Cashiers (from 1694 to date), as well as digitised sources that include Court of Directors' minutes from 1694–1989. There's also a War Gallery with images of plaques and panels recording staff who fell in both world wars.

Banking: Bank archives often contain records of other banks and predecessor companies acquired in the past. So the RBS Heritage Hub (heritagearchives.rbs.com), for example, contains information about all British and Irish banks that became part of RBS, including an overview of archives which you can browse alphabetically or geographically. There's also RBS Remembers (rbsremembers.com) commemorating the centenary of the First World War and the employees who fell – including forty-five men who died on the first day of the Somme.

The Archive of Lloyds Banking Group (lloydsbankinggroup.com/our-group/our-heritage/our-archives/) has material dating back to 1695. Potential sources for family historians include staff records (registers, salary records, report books, widow and orphan fund records) and minute books, sometimes with details of appointments and retirements, staff rolls of honour from both world wars and even some customer records.

For details of the archives of the Hongkong and Shanghai Banking Corporation (HSBC), which opened for business in Hong Kong in March 1865, go to hsbc.com/about-hsbc/company-history/hsbc-archives.

This just scratches the surface – John Orbell and Alison Turton, authors of *British Banking: A Guide to Historical Records* (Routledge, 2001), estimate there are more than 700 archive collections maintained by banks, county record offices, universities and local libraries.

Useful websites

Bank of England (bankofengland.co.uk/about/pages/history/default.aspx)

Coutts (coutts.com/about-us/history/)

HSBC Archives (hsbc.com/about-hsbc/company-history/hsbc-archives)

Lloyds Archives (lloydsbankinggroup.com/our-group/our-heritage/our-archives/)

RBS Heritage Hub (heritagearchives.rbs.com/use-our-archives/your-research/british-banking-history.html)

Bankruptcy: *See* 'Debtors and bankrupts'

Bankruptcy, Court of: This was established in 1832, where creditors could petition the Lord Chancellor for a Commission of Bankruptcy. Ten years later district courts were established for areas outside London. TNA has most records for the London courts, while districts court records will be found at local archives. So you could do worse than starting with TNA's Discovery (discovery.nationalarchives.gov.uk).

Banns: Banns of marriage are the public announcement in a Christian parish church or in the town council of an impending marriage. Their purpose is to give anyone the opportunity to raise any potential impediment to the marriage and traditionally the calling of banns takes place on three successive Sundays.

After 1754, parishes in England and Wales were also required to keep registers of banns and the resulting 'banns books' are often found at county record offices and contain information not found on the marriage licence itself.

In Scotland the proclamation of banns was the notice of contract of marriage, read out in the kirk before the marriage took place. Couples or their 'cautioners' (sponsors) were often required to pay a 'caution' or security to prove the seriousness of their intentions.

Forthcoming marriages were supposed to be proclaimed on three successive Sundays, but all three proclamations could be made on the same day for a fee. Scottish OPR Banns and Marriages can be explored via ScotlandsPeople. But the site urges caution: 'Do not expect too much from OPR banns & marriages records. The amount of information recorded can be variable and most entries contain very little detail.

At best: date(s) of the proclamation of intended marriage and/or date of marriage, names of bride and groom and their parish of residence, sometimes the occupation of the groom and occasionally the name of the bride's father.

At worst: the names of the bride and groom recorded along with the fee paid in caution.'

(*See also* 'Marriage licences', 'Marriage certificates', 'Marriage bonds and allegations'.)

Baptisms: Religious ceremony where water is poured or sprinkled over an individual symbolising purification and admission to the Christian Church. Baptisms are usually performed on infants and accompanied by the naming or Christening of the child. To begin with, burials, marriages and baptisms were all recorded together within single-volume registers. Although they had been separated by the nineteenth century, it was Rose's Act of 1812 which further fixed the format of the baptism register so that fathers' occupations were also recorded. (*See also* 'Parish Registers'.)

Baptists: A group of denominations that believe baptism should be performed only for professing believers – as opposed to infants. The first English Baptist church met in Spitalfields in 1612. The Baptist Missionary Society was founded in 1792.

Useful websites
Angus Library and Archive (theangus.rpc.ox.ac.uk/)
Baptist Historical Society (baptisthistory.org.uk)
Lists important repositories of Baptist records.
Baptist History & Heritage Society (baptisthistory.org)
Dr Williams's Library (dwlib.co.uk)
Strict Baptist Historical Society (www.strictbaptisthistory.org.uk)

Barkman: A worker who tanned leather using tree bark.

Baron/Baroness: The lowest rank of the peerage.

Barony: Irish land divisions run as follows Province > County > Barony > Parish > Townland. Although baronies were made obsolete in 1898, they were used to describe different areas in many genealogical sources including land surveys. These often span multiple civil parishes and counties.

Barque: A type of ship with three or more masts.

Barrington registers: These come from the diocese of Durham from between 1798 and 1812. They are named after the Right Revd Shute Barrington, who ordered that more detailed information should be kept in baptism and burial registers. The baptism entries from this period give date of baptism, name of the child, date of birth (often omitted from other baptism registers), position in the family, as well as the occupation and abode of the father and the maiden name and place of origin of the mother. Meanwhile, Barrington burial registers give the name and abode of the deceased, parentage, occupation, the date of death, date of burial and age.

Bassett, Miles: A troubled gent whose seventeenth-century will is one of the more famous examples of probate bile, today preserved within the NLW's probate collection. 'And [I could put] as little confidence in my crabbed churlish unnatural, heathenish, and unhuman sonne inlawe Leyson Evans and Anne his wife; I never found noe love, shame nor honestie with them. … but basenesse and falsehood, knaverie and deceipt in them all, ever unto me … they were my greatest Enemies, I had no comfort in anie of them, but trouble & sorrow ever, they sued me in Londone in the Exchequier and in the Comonplease, and in the Marches at Ludlowe, and in the greate Sessions at Cardiff and thus they have vexed me ever of a long time.'

Bastardy: Until the passing of the New Poor Law, the parish was responsible for the welfare of its parishioners. Like settlement examinations, which were records created as the parish tried to ascertain if a person had the right to settlement in the parish, and therefore the rights to claim poor relief from that parish, so the records of bastardy were created during a process in which the parish would try to establish the father of an illegitimate child. The idea was that if they ascertained the identity of the father, he, and not the parish, would become responsible for providing for the child. The system created all sorts of records including bastardy bonds, bastardy examinations and pauper settlements. These records are often grouped together with Poor Law/'parish chest' material, or among quarter sessions records. The bastardy bond (also known as a 'bond of indemnification') was the father's guarantee of responsibility for the child. This London Lives page (www.londonlives.org/static/Bastardy.jsp) explores some bastardy case studies and includes a register of bastardy examinations.

Bastle: A kind of fortified farmhouse – particularly associated with the Anglo-Scottish borders during the seventeenth century.

Bath Blitz Memorial Project (bathblitz.org): Project to commemorate the attacks on Bath in April 1942 which killed more than 400 people and saw 19,000 buildings destroyed or damaged.

Batt maker: Maker of wool wadding used in mattresses.

Battle of Aubers Ridge: Disastrous Western Front offensive that took place in May 1915. Four VCs were awarded for actions at the battle. One noted casualty was New Zealand-born tennis star Anthony Wilding, winner of eleven Grand Slams.

Battle of Britain Clasp: The official clasp awarded to all combatants and other personnel who served during the Battle of Britain. Via the Battle of Britain Memorial website (battleofbritainmemorial.org) you can search a database of all those awarded the clasp.

Bawdy courts: Slang term for the network of Church courts that existed alongside civil/criminal courts. They heard, among cases relating to Church administration of probate, matters relating to defamation, drunkenness and divorce – meaning the content could often be quite racy.

Beadle: A minor town or lay church official with the power of punishing petty offenders.

Beamish Museum: beamish.org.uk

BEDFORDSHIRE:
Bedfordshire & Luton Archives (bedfordshire.gov.uk/archive/)

Has a collection of records of the now defunct brick-making industry, principally those of the London Brick Company and its predecessors and subsidiaries. The National Cataloguing Grant-funded 'Paths to Crime' project saw the cataloguing of Quarter Sessions Rolls for Bedfordshire from 1830–1900. (The Bedfordshire Quarter Sessions Rolls up to 1831 had been catalogued before.)

Bedfordshire Gaol register database (apps.bedfordshire.gov.uk/grd/)

Bedfordshire FHS (bfhs.org.uk)

Belfast Burials (belfastcity.gov.uk/community/burialrecords/burialrecords. aspx): Here you can search Belfast burial records from three cemeteries dating back to 1869. You can also purchase images of the original burial record.

Bench mark: Originates from the horizontal marks made in stone structures to form a 'bench' or level.

Benefice: A Church appointment or ecclesiastical living – typically property and income for Church duties carried out.

BERKSHIRE:

Berkshire Record Office (www.berkshirerecordoffice.org.uk)

Holds probate records from 1480–1857, as well as settlement and removal papers, apprenticeship indentures, bastardy orders and records of over 800 schools, hospitals and other institutions. Its New Landscapes website (www.berkshireenclosure.org.uk) allows users to explore maps and land awards showing the process of enclosing common fields between 1738 and 1883.

Berkshire FHS (berksfhs.org.uk)

BERWICKSHIRE:

Archives of Scottish Borders (www.heartofhawick.co.uk)

Eyemouth Museum (eyemouthmuseum.org)

Borders FHS (bordersfhs.org.uk)

Bethlem Royal Hospital: Founded in 1247, this was the first institution to specialise in the treatment of mental illness. It was known by the nickname Bedlam, which came to mean out of control uproar or confusion. The hospital was established near Bishopsgate – just beyond the City of London – moving to Moorfields, then Southwark before finally settling in West Wickham in 1930.

Its treatment of patients was hotly debated in medical circles during the eighteenth and nineteenth centuries. Andrew T. Scull, in *Masters of Bedlam: The Transformation of the Mad-Doctoring Trade* (Princeton University Press, 1996), quotes Alexander Cruden writing in *The London Citizen Exceedingly Injured* (1739): 'But is there so great Merit and Dexterity in being a mad Doctor? The common Prescriptions of a Bethlemitical Doctor are a Purge and a Vomit, and a Vomit and a Purge over again, and sometimes a Bleeding, which is no great mystery.'

Things came to a head in a 1815 Parliamentary Inquiry, when Quaker reformer Edward Wakefield visited Bethlem, publicising the awful conditions, haphazard organisation and cruelty – all in stark contrast to Quaker-run York Retreat, founded in 1796, which was a beacon of a new more progressive approach to lunatic care. Wakefield particularly drew to attention to one notorious case – that of American marine James Norris who had been continuously restrained, with an iron ring around his neck, for twelve years. The scandal led to the resignation of Principal Physician Thomas Monro in 1816 – ending a 125-year Monro dynasty at the hospital.

You can find out more via the Bethlem Museum of the Mind (museumofthemind.org.uk). The website has plenty of advice for researchers, as well as digitised records and a selected index. Salary Books and Character Books, in particular, may contain references to your ancestors.

Betrothal: A simple betrothal before witnesses was all the ceremony required for a marriage in the Early Modern period.

Birmingham Archdiocesan Archives (birminghamarchdiocesanarchives. org.uk): A good example of a Roman Catholic archdiocesan archive. This is the repository for all parishes in the archdiocese which comprises Staffordshire, Warwickshire, Worcestershire and Oxfordshire. There are currently 56,000-plus records in the searchable online index.

Birth certificates: Full birth certificates include the name, date and place of birth, the father's name (if given at the time of registration), his place of birth and occupation, as well as the mother's name, place of birth, maiden surname and (after 1984) occupation. The name and maiden name can help you track down the mother's parents, and from the September quarter of 1911 the mother's maiden name is included in the General Register Office (GRO) index.

Remember, if a father's name is missing from a birth certificate it may mean that the baby was illegitimate. Before 1875 a woman could name any man as the father without providing evidence. If there's a line through the name column, it means no name was given at the time of registration. Remember too that English/Welsh birth registrations made before 1969 do not include details of the parents' place of birth or mother's occupation. (For more information see the various 'Civil registration' entries.)

Births (civil registration): When the new system of civil registration launched in 1837, births and deaths were the responsibility of the local registrar (the clerk of the Board of Guardians), while clergy of the Church of England would register marriages. The job entailed travelling through the district to record all births within six weeks of arrival and deaths within five days of departure. Registrars were paid per registration, but there was resistance to the system, and some individuals were missed from both official birth and death records from this period. However, more robust laws introduced in 1874 made it compulsory to report births and deaths, and there was a system of fines imposed for any late registration. Always remember that the quarter refers to the date the event was registered, not the date the birth occurred. Births were frequently registered late, so someone born at the end of July, for example, might not appear until the September quarter, or even later.

Bishops' transcripts: Contemporary copies of parish registers made by the parish priest and sent annually to the archbishop. They were introduced in 1598 and offer genealogists a second chance – where you find a frustrating gap in the original parish records, it may often be the case that the bishops' transcripts survives. Bishops' transcripts sometimes recorded less detail than the original registers. They become less common from 1837 and had ceased altogether by the 1870s. BTs survive in diocesan collections – normally found within county record offices – and lots of collections have been transcribed, indexed and/or digitised over the years. You can find lots of examples online via Ancestry, Findmypast et al. FamilySearch, for example, has collections from Durham, Kent, Cambridgeshire, Sussex and more.

Black Presence in Britain (blackpresence.co.uk): The section on slave narratives includes the *History of Mary Prince, a West Indian Slave*. This was the first account of the life of a black woman to be published in England (in 1831), which had a galvanising effect on the anti-slavery movement.

Blackamoor: An archaic term for a black African or dark-skinned person.

Blacksmiths Index (blacksmiths.mygenwebs.com/): Online index of blacksmiths, cartwrights, wheelwrights, farriers and iron workers, and other related crafts and occupations, compiled mainly from UK census material.

Bletchley Park (bletchleypark.org.uk): Home to Britain's Second World War codebreakers, administered by the government's Code and Cypher School.

Blitz: The word Blitz derives from the German word for 'lightning' and particularly refers to the frequent German bombing raids carried out on the UK in 1940 and 1941. Although 'the Blitz' is associated with raids on Greater London, it is also attached to any major city that suffered multiple attacks during the war. The worst single raid on Coventry took place on Thursday, 14 November 1940, killing more than 550 people and decimating large portions of the city, including the Cathedral. There was also the so-called 'Baedeker Blitz' – a series of raids on English cities of cultural rather than military significance, named after the Baedeker guide books. These attacks were in response to Bomber Command's raid on the medieval port Lübeck in March 1942.

Useful websites

Bath Blitz (bathblitz.org)

Bomb Sight (bombsight.org)

Bombs Over Bucks (www.buckscc.gov.uk/leisure-and-culture/centre-for-buckinghamshire-studies/online-resources/bombs-over-bucks/)

Bristol Blitz (bristolblitzed.org)

Clydebank Blitz (educationscotland.gov.uk/scotlandshistory/20thand21st centuries/worldwarii/clydebankblitz/)

Coventry Blitz (historiccoventry.co.uk)

Flying Bombs and Rockets (flyingbombsandrockets.com)

Greater Manchester Blitz Victims (www.greatermanchesterblitzvictims. co.uk)

Hull Blitz (hullblitz.org)

IWM (iwm.org.uk/history/the-blitz)

Liverpool Blitz (liverpoolblitz70.co.uk)

Portsmouth Blitz (portsmouthblitz.co.uk)

West End at War (westendatwar.org.uk)

York Air Raids (yorkairraids.wordpress.com)

BMDIndex (bmdindex.co.uk): An index to birth, marriage and death records from 1837–2005 as published by the GRO – around 255 million events. At time of writing the site offered a simple '£5 for three months' payment option.

BMD Registers (bmdregisters.co.uk): Source of Nonconformist BMDs, drawn from TNA collections. There are also births, marriages and deaths on British-registered ships (1854–91), foreign registers and returns (1627–1960), and non-parochial registers from French, Dutch, German and Swiss churches in London and elsewhere.

Boatswain/Bo'sun: Ship's officer in charge of rigging and sails.

Bodleian Library (bodleian.ox.ac.uk): The main research library of the University of Oxford, one of the oldest libraries in Europe and the second largest in Britain (after the BL).

Boer War: Two separate Boer wars were fought between the British Empire and two independent Boer states – the Republic of Transvaal and the Orange Free State. The first took place in 1880–1. The one commonly referred to as the 'Boer War' is the second, which took place between 1899 and 1902. Online the best starting point is the Anglo Boer War (angloboerwar.com), which boasts more than 400,000 soldiers' records, a bustling forum, free-to-view books, images and articles. Some commercial collections include the Ancestry/TNA-partnered Campaign Medals 1793–1949, which also has UK Casualties of the Boer War which records 55,000 British soldiers killed, captured or wounded. Findmypast has a Boer War database drawn from various sources, which should reveal an individual's unit and any medals/awards won. The Register of the Anglo-Boer War (casus-belli.co.uk) hosts the Anglo-Boer War Memorials Project, recording memorials across the world and currently with nearly 300,000 names.

Boer War Roll of Honour (roll-of-honour.com/Boer/): This page tells you more about the Boer Roll of Honour database. There are also details of Boer War memorials across the UK.

Bomb Sight (bombsight.org): A mapped 'bomb census' of the London Blitz.

Bomber Command: Controlled the RAF's bomber forces from 1936–68. Via the official RAF website you can find information about Bomber Command squadrons (www.raf.mod.uk/history/bombercmdsquadrons. cfm) and there are also sections on famous raids and group commanders. You can find out more about Second World War aircrews and ground crews via rafbombercommand.com. There's also www.bombercrew. com, www.bomberhistory.co.uk and dambustersblog.com.

Bona notabilia: A term that you may come across in probate material – it means 'notable goods', and was used when an estate was valued at £5 or more.

Booth, Charles: Social researcher and reformer (born 1840) whose most famous work was *Life and Labour of the People in London*, which documents late Victorian working class life in the capital. You can find out more via the Charles Booth Online Archive (booth.lse.ac.uk), which includes images of the original Stepney Union casebooks, drawn from the survey.

Border marriages: This succinct summary comes from NRS (at nrscotland.gov.uk/research/guides/birth-death-and-marriage-records/ irregular-border-marriage-registers): 'Marriage by declaration in front of two witnesses was legal in Scotland but in 1753 a law banned such irregular marriages in England. This led to couples crossing the Border to marry at places like Gretna Green, Coldstream, and Lamberton Toll. The marriages were carried out by "priests" who also provided witnesses. Lord Brougham's Act (an Act for Amending the Law of Marriage in Scotland 1856, 19 & 20 Vict, c96) finally put paid to the practice.' You can explore records of border and runaway marriage records via the NRS Historical Search Room (located on the first floor of General Register House) or the ScotlandsPeople Centre.

Boroughs: Borough status gave towns and regions specific rights and powers, officials and quarter sessions courts, independent from the parent county. In medieval England there was also a distinction between a seigneurial borough – granted a degree of self-government by the local lord of the manor – or the fully incorporated boroughs – granted its privileges directly from the king via a Royal Charter. An Act of 1835 introduced town-level municipal boroughs, the Local Government Act 1888 established county boroughs, while in the 1890s London parishes were reorganised into new metropolitan boroughs.

Borthwick Institute for Archives: Specialist archive service of the University of York. It has a number of important genealogical resources including probate records, parish registers, bishops' transcripts and marriage bonds. The probate archive contains the wills, inventories, administration bonds and other related records proved in the Prerogative and Exchequer Courts of York between 1389 and January 1858, and those proved in a number of smaller Peculiar Courts which fell outside this jurisdiction. The series is only broken for the period of the Commonwealth (1653–60) when probate business was removed to a central court in London. The Borthwick's probate archive is the largest outside TNA. The diocese covered the whole of Yorkshire (except for the north-western part of the county which formed the Richmond archdeaconry, the records for which are mostly in West Yorkshire Archives, Leeds). Remember too that the Prerogative Court of York granted probate where the deceased left goods in more than one jurisdiction within the northern province, covering the counties of Cheshire, Lancashire, Westmorland, Cumberland, Northumberland, Durham, Yorkshire and Nottinghamshire.

Bottle of beer: In Meirionnydd Record Office in Gwynedd, Wales, there's a burial register from the year 1844 which records the burial of a young cabin boy whose body was found washed up on the shore. As his name was unknown the entry reads simply 'Bottle of Beer', as one was found in his jacket pocket.

Bottomer: Someone employed at the bottom of a mine shaft – often overseeing the loading of cages.

Boundary changes: When searching for any record of your ancestor, it's important to know the when and the where. Your ancestor may have lived in the same home for their entire life. But during that time civil and ecclesiastical boundaries may have shifted beneath their feet. From a practical research perspective this means that many a local source may reside in different collections within the same archive, or survive in several different archives. A good example is Yorkshire. Yorkshire is already unique thanks to its traditional Ridings divisions. Then in 1974, during the great administrative re-shuffle, some North Riding parishes were transferred to County Durham, while the former West Riding areas of Harrogate, Ripon and the Skipton joined up with parts of the East Riding to form the newly created county of North Yorkshire. Today records of that part of North Yorkshire that was formerly part of the East Riding are held by the East Riding Archive Service in Beverley. And the North Riding archives holds records relating to parts of the former North Riding lost to Durham and Cleveland/Teesside under the boundary changes of 1974. So depending on when and where a record was created, it might potentially reside at the North Yorkshire County Record Office, the Teesside Archives in Middlesbrough, Durham County Record Office or the Borthwick Institute at York University.

With all that said, don't get in a flap – in general, most records normally remain with the archives of the counties they were originally in.

Bowker: A bleacher of yarn.

Bowyer: A maker of bows.

Boyd's Marriage Index: One of the most famous resources at the SoG. The original marriage index was compiled by Percival Boyd. Born in 1868, Boyd joined the SoG in 1922, becoming a fellow in 1926 and serving on the executive committee for twenty-two years. The original index was announced to SoG members in 1925. It contains entries that range from the start of parish registers (1538) right up to the start of civil registration (in 1837). The entries were drawn from registers, bishops' transcripts, marriage licences and banns. In all the index includes marriages from more than 4,320 parish registers. Coverage, both by area and time, is patchy. The SoG guide to the index (sog.org.uk) estimates that the 7 million entries represent around 15 per cent of all pre-1837 English marriages. The marriage record entries contain the first and last name of the bride and groom, the year, county and parish where the marriage took place, and source of the record. The index is currently available online via Findmypast.

Brachygrapher: Obsolete term for a shorthand stenographer.

Brasil: A red dye made from the brazilwood tree.

BRECONSHIRE:
Powys Archives (archives.powys.gov.uk)
Powys FHS (powysfhs.org.uk)

Brewers and publicans: Records relating to the brewing trade tend to reside in local county record offices. From the sixteenth century anyone keeping an inn or alehouse had to apply to the Justices of the Peace for permission, and pub landlords had to make a recognisance or bond that they would operate an orderly boozer. Other potential sources include trade and street directories, and brewery records may be kept either by the brewery or may be deposited in the local archives. Remember too that apprenticeship records relating to brewing may exist. A good place to start your search for relevant material is discovery.nationalarchives. gov.uk. The Brewery History Society (breweryhistory.com) has an online gazetteer of pre-1940 breweries. The Scottish Brewing Archive (archives. gla.ac.uk/sba/default.html) has an alphabetical list of breweries and associated firms whose records are held here.

Useful websites
Beamish Museum (beamish.org.uk)
Brewery History Society (breweryhistory.com)

Guinness Archive Index (guinness-storehouse.com/en/genealogysearch.aspx)

Lost Pubs Project (closedpubs.co.uk)

National Brewing Library (brookes.ac.uk/library/speccoll/brewing.html)

Pub History Society (pubhistorysociety.co.uk)

Brewers Hall (www.brewershall.co.uk/history-and-treasures/): The earliest reference to an organised group of brewers in the City of London was in 1292, but it wasn't until 1438 that they were incorporated as a livery company. Unlike most ancient livery companies, the Brewers' Company has remained close to its trade and boasts some of the oldest continuous records of any livery company – it still possesses the memorandum book of William Proland who was Clerk to the Company from 1418–40, and which contains some of the earliest examples of official written English.

Brewster session: An annual session of the quarter sessions that dealt with granting licences to sell alcohol.

BRISTOL & AVON:
Bristol Record Office (bristolmuseums.org.uk/bristol-record-office/)

Bristol Record Office looks after records of the Diocese of Bristol from 1552, parish registers and records for the Bristol Archdeaconry (including parts of South Gloucestershire and North Somerset) and courts material. Teams of volunteers have also compiled lots of indexes and transcripts to records held in the Bath collections, including parish registers and the Borough Sessions Court. Volunteers have also indexed the *Bath Chronicle* newspaper.

Bristol & Avon FHS (bafhs.org.uk)

Britain From Above (britainfromabove.org.uk): Explore high-resolution aerial images taken between 1919 and 1953. You can search by place name, map or year, and register to provide information about the images.

Britain's Small Wars (britainssmallwars.co.uk): Fascinating website that compiles detailed histories of the more obscure conflicts from the past 200 years. These include:

1799	The Invasion of North Holland
1826	The Siege of Bhurtpore, India
1834–9	The First Carlist War, Spain
1845–6	The First Sikh War, Punjab
1848	The Matale Rebellion, Sri Lanka

1863–4	Waikato War, New Zealand
1864	The Tauranga War, New Zealand
1879	The Zulu War, South Africa
1881–99	The Mahdist Wars, Sudan
1885	The North-West Rebellion, Canada
1900	Boxer Rebellion, China
1915	The Singapore Mutiny

British Agricultural History Society: bahs.org.uk

British Association for Local History: www.balh.org.uk

British Association of Paper Historians: baph.org.uk

British Dental Association Museum (www.bda.org/museum): The website includes details of the John McLean Archive – an oral history project that gathers reminiscences covering topics such as the start of the National Health Service and dental education. There's also some research advice including a 'Was Your Ancestor a Dentist?' factsheet.

British Evacuees Association: evacuees.org.uk

British Film Institute: Charitable organisation that promotes and preserves film and television in the UK, founded in 1933. BFI has drawn together thousands of archival films from all over the UK, which you can explore via the www.bfi.org.uk/britain-on-film player. You can search by keyword, parent film archive or explore the Britain on Film map. Details of the BFI National Archive are at bfi.org.uk/archive-collections, and there's Screenonline (screenonline.org.uk) and Colonial Film (colonialfilm.org. uk), subtitled 'Moving images of the British Empire', with details of 6,000 films.

British & Foreign School Society Archive: bfss.org.uk/archive/

British GENES Blog (britishgenes.blogspot.com): Newsy blog from genealogist Chris Paton.

British History Online (british-history.ac.uk): Offers access to Victoria County History volumes and a number of useful and sometimes name-rich sources often helpful in researching the elite classes. These include the Catalogue of Ancient Deeds and Feet of Fines, and the Calendars of State Papers, which give details of appointments, titles, inheritance and marriages. It also hosts historic maps of London from before 1800 and maps from the nineteenth-century series of the Ordnance Survey, including the complete 1:10,560 series and selected areas of the 1:2,500 series.

British Home Children in Canada (canadianbritishhomechildren. weebly.com): Has data relating to approximately 118,000 children sent to Canada from the UK under the Child Immigration scheme (1863–1949).

British Jewry (www.british-jewry.org.uk): Hosts several databases from the Portsmouth circumcision database to the vast Leeds Database.

British Library: Created in 1973 as a result of the British Library Act 1972 – before this the library had been part of the British Museum. As the legal deposit library it receives copies of all books published in the UK and Ireland. The Newsroom is the BL's dedicated newspaper research space in the St Pancras building. (*See* Newspapers.)

British Medal Forum (britishmedalforum.com): Covers British, Canadian, Australian, New Zealand, Indian, South African and all Commonwealth medals.

British Music Hall Society: britishmusichallsociety.com

British Nationality Act 1948: Thanks partly to post-war labour shortages, between the years 1948 and 1962 there were no restrictions on immigrants from Commonwealth countries, and the British Nationality Act of 1948 made it relatively simple for migrants to obtain citizenship. Certificates of citizenship issued by the Home Office from this period have also survived and can be found at TNA in HO 334.

British Newspaper Archive (britishnewspaperarchive.co.uk): This Findmypast website is built on collections preserved by the BL. It reached 15-million pages from 661 titles in mid-2016, from national and local newspapers, to specialist periodicals. Searching is free, but it costs to view the resulting images, although free access is available in many archives and libraries. At time of writing one month's access cost £12.95.

British Optical Association Museum (college-optometrists.org/en/ college/museyeum/): Offers a research service for family historians interested in opticians (optometrists) from the 1890s onwards.

British Pathé (britishpathe.com): Explore newsreels, video and archive film footage and stills.

British Record Society (www.britishrecordsociety.org): Society founded in 1889 which compiles, edits and publishes indexes, calendars and transcripts of historical records in public or private custody throughout Great Britain. For many years it concentrated on producing indexes to English probate records. Recent publications include a three-volume index to wills and administrations in Wiltshire, and members are also publishing transcripts of seventeenth-century hearth tax returns.

British Telecom Digital Archives (www.digitalarchives.bt.com): Various searchable resources including almost half a million photographs, reports and items of correspondence from the archives going back to 1846.

British Transport Police History Group (btphg.org.uk): Lists recipients of various honours, decorations and medals.

Broadcloth: A dense, plain woven cloth.

Broadside: A large printed sheet with popular ballads, news, events, proclamations or advertisements. Via NLS's Word on the Street site (digital. nls.uk/broadsides/) you can explore a collection of nearly 1,800 broadsides. One famous example from America was the Dunlap broadside – the first publication of the Declaration of Independence in 1776.

Brown, Lancelot 'Capability': The tercentenary of landscape architect Capability Brown's birth was celebrated in 2016. To mark the event the RBS's online Heritage Archive reproduced the ledger pages containing the bank accounts of Lancelot Brown and his executors from when he was a customer of Drummonds Bank from 1753 until his death thirty years later. According to capabilitybrown.org: 'Brown offered a number of different services to his clients: for a round number of guineas, he could provide a survey and plans for buildings and landscape, and leave his client to execute his proposal; more frequently he provided a foreman to oversee the work, which would be carried out by labour recruited from the estate. Even in 1753, when he opened his account with Drummond's Bank, Brown was employing four foremen and by the end of the decade he had over twenty foremen on his books. Finally, he could oversee and refine the work himself, usually by means of visits for a certain number of days each year.'

Browsers: Always keep your web browser up to date, if only for security reasons. It's also a good idea to have more than one browser for when things aren't working properly – a website that clunks up against Internet Explorer might be perfectly happy within Google Chrome.

Buckie & District Fishing Heritage Centre: buckieheritage.org

BUCKINGHAMSHIRE:
Centre for Buckinghamshire Studies (www.buckscc.gov.uk/leisure-and-culture/centre-for-buckinghamshire-studies/)

The Centre for Buckinghamshire Studies has microfiche copies of the annual National Probate Index. It also looks after around 35,000 Buckinghamshire wills, and you can search and order copies via an online wills database.

Buckinghamshire FHS (bucksfhs.org.uk)

Buckinghamshire Remembers (buckinghamshireremembers.org.uk)

Database of First World War casualties listed on Buckinghamshire war memorials.

BuildingHistory (buildinghistory.org): Useful website full of concise advice aimed at researching buildings and house history.

Bumboat: Small vessel used to ferry objects to and from ships moored off shore.

Burgess rolls: Burgess rolls and books often survive within county or borough collections. Admission as a burgess was usually obtained by birth in the town, descent from a burgess, serving as an apprentice to a burgess or by purchase. Burgess books list those admitted as burgesses together with relationships to previously admitted burgesses and sometimes names and ages of children. Shropshire Archives, for example, has burgess books for Shrewsbury, Bridgnorth, Ludlow, Much Wenlock and Oswestry (shropshirearchives.org.uk).

Burgh: The Scottish equivalent of the borough. The earliest royal burghs date from the twelfth-century reign of King David I. The Aberdeen City and Aberdeenshire Archives has a Charter of King William the Lion of c. 1190, which grants the Burgh of Aberdeen the right to its own guild of merchants. Burghs continued to be the principal subdivision of Scotland after the Acts of Union 1707, then during reorganisation in 1889 they were categorised as large burghs or small burghs.

Burgh Records Database Project (abdn.ac.uk/aberdeen-burgh-records-database/): Pilot project run by Aberdeen University which allows users to search across text and images of 100 pages of an Aberdeen council register.

Burial grounds: Before the 1850s burials were recorded in the registers of Anglican parish churches or in some Nonconformist chapels. An Act of 1853 enabled local authorities or private companies to purchase and use land for the purpose of burial.

Useful websites

Belfast Burials (belfastcity.gov.uk/community/burialrecords/burialrecords. aspx)

Burial Inscriptions (burial-inscriptions.co.uk)

DeceasedOnline (deceasedonline.com)

GraveMatters (gravematters.org.uk)

Interment.net (interment.net)

Burial registers: It's fair to say that even after the standardisation of baptism and burial registers of 1812, burial registers can be rather disappointing. They often omit any reference to relatives, and 'abode' is often nothing more than the name of the parish. However, they do sometimes contain comments by the parish priest. Burial registers (along with baptisms and marriages) were first ordered to be kept from the 1530s, but they don't always survive from this date. Detail may vary depending on the incumbent or clerk who kept them, and some external influences, particularly the Civil War, resulted in gaps.

Burke's Peerage: Record of the genealogy and heraldry of the peerage, baronetage, knightage and landed gentry, established in London in 1826 by Irish genealogist John Burke. Much of the material online (burkespeerage.com) is only accessible by subscription, but there are free sections with detailed pedigrees of prominent royal families.

Burler: Someone who removes threads, knots, lumps and other imperfections from cloth.

Business Archives Council of Scotland (www.gla.ac.uk/services/ archives/bacs/): Established in 1960 to preserve records of Scottish business and industry.

BUTESHIRE:

Argyll & Bute Archives (argyll-bute.gov.uk/community-life-and-leisure/ archives)

Bute Museum (www.butemuseum.org.uk/archives/)

Glasgow & West of Scotland FHS (gwsfhs.org.uk)

Butt: A measure of liquid – usually wine or ale – equivalent to around 126 imperial gallons.

C

CAERNARFONSHIRE:
Gwynedd Archives Service (gwynedd.gov.uk/archives)

Runs the Caernarfon and Meirionnydd record offices.

Gwynedd FHS (gwyneddfhs.org)

CAITHNESS:
Highland Archives Service (highlandarchives.org.uk/caithness.asp)

Caithness FHS (caithnessfhs.org.uk)

Highland FHS (highlandfamilyhistorysociety.org)

Calendar: The Gregorian or Western calendar was introduced in October 1582 by Pope Gregory XIII to halt the gradual drift of the Julian calendar. Countries adopted the change at different times – Britain adopted the Gregorian calendar in 1752, by which time there was a difference of eleven days between the two calendars. As a result 2 September 1752 was followed by 14 September 1752.

Calendars: Chronological lists of documents or manuscripts, often with annotations and excerpts from the original documents.

Calendars of State Papers: Summaries of a series of handwritten documents relating to the administration of England, and its foreign relations, in the early modern period. The originals are at TNA and you can explore the majority of these via British History Online (british-history. ac.uk). They're potentially useful for family historians as they give details of appointments, titles, inheritance and marriages of the elite classes.

CAMBRIDGESHIRE:
Cambridgeshire Archives (cambridgeshire.gov.uk/info/20011/archives_ archaeology_and_museums/177/archives_and_local_studies)

Looks after records of local courts, hospitals, Poor Law unions, turnpike trusts and coroners, as well as businesses and charities, ancient manors and estates, local societies and organisations. In addition, there are the parish and Nonconformist records, and wills and inventories from the Ely Consistory and Archdeaconry Courts.

Camdex (camdex.org)

Index of births, marriages, civil partnerships and deaths in Cambridgeshire.

Cambridgeshire FHS (cfhs.org.uk)

Cambridgeshire Records Society (cambsrecordsociety.co.uk)

CANADA:
Archives Canada (www.archivescanada.ca)

Library and Archives Canada (www.bac-lac.gc.ca)

Canada, migration to: Child emigration peaked from the 1870s until 1914 – about 80,000 children were sent to Canada alone during this period. There are TNA-held Colonial Office reports on pauper child emigrants resident in Canada (1887–92). These comment on condition, health, character, schooling and church attendance of each child, and also the children's own views of their new homes. They also record the union or parish from which they were sent, as well as each child's name, age and host's name and address.

British Home Children in Canada (canadianbritishhomechildren. weebly.com) has data relating to approximately 118,000 children sent to Canada from the UK under the Child Immigration scheme (1863–1939). (*See also* 'Child migration'.)

Canon: A cleric living with others in a clergy house.

Canterbury Cathedral Archives (archives.canterbury-cathedral.org): Holds records of the Diocese of Canterbury, individual parishes in the Archdeaconry of Canterbury, records of Canterbury City Council (and its predecessors), as well as archives of various organisations, businesses and individuals in the area.

Cantref/cantred: The cantref/cantred or commote is a traditional and now largely obsolete unit of land in Wales.

Cappers: Another term for hatmakers.

CARDIGANSHIRE:

Ceredigion Archives (archifdy-ceredigion.org.uk)

The archive in Aberystwyth has a run of material chronicling the rise and fall of Pwll Roman Lead Mine in north Cardiganshire, with monthly running costs and ledgers detailing men employed on particular days of the week, sometimes showing specific jobs they were paid to carry out.

Cardiganshire FHS (cgnfhs.org.uk)

Dyfed FHS (dyfedfhs.org.uk)

CARMARTHENSHIRE:

Carmarthenshire Archives Service (www.carmarthenshire.gov.uk/english/leisure/archives/pages/archivesrecords.aspx)

Dyfed FHS (dyfedfhs.org.uk)

Cartulary: A medieval manuscript volume or roll containing transcriptions of documents relating to the foundation of ecclesiastical establishments.

Castle Garden (castlegarden.org): The main immigration processing centre into the US before the foundation of Ellis Island. This website provides a database of 11,000,000 individuals recorded between 1820 and 1892.

Catalogues: All archives should maintain at least a basic catalogue. Most are online – either through their own dedicated catalogue website, or through multi-archive catalogues. They are designed to help you find relevant documents, note down references so you can then request to view the documents in the research/reading room. The level of detail within each description varies a great deal. Most will give a reference or finding number, a title and date. Some may simply describe the scope and content of a collection of documents, others may detail each document within a larger collection, others may include still further detail with complete transcriptions of the contents and name indexes, others may even lead to digitised copies of the documents themselves. Most have some kind of help or FAQ section, and remember that putting "double quotes" around search requests should lead to an exact answer. Some important multi-archive catalogues include TNA's Discovery (discovery. nationalarchives.gov.uk), Archives Wales (archiveswales.org.uk) and the Scottish Archive Network (scan.org.uk). For more search tips see 'Search tools and commands'.

Catholic Church for England & Wales (catholic-ew.org.uk): This website is useful for tracking down details of Catholic diocesan archives.

Catholic Family History Society (www.catholic-history.org.uk/cfhs/): Produces a large number of transcriptions.

Catholic Heritage (www.catholic-heritage.net): Project to provide a single catalogue to diocesan archives, bishops' conferences, seminaries and religious orders.

Catholic National Library (catholic-library.org.uk): Most Mission Registers (listing baptisms, confirmations, marriages, deaths) remain in the custody of parish priests, but many have been transcribed and indexed by the Catholic FHS and deposited here. The website has a page listing county by county coverage of all the registers and there is also an online catalogue.

Catholic Parish Registers in Ireland: NLI originally made microfilm copies of registers from most Catholic parishes in Ireland and Northern Ireland during the 1950s and 1960s. These contain baptisms and marriages from Catholic parishes up to 1880. The coverage dates of the registers vary from back to the 1740s in some city parishes in Dublin, Cork, Galway, Waterford and Limerick, to the 1780s in counties such as Kildare, Wexford, Waterford and Kilkenny. Registers for parishes along the western seaboard do not generally begin until the 1850s. Christenings generally took place as soon as possible after children were born, sometimes on the same day. The records include the date of baptism, names of child, father, mother (with maiden surname in later records) and the sponsors or godparents. Marriage records provide the date, names of the bride, groom and witnesses. Meanwhile burials would record the name of the deceased, date of burial and sometimes an occupation or residence (townland). Later years often include the age at death and for children at least one of the names of the parents, usually the father. You can view digital images free of charge via registers.nli.ie.

Catholic Record Society: catholicrecordsociety.co.uk

Catholic Relief Act: These Acts, of 1778 and 1791, permitted Catholics to own land and removed many restrictions placed on Catholic priests, including the threat of imprisonment. The latter Act also allowed Catholic clergy to say Mass.

Catholic research: Following the sixteenth-century Act of Uniformity, Catholics faced fines, imprisonment and persecution for practising their faith. As a result very few records from this era were maintained and, as with Nonconformists, Catholics frequently appear in Anglican sources. All marriages from between 1754 and 1837 had to be Church of England to be legally valid, for example. And, as noted in the GenGuide page relating to Catholic research, it was 'not uncommon for the Anglican minister to mark an entry in the register with "papist" or "recusant"'.

From the mid-nineteenth century Catholic registers become more commonplace and also give more genealogical detail than their Anglican counterparts. Catholic baptism registers will usually show the names of godparents. Remember too that most Catholic registers are in the custody of the parish.

TNA material within RG 4 includes births, baptisms, deaths, burials and marriages for some Roman Catholic communities in Dorset, Hampshire, Lancashire, Lincolnshire, Northumberland, Nottinghamshire, Oxfordshire and Yorkshire. These are available to search via BMDRegisters.co.uk or TheGenealogist.co.uk.

The Catholic Family History Society (www.catholic-history.org.uk/ cfhs/) has produced a large number of transcriptions, and the Catholic National Library (catholic-library.org.uk) has transcribed mission registers listing baptisms, confirmations, marriages and deaths. The Manchester & Lancashire FHS (mlfhs.org.uk) has produced an index to Catholic parish registers for Manchester. ScotlandsPeople gives access to Catholic registers from all Scottish parishes in existence by 1855 – this is drawn from registers looked after by the Scottish Catholic Archives (www.scottishcatholicarchives.org.uk).

Birmingham Archdiocesan Archives (birminghamarchdiocesan archives.org.uk) is an example of a regional Catholic diocesan archive and is in fact the repository for all parishes within the archdiocese – comprising Staffordshire, Warwickshire, Worcestershire and Oxfordshire. There are currently 56,000-plus records in the searchable online index. There's also the Westminster Diocesan Archives (rcdow.org.uk/diocese/archives/) and the Leeds Diocesan Archives (dioceseofleeds.org.uk/archives/). You can explore holdings in a number of Catholic archives and libraries via Catholic Heritage (www.catholic-heritage.net). The SoG (sog.org.uk) looks after some transcribed/indexed Catholic registers and has an index of Catholic nuns (1598–1914).

Away from parish-level events, other records to watch out for include Association Oath Rolls, Protestation Oath Returns, Recusant Rolls, Returns of Papists and Sacrament Certificates.

Useful websites

Catholic Church for England & Wales (catholic-ew.org.uk)

Catholic Heritage (www.catholic-heritage.net)

Catholic National Library (catholic-library.org.uk)

Catholic parish registers at NLI (registers.nli.ie)

Cause Papers Database (hrionline.ac.uk/causepapers/): This is a free database of Cause Papers in the Diocesan Courts of the Archbishopric of York (1300–1858). The original documents are held in the Borthwick Institute for Archives at the University of York. These Church courts generally dealt with cases relating to failure to attend church, drunkenness, divorce and probate.

Cemeteries: Cities and larger towns have public cemeteries or crematoria, as opposed to parochial graveyards. The first public cemeteries were opened in the first half of the nineteenth century in response to the health risk caused by overcrowding of churchyards. The Exeter Higher Cemetery, for example, was opened in 1866, since when more than 70,000 people have been buried here. Most public cemeteries are administered by the local council. Burial registers from public cemeteries may reside with the local council, or be retained at the cemetery office itself. The kinds of records that survive include registers of graves, register of interments, letters and minutes relating to the local burial board and more. Many have their own websites with details of how to contact the cemetery office, and some have placed indexes or burial databases online (particularly useful as cemetery registers were usually arranged in chronological rather than alphabetical order). In addition there are specialist subscriptions sites – the best known being DeceasedOnline (deceasedonline.com) – that have increasing quantities of burial data from public cemeteries from across the UK.

Census: Census returns allow you to confirm key facts about an individual – such as occupation, age and family, relationships and living arrangements – as well as making deductions about status, the household and the wider community. It also allows us to confirm or contradict family stories that may have become separated from the absolute truth in continuous retelling. Although not an example from these shores, the Marx brothers would often paint a picture of poverty when describing their upbringing, making endless jokes about their father being a useless tailor. However, the 1905 census of New York allows us (or specifically Simon Louvish writing in *Monkey Business: The Lives and Legends of the Marx Brothers* (Groucho Marx, 2003)) to strip away the myth, and uncover a family that in reality flourished in a fairly well-to-do New York suburb.

Assuming you find your family in each census, these records can give you a decade by decade snapshot of their lives. They also offer vital information to help you track down references in other sources, such as civil registration records of births, marriages and deaths.

The census system began in 1801, but becomes genealogically useful from 1841 – prior to that the census was little more than a headcount.

Although broadly speaking more data was recorded as time went on, the system remained largely unchanged through most of the nineteenth century. From 1841–1901, a schedule was completed for each household, which was then collected by the enumerator, who copied the information into enumeration books. It is these books that form the basis of what is now available to explore on and offline. In 1911 all household schedules were kept and the enumerators produced summary books which listed every address, including unoccupied buildings, and only contain the names of the head of each household.

Details of where you can access census material appear below, but most record offices and local history libraries will hold microform copies of the census returns for the area, and most will offer free access to census data on the likes of Ancestry or Findmypast. The network of Family History Centres operated by the LDS Church (familysearch.org/locations/) also offers census material on microfilm.

Census (1801–31): The first censuses of Great Britain were simple headcounts which did not record any names of individuals. The second census, for example, was taken on Monday, 27 May 1811 and recorded a population of around 12.6 million people.

Census (1841): The first genealogically useful census in that it names every individual within each household. The census forms recorded the names, age (rounded down to the nearest five years for those aged 15 or over), gender and occupation. There was a yes/no to whether they were born in the county in which they were enumerated, and whether they were born in Scotland, Ireland or 'Foreign Parts'.

Census (1851): This census recorded full names (often initials for middle names), relationship to the 'head of the household', marital status, age, sex, occupation, county/parish of birth, country of birth (if outside England and Wales), whether they suffered from certain medical disabilities and information about the dwelling itself. This was also the first census where special schedules were drawn up for vessels and enumeration books were completed for workhouses, barracks and hospitals.

Census (1891–1901): These censuses include entries for employment status, record the number of rooms in houses, and list languages spoken by individuals in Wales, Scotland and Ireland.

Census (1911): The first census where the household schedules themselves were kept. Unlike previous censuses, these were not copied into enumeration books, but instead summary books were compiled listing every address – but only the names of the head of each household. Alongside what had become 'usual' census data, the 1911 survey also recorded a married woman's 'fertility in marriage' – length of present marriage and number of children born of that marriage, living or deceased – as well as more detailed occupational data, and extra detail on nationality and the exact birthplaces for people born in Scotland or Ireland.

Census in Ireland: You can explore, free of charge, the complete census of Ireland 1901/1911 via NAI's dedicated website at census.nationalarchives. ie. Alongside the complete 1901 and 1911 censuses, this has fragments and substitutes for previous years. As so much of Ireland's original census material has not survived, you will often hear about references to 'census substitutes' – records that can function as a kind of proto-census where none exists. The most famous of these is the Griffith's Valuation (see separate entry), a full-scale valuation of property published in 1847 and 1864. It remains one of the most important genealogical sources for research into nineteenth-century Ireland.

Census in Scotland: Returns for Scotland are almost identical in format to those for England and Wales, except for the census of 1911, when similarly detailed information was gathered, but was then copied into enumeration books as in previous years. This was the twelfth census of Scotland and it was taken on the night of Sunday, 2 April. All people who were alive after midnight were enumerated and people on board boats or barges were enumerated if the vessel was 'within the limits of the jurisdiction of His Majesty's Customs'.

To begin with birthplaces were less specific than in later years. So, like the English and Welsh counterpart, the Scottish census of 1841 recorded only whether or not the person was born in the county where the census took place, and whether the person was English, Irish or Foreign. As noted on the excellent ScotlandsPeople website: 'Enumerators were instructed to record occupations in an abbreviated form, e.g. H.L.W. denoted handloom weaver.'

ScotlandsPeople has indexes and images of the census records from 1841–1911 (and transcripts are available on Findmypast and Ancestry). At time of writing a credit system is operating where each time you conduct a search you are told how many records have been found, and you have the opportunity to re-define/narrow the search. Then if you decide to display the results, a single page of twenty-five results costs one credit, then viewing a record image costs five credits.

Census indexes: Every census for England and Wales has been indexed. FamilySearch.org has a complete index and transcription of the 1881 census, as well as indexes to the remaining censuses (1841–1911) for England and Wales. Ancestry and Findmypast have the census material from 1841–1911 inclusive, and TheGenealogist also offers various census transcripts and images from 1841–1911. Family history societies have produced transcriptions of local census material and other census-like sources. Most archives and libraries offer free access to websites such as Ancestry, meaning you can also search nationwide census material. There's also partial census transcripts for England, Wales and Scotland free of charge on FreeCEN (freecen.org.uk).

Census milestones:

1801   The census has been taken every ten years since 1801 with the exception of 1941.

1841   The first census to list the names of every individual.

1891   The census asked about language spoken in Wales, from 1891, and in the Isle of Man, from 1901.

1911   The first where the army overseas was enumerated.

1921   The 1921 census, and the following censuses, are kept by the Office for National Statistics. They will be made available 100 years after the date they were conducted.

1939   The 1939 Register is the nearest to a census of England and Wales between 1921 and 1951. The 1931 census for England and Wales was destroyed during the Second World War and no census was taken in 1941.

Census dates: 1841 (6 June), 1851 (30 March), 1861 (7 April), 1871 (2 April), 1881 (3 April), 1891 (5 April), 1901 (31 March), 1911 (2 April), 1921 (19 June).

Census tips:
1. If someone appears to be missing, make sure you try searching by spelling variations. Also try to think about how the name might sound phonetically – this can help you guess how the writer might have spelt it.
2. Wider family networks would often live closer to each other than they tend to today – it may be worth searching for family members in nearby streets or neighbourhoods.
3. The forenames/Christian names may not match up with those given in parish or civil registration records – people may have been known by a nickname or middle name.
4. Always double check that you are searching in the right parish – always watch out for confusion caused by the difference between civil and ecclesiastical parishes.
5. Don't rely on an age given in the census – treat it with a healthy scepticism. It was common to lie about, or be unaware of, one's exact age.
6. Remember that house numbers were rarely given in earlier census years. Indeed, you may find that in smaller villages only the name of the village or hamlet is recorded.

Census websites:
Ancestry UK Census Collection: search.ancestry.co.uk/search/group/ukicen

Census of Ireland 1901/1911 (census.nationalarchives.ie): Also includes surviving fragments for previous years.

FamilySearch (familysearch.org): Has material relating to all the available censuses of England and Wales from 1841 – but what is available where varies. You can explore all of the 1881 census, but for 1911, for example, you can use the index that has been provided by affiliate partner Findmypast, and the index links to images on their website – available for a fee. Findmypast has material from the 1841–1911 censuses, as well as the 1939 Register, a census-like register of more than 40 million Britons alive on Friday, 29 September 1939.

FreeCEN (freecen.org.uk): Partial census data for 1841–91, excluding 1881.

TheGenealogist: thegenealogist.co.uk

ScotlandsPeople (scotlandspeople.gov.uk): Census returns for Scotland from 1841 to 1911.

UK BMD (ukbmd.org.uk): Lists some sites providing transcriptions of census material.

Center for Jewish History (www.cjh.org): Home of five pre-eminent Jewish historical institutions based in New York.

Chain: A chain, as a unit of length, measures 66ft or 22yd and was first invented by English clergyman and mathematician Edmund Gunter in 1620. Other archaic measurements to watch out for include: link, furlong, rod, rood and pole.

Chaldron: An obsolete measure of volume, typically used to describe amounts of coal.

Chancel: Part of a church near the altar typically separated from the congregation by steps or a screen.

Chancery: The Court of Chancery had jurisdiction over trusts, land law, the administration of the estates of lunatics and the guardianship of infants, and held pre-eminence over the common-law courts. It sat at Westminster Hall from the 1300s until its dissolution in 1873 and its records are at TNA.

Chandler: The head of the chandlery (wax, candles, soap) in households and ships.

CHANNEL ISLANDS:
(Jersey, Guernsey, Alderney, Sark, Herm)
Alderney Society (alderneysociety.org/museum_collections.php)
Channel Islands FHS (jerseyfamilyhistory.org)
Genuki, The Channel Islands (chi.genuki.weald.org.uk)
Guernsey Archives (www.gov.gg/islandarchives)
Jersey Archive (jerseyheritage.org/places-to-visit/jersey-archive)
La Société Guernesiaise (societe.org.gg/sections/familyhistory.php)
Priaulx Library (priaulxlibrary.co.uk)

Chapelry: A small parochial division of a large, populated parish, served by a chapel of ease. Chapels of ease were smaller places of worship created for parishioners too far from the main place of worship. A chapel of ease would keep its own parish register of baptisms and burials, and, where authorisation was granted, marriages. In particular, Lancashire, Yorkshire, Cheshire and Greater London have many parishes divided into many more chapelries. The largest parish in England is the one served by Manchester Cathedral – within its bounds there are over 150 smaller chapels.

Chapels Society (chapelssociety.org.uk): Focuses on the history and architecture of Nonconformist places of worship.

Chaplain: A priest serving a family, private body or institution.

Charles Booth Online Archive (booth.lse.ac.uk): Explore Booth's famous survey of life and labour in London (1886–1903).

Charnel house: A building where skeletal remains unearthed while digging graves in churchyards were stored.

Chartism: The umbrella term for a political movement that flourished in Britain between 1838 and 1848. It was born out of the Reform Act 1832, which gave the vote to a section of the male middle classes, but not the working classes. Amid unrest and increasing radicalism, a committee of MPs and working men published the 'People's Charter' in 1838, which stipulated six aims (including universal male suffrage and no property qualification for MPs) and gave the movement its name. Although Chartism ultimately disappeared having failed to achieve these goals, it paved the way for a new generation of politicians, trade unionists and political agitators to continue the fight for a fairer democratic system.

Chartist Ancestors (chartists.net): Fascinating website that explores the history of the Chartist movement, in particular the three great petitions of 1839–48. There's also a useful blog at chartist-ancestors.blogspot.co.uk.

Charwoman: Cleaner or worker, who was usually employed by the hour, as opposed to 'live-in' domestic service.

Chattel: A personal possession. In law it was used to describe property other than freehold land.

CHESHIRE:
Cheshire Archives & Local Studies (archives.cheshire.gov.uk)

The designated repository for records of the 400 or so parishes in the diocese of Chester. It is also home to the more detailed Dade registers, which continued to be kept for Witton until 1862. The website includes a Railway Staff Database of 25,000 names going back to 1869 drawn from 17 staff registers from 4 railway companies – Cambrian Railway, Great Western Railway, London & North Western Railway and London & North Western and Great Western Joint Railway.

Family History Society of Cheshire (fhsc.org.uk)

Cheshire Probate Records, 1492–1940 (familysearch.org/search/collection/1589492)

Chief beneficiaries: The individuals in a will who were given the majority of the wealth – usually members of the immediate family.

Child migration: The Poor Law Amendment Act of 1850 allowed Boards of Guardians to send children under 16 overseas. Records of specific cases are most likely to survive within records held in local archives. Aberdeenshire archives' General Registers of the Poor for Peterhead contains an entry relating to 4-year-old Elspet Niddrie, whose dying mother and adult half-sister were unable to care for her, so she was sent to an aunt who had emigrated to America in 1904. The case ends with the Inspector of the Poor writing: 'Passage paid to Boston USA and sent to Aunt … sailed today on Allan Liner Numidian'.

There are TNA-held Colonial Office reports on pauper child emigrants resident in Canada (1887–92). Useful information may also be found within locally held Poor Law collections, as well as records of Dr Barnardo's Homes, the Overseas Migration Board and the Big Brother emigration scheme. (*See also* 'Home Children' and 'Canada, Migration to'.)

Childrenshomes (childrenshomes.org.uk): Useful sister site to work houses.org, which gives details of orphanages, homes for those in poverty or with special needs, reformatories, industrial and approved schools, training ships and more.

Children's Overseas Reception Board: In June 1940 the Children's Overseas Reception Board was set up to administer offers from Canada, Australia, New Zealand, South Africa and the US to care for British children in private homes. The evacuation scheme stopped following the *City of Benares* tragedy in September 1940. The *City of Benares* was carrying ninety Children's Overseas Reception Board evacuees to Canada when it was torpedoed by a German submarine. Those lost included seventy-seven children. The sinking caused public outrage in Britain and led to the total cancellation of the CORB scheme. You can search TNA's Discovery by name for case histories of all individuals evacuated through the scheme.

Christenings: *See* 'Baptisms'.

Church in Wales: The Welsh Church Act 1914 saw the Church of England separated and disestablished in Wales and Monmouthshire, leading to the creation of the Church in Wales.

Church of England court hierarchy: Archbishop's or Prerogative Courts > Bishop's or Consistory and Commissary Courts > Archdeacon's or Archdeaconry Courts > Peculiar Courts.

Church of England Record Centre (lambethpalacelibrary.org): Has records of the National Society for Promoting Religious Education, established in 1811, which includes indexes of school teachers (1812–55). Alongside collections that relate to church buildings and property, Church legislation and policy making since 1919 (through the Church Assembly), commissions of enquiry, there's also material relating to the work of various Christian organisations and financial assistance given to parish clergy – including endowments to benefice capital and loans for parsonage houses by the Queen Anne's Bounty (1704–1948), the Ecclesiastical Commissioners (1836–1948) and the Church Commissioners since 1948.

Church of Ireland (Anglican Church): The largest Christian denomination in Ireland is Roman Catholicism, the second is the Church of Ireland. Church of Ireland parochial records are often still with the relevant parish, although many (originals, copies and microfilmed examples) are held at NAI. PRONI also has copies of Church of Ireland registers for the dioceses of Armagh, Clogher, Connor, Derry, Dromore, Down, Kilmore and Raphoe. Many registers were destroyed, especially in the fire at the Public Record Office in 1922. Some survivors have been digitised and are available via the expanding Anglican Record Project (www.ireland.anglican.org/arp).

Church rates: Tax levied on each parish householder to maintain the church. These rates were set by churchwardens. The tax was brought to an end by the Compulsory Church Rates Abolition Act passed in 1868, although it continued on a voluntary basis. Surviving records are normally found at local record offices.

Churchwarden's accounts: Churchwarden's accounts can be hard to use as they are rarely indexed or transcribed (although it's always worth seeing what has been produced by the local family history group). They are often the earliest surviving records within a parish collection. Wardens were in charge of the maintenance of the church itself, which can sometimes produces snatches of name-rich information. The accounts for Great Dunmow of 1538 (held at Essex Record Office), for example, include a list of subscribers contributing to a new bell clapper. Churchwardens often had to present any wrongdoings at quarter sessions, including failure to attend church, drunkenness or other undesirable behaviour – the kinds of cases that might reach the Church courts.

Cinque Ports: Derived from the Norman French meaning simply 'Five Ports', the Cinque Ports are a series of coastal towns in Kent and Sussex – Dover, Hastings, Hythe, New Romney and Sandwich. The group was expected, by Royal Charter, to provide ships for the Crown, in return for exemption from certain taxes, the ability to levy tolls and other privileges of self government.

Civil registration: Civil registration in England and Wales began on 1 July 1837 – before that date only churches recorded births, marriages and deaths. Today these civil registration records are the first and most valuable genealogical tool for fixing an individual's life events.

Civil registration took place within registration districts that had been drawn up three years earlier for the new system of Poor Law unions. Each district was divided into sub-districts – and had a Registrar of Births and Deaths.

Every quarter the superintendent registrars would send copies of registrations to the Registrar General in London. So the registration districts hold the original birth and death records, and the GRO holds copies. (There were originally twenty-seven registration districts in England and Wales, but this was increased to thirty-three in 1852.)

As registrations came in, alphabetical indexes were compiled on a quarterly basis. It is these quarterly civil registration indexes that are generally referred to as the GRO indexes (named after the General Register Office). There are various on and offline sources where you can begin to search the GRO indexes for England and Wales – from regional indexes produced by local register services or genealogical groups, to nationwide indexes through commercial bodies. (*See also* 'Civil registration indexes'.)

Civil registration certificates: Events were recorded on certificates – one copy retained by the registrar, the other given to whoever was supplying the information. Aside from any certificates that might survive in your family archive, the data should exist in two places – the original records held at the local level, and the copies held centrally.

Once you do have a match in the GRO indexes you can order a copy of the certificate from the GRO (gro.gov.uk) or the local register office relevant to the certificate.

Even if you don't manage to find an index reference number in FreeBMD or any other source, you can still request a copy online provided you have sufficient information to identify the entry. You will need to supply the date of event, if you have it. If not you enter 01/01/YYYY and staff search the specified year and one year either side. Ordering full certificates with or without GRO index reference supplied costs £9.25 – although without takes longer.

Civil registration dates: Civil registration began in England and Wales in 1837, Scotland in 1855 and Ireland in 1864.

Civil registration indexes: There are lots of places, on and offline, where you can search civil registration indexes, also known as the GRO indexes, including commercial/pay-per-view websites such as Ancestry, Findmypast and TheGenealogist.

Using FreeBMD.org.uk (a project to transcribe civil registration indexes of births, marriages and deaths for England and Wales), you enter your ancestor's surname, first name(s) and then choose to search birth, marriage or death indexes.

If it's a common name you may need to narrow your search by year of event, registration district, etc. Wildcards and multiple selections can also be used: such as selecting several registration districts simultaneously.

Returned search results include the following information: event, quarter and year; surname; first name(s); registration district; volume number; page number. In addition, you will notice that the website also offers the ability, in many case, to see scanned images of the original index pages.

In general, the more parameters you specify the more precise the results will be, but remember that if you narrow results too far, and are using some piece of information that turns out to be incorrect, the more likely you are to miss the individual you are looking for. So a name that has been misspelt in the original records, or an incorrect birth date, could lead you to miss an entry.

Also, the quarter refers to the date the event was registered NOT the date it occurred. Births were frequently registered late – so make sure you look in the following quarter(s) after the actual birth date. Also take care specifying the district or county – especially if you are researching a densely populated, urban area.

The GRO only started adding data like date of birth, mother's maiden name and spouse name later in the creation of the index. So searching for information by a mother's maiden name will not return any records prior to September 1911.

Civil registration, Ireland: Although registration of Protestant marriages began in 1845, country wide registration was not extensive in Ireland until 1864. As with England and Wales, the new registration districts were based on the boundaries of the existing Poor Law unions.

For all of Ireland, the General Register Office in Roscommon has records of births, deaths (both 1864–1921) and marriages (1845–1921), and for the Republic of Ireland from 1921 to present. For Northern Ireland (the counties of Antrim, Armagh, Derry, Down, Fermanagh and Tyrone only) the General Register Office for Northern Ireland has records of births, deaths (both 1864 onwards), adoptions (1931 onwards) and marriages (1845 for non-Roman Catholic marriages, all marriages from 1864).

You can order a photocopy of an entry in any register from the General Register Office or purchase an official certificate via certificates. ie. You can also access some civil registration data free or on a pay-as-you-go/subscription basis via Ancestry, Findmypast, rootsireland.ie, familysearch.org or irishgenealogy.ie.

Civil registration quarters:

March quarter: registrations in January, February and March.

June quarter: registrations in April, May and June.

September quarter: registrations in July, August and September.

December quarter: registrations in October, November and December.

The quarter refers to the date the event was registered not the date it occurred. Births in particular were often registered late. Someone born at the end of September, for example, may well appear in the December quarter.

Civil registration, Scotland: The system started later than in England and Wales, but the records are slightly more detailed. Registers were kept in Scotland from 1 January 1855.

Alongside what might be termed the usual information, Scottish birth registers also recorded place and time of birth, parents' names (including maiden name), father's occupation, name of informant and relationship to child, and date and place of marriage. At launch even more details were included: in 1855 there was information on siblings and the ages and birthplaces of both parents, as well as their usual residence and date and place of their marriage (although such details were soon dropped). Marriages included the date and place of marriage, name and occupation of both fathers, the name and maiden name of both mothers. Finally, death certificates included spouse's name, parents' names, occupations and whether they were deceased, cause of death, duration of last illness, doctor's name and details of the informant.

Civil Registration indexes for Scotland are available on a pay-per-view basis via ScotlandsPeople (scotlandspeople.gov.uk). These include scans of microfiche copies of the original register pages. Although remember that birth records less than 100 years old, marriage records less than 75 years old and death records less than 50 years old are deemed 'modern day records' and so you will need to order an 'extract' copy (£12 per extract).

Civil War: The English Civil War was a near decade-long struggle between Parliamentarians and Royalists over England's government between 1642 and 1651. A national system of civil registration was introduced which led to fewer entries being recorded in parish registers. In addition, the war disrupted the probate process as Parliament abolished ecclesiastical courts in 1653 (restored in 1661). Wills proved during this period are filed at the PCC.

CLACKMANNANSHIRE:

Clackmannanshire Archives (clacksweb.org.uk/culture/archives/)

Central Scotland FHS (csfhs.org.uk)

Clandestine marriages: Records of Clandestine Marriages and Baptisms in the Fleet Prison, King's Bench Prison, the Mint and the May Fair Chapel ranging from 1667–*c.* 1777 are held at TNA (in RG 7). Almost 900,000 unlicensed marriages from the Clandestine Marriage and Baptism Registers are available via Ancestry, and indexes can also be found via www.BMDregisters.co.uk/www.thegenealogist.co.uk. Mark Herber, author of the excellent reference work *Ancestral Trails* (The History Press, 2005), has also produced volumes of transcriptions of clandestine marriages, which are also available on CD.

Clangers: A traditional nickname for people from Bedfordshire, derived from the local pasty like dish, comprising a suet crust pastry with savoury filling at one end, sweet at the other.

Clarendon Code: This comprised a series of four Acts passed between 1661 and 1665 that further reduced the powers of Nonconformists. For example, the 1661 Corporation Act barred Nonconformists and Catholics from official posts – unless they took the sacrament of holy communion at an Anglican service.

Clergymen: In genealogical circles clergy generally refers to clergy who operated in Christian denominations, including the Anglican and Roman Catholic churches. When researching individual clergy some useful libraries and resources include Lambeth Palace Library's (lambethpalacelibrary.org) Church of England collection and the Church of England Record Centre. There's also the Clergy of the Church of England Database (theclergydatabase.org.uk) and Crockford's Clerical Directory (www.crockford.org.uk). The Catholic FHS (catholicfhs.co.uk) has some useful advice for researching Catholic ministers.

Useful websites
Cause Papers Database (hrionline.ac.uk/causepapers/)
Clergy of the Church of England Database (theclergydatabase.org.uk)
CCEd launched in 1999 and draws on data from over fifty archives in England and Wales. It brings together biographical data of clergymen between 1540 and 1835, as well as information on dioceses, lists of bishops and locations where clergy served.
Crockford's Clerical Directory (www.crockford.org.uk)

Clerks of the peace: In charge of keeping records at the quarter sessions.

Clinical Notes (www.clinicalnotes.ac.uk): Searchable database of medical case notes dating back to the seventeenth century.

Cloth lapper: Cleaned cotton before the sheets were fed into carding machines.

Clubmen: Bands of vigilantes who would protect their farms, crops and livestock from plundering armies during the English Civil War.

Coal Mining History Resource Centre (cmhrc.co.uk): Has the National Database of Mining Deaths dating back to the 1600s.

Coastguard officers: The Coastguard was formed in 1822 by the amalgamation of three anti-smuggling services: the Revenue Cruisers, Riding Officers and Preventive Water Guard. You can browse and download Coastguard establishment books and registers (1816–1947) for free via 'TNA's Discovery catalogue. According to the TNA research guide on the subject, after 1856 'the duties of the Coastguard were defending the coast, providing a reserve for the RN, and preventing smuggling'.

Coastguard ranks: chief officer, boatman, chief boatman, permanent extraman, commissioned boatman, temporary extraman.

Coat of arms: Unique heraldic design on an 'escutcheon' (shield), tabard or surcoat. The common misconception is that a coat of arms is linked to a single surname. As the College of Arms FAQ stresses: 'There is no such thing as a "coat of arms for a surname". Many people of the same surname will often be entitled to completely different coats of arms, and many of that surname will be entitled to no coat of arms. Coats of arms belong to individuals. For any person to have a right to a coat of arms they must either have had it granted to them or be descended in the legitimate male line from a person to whom arms were granted or confirmed in the past.'

Cod placer: Someone who supervised the placing of pottery in kilns or ovens.

Codicil: A document that modifies or revokes all or part of a will.

Coffer: A strongbox or chest for holding valuables. The original sixteenth-century orders that clergy should begin keeping parish registers detailed that the records had to be stored in a 'sure coffer' with two locks.

Cognate: In law this noun is used to describe a blood relative on the mother's side.

Collage (collage.cityoflondon.gov.uk): Has more than 250,000 images of London and surrounding areas from the 1860s–1980s from collections at the LMA and the Guildhall Art Gallery.

College of Arms (college-of-arms.gov.uk): The College of Arms is the best place to familiarise yourself with the heritage, history and peculiarities of heraldry. Via Resources there's an FAQ section and the Roll of the Peerage, while from Services you can learn how to prove a right to arm, while the About Us section has details of records and collections held here.

Collier: This word was used to describe a miner, a ship for transporting coal and later a worker who produces charcoal.

Combination Act 1799: Effectively outlawed 'combining' (or unionising) to gain better working conditions. In 1824/25 Combination Acts were repealed, so trade unions were no longer illegal. There was also the Unlawful Oaths Act 1797, passed in response to the Spithead and Nore mutinies by sailors of the RN, which prohibited the swearing of secret oaths – this was the Act under which the Tolpuddle Martyrs would be tried.

Commissioned officer: A RN commissioned officer (as opposed to a warrant officer) was someone who became an officer by being awarded a royal commission, usually after passing an examination. Commissioned officers include admirals, commodores, captains, commanders and lieutenants. (*See also* 'Navy' for details of RN service records.)

Commonwealth War Graves Commission: Since 1917 the CWGC has cared for cemeteries and memorials in 154 countries. The CWGC's casualty database is the official record of the war dead, and a vital research tool for military historians and genealogists. The Commission was founded by Fabian Ware as the Imperial War Graves Commission, changing its name in 1960. Their most important work is maintaining the graves and memorials of the fallen, commemorated uniformly and equally, irrespective of rank or race. At the heart of the CWGC website is the database of 1.7 million men and women of the Commonwealth forces who died, and the 23,000 cemeteries, memorials and other locations worldwide where they are commemorated. You can filter results by regiment, service number, unit and rank. There are also collections of digitised documents relating to grave registration, exhumation, verification, headstones and more. The CWGC records details of the 67,000 Commonwealth civilians who died 'as a result of enemy action' in the Second World War. The In From the Cold project (infromthecold. org) focuses on tracking down records of individuals omitted from the register.

Companies: A company can be incorporated by Royal Charter, Act of Parliament or by registration with the Register of Companies. There's a NRS guide to the subject at nrscotland.gov.uk/research/guides/company-registration-records, and a more general guide to businesses at TNA (www. nationalarchives.gov.uk/help-with-your-research/research-guides/

businesses/). TNA has Companies Registration Office records in series BT (1844–1980) with information about the registration and dissolution of companies. Similarly, NRS holds registers which can be consulted in the Historical Search Room and are included in the catalogue.

Compton Census: A census taken in 1676 to determine religious affiliation, although sadly no individual names are recorded. It is named after Bishop of London Henry Compton.

Confectioners: The Borthwick Institute in York holds business archives that are particularly strong in relation to confectioners. The Rowntree Mackintosh (1862–1969) and Terry's (1767–2005) archives reflect York's central contribution to the confectionery trade. They contain a wide variety of records including minutes, accounts, market research reports, production papers, staff records, photographs and impressive advertising material, providing valuable insights into all aspects of business activity.

Conisbrough Manor, Lives and Livelihoods (hrionline.ac.uk/conisbrough/): Gives a fascinating insight into life for the community that surrounded a country manor.

ConnectedHistories (connectedhistories.org): Vast hub, funded by the Joint Information Systems Committee which gives access to various digital repositories of British history sources from between 1500 and 1900. It's designed as a single federated search that allows searching of names, places and dates within the likes of digital library British History Online (including the Victoria County History), the Proceedings of Old Bailey Online, London Lives, Convict Transportation Registers Database, the Clergy of the Church of England Database and the Charles Booth Archive. Many of these resources are free. Some, such as British Newspapers 1600–1900, are subscription-based.

Consanguinity: Blood relationship.

Conscientious Objectors: People who for reasons of conscience objected to serving in the armed forces. During the First World War there were roughly 16,000 men who were officially recorded as Conscientious Objectors (COs). Remember, this figure would not include those who were declared unfit for service or who worked in reserved occupations. As the refusal to bear arms is central to Quaker beliefs, you may find references to Quakers in the records of Conscientious Objectors, held by TNA. There's a fascinating article by Margaret Brooks on the subject via the IWM website (at www.iwm.org.uk/history/conscientious-objectors-in-their-own-words). She writes: 'The number of COs may appear small compared with the six million men who served, but the impact of these men on public opinion and on future governments was to be profound.'

Records that do survive are often at local record offices, but TNA has nominal lists of appeals (1939–62) in LAB 45 which is searchable via the Discovery catalogue. You can also search case papers from the Middlesex Appeal Tribunal (1916–18), and NAS has similar records for Midlothian.

Contumacy: Refusal to obey a court order or summons.

Conventicle Act: An Act of 1662 which tightened the laws restricting Nonconformist worship. Now it was illegal for Catholics or Nonconformists to worship even within private houses where more than four outsiders were present.

Convicts to Australia (members.iinet.net.au/~perthdps/convicts/): Website with lots of advice about researching records of convicts transported to Australia, as well as transcribed lists of the First, Second and Third Fleets.

Co-Operative Archive (www.archive.coop): The National Co-operative Archive is based in Manchester. The website has lots of material that you can browse online including records of Co-Operative societies, the women's guild, the Co-Operative Union, periodicals and more. You can also find out more about the associated Rochdale Pioneers Museum (www.rochdalepioneersmuseum.coop).

Coram, Thomas: Pioneering philanthropist who created the London Foundling Hospital for abandoned children – the foundation stone was laid in 1742. It is said to be the world's first incorporated charity.

Cordwainer: A shoemaker. The Worshipful Company of Cordwainers (cordwainers.org) is one of the oldest livery companies in the City of London, with roots back to 1272.

Corn Laws: These placed restrictions and tariffs on imported grain, designed to keep prices high to favour domestic farmers. The Anti-Corn Law League was formed in 1838 and the Corn Laws repealed in 1846.

CORNWALL:
Cornwall Record Office (cornwall.gov.uk/community-and-living/records-archives-and-cornish-studies/)

The county's archives include parish and Methodist registers, and more than 65,000 probate records dating back to the sixteenth century. Bodmin Gaol registers contain the names of thousands of nineteenth-century individuals, along with information on their crimes, physical descriptions and behaviour.

Cornwall FHS (cornwallfhs.com)

Coroner's inquest: If your ancestor died in unexplained circumstances there may have been a coroner's inquest. Up to 1752 coroners handed records to assize judges (which were eventually transferred to TNA). But inquests held between from 1860 were filed through the quarter sessions – meaning those that survive will usually be at local archives. Other important potential sources of information are local and national newspapers, which tended to run reports into unexpected, suspicious or newsworthy deaths. Indeed, the newspaper report of an inquest may be the only record that survives.

PRONI looks after coroners' records from 1872–1997, and 6,206 files/papers relating to inquests are now referenced via the online Name Search (www.proni.gov.uk/index/search_the_archives/proninames/coroners__inquest__papers_-_whats_available.htm). The database entries contain name, address, date of death and date of inquest of the deceased. The actual papers themselves record much more information such as the name of the coroner, circumstances of death and names of jurors. London Lives has this page on Coroners' Inquests into Suspicious Deaths (londonlives.org/static/IC.jsp), where you can freely explore digital images and transcriptions from around 5,000 eighteenth-century inquests from the City of London, Middlesex and Westminster. In Scotland the equivalent to coroner's inquests are the Fatal Accident Inquiries, which were processed through the sheriff courts. There's a useful guide available via NRS (nrscotland.gov.uk/research/guides/fatal-accident-inquiry-records).

Other websites include Salisbury Inquests (salisburyinquests.wordpress.com), Hertfordshire Coroners' Inquests (hertsdirect.org/services/leisculture/heritage1/hals/famhist/coroner/) and the Sussex Record Society site gives free access to Notes of Post Mortem Inquisitions Taken In Sussex 1485 and 1649 (sussexrecordsociety.org). Finally there's TNA's guide at: nationalarchives.gov.uk/records/looking-for-person/coroners-inquests.htm.

Cottager: Another name for a rural labourer.

Cotter: The Scottish term for a peasant farmer.

Cotton Factory Times: This newspaper was, in the words of Alan Fowler and Terry Wyke (lancashirecottoncartoons.com), the public voice of the principal Lancashire cotton trade unions – the Spinners, the Weavers and the Cardroom operatives. It was first printed in 1885 as a weekly newspaper and ran until 1937. You can find out about places where the journal survives (such as Manchester University's Special Collections and the Tameside Local Studies Library) via TNA's Discovery. Also at lancashirecottoncartoons.com you can view cartoons featured in the newspaper drawn by Sam Litton.

Cotton Famine: The Lancashire Cotton Famine of the 1860s was caused by the blockade of ports during the American Civil War – which disrupted the flow of cotton to Lancashire leading to mass unemployment as mills closed down. Archives in the cotton districts may have material relating to the support given to those thrown out of work.

County archives: Network of institutions that generally look after county, borough, town, parish and other local government records, parish chest material, electoral registers, tax records, photographic collections, local newspapers, records of institutions such as hospitals and schools, court material, records of individuals, families and charities. They will normally offer banks of microfilm/fiche readers and lines of computers, usually offering free online access to commercial websites such as Ancestry and sometimes to internal digital finding aids. Alongside these 'usual' sources, there will be collections unique to the area such as local business records or collections relating to individuals. You can find archives from across all of the UK using TNA's Discovery (discovery.nationalarchives. gov.uk/find-an-archive). For information about the different regional archives that can be found across Scotland, try the Scottish Archive Network (www.scan.org.uk).

County Asylums Act 1808: Established a network of county level institutions to care for people with mental health problems (although many counties failed).

County councils: Created by the Local Government Act 1888. They took over many administrative functions that had previously been overseen by quarter and petty sessions.

Court of the Lord Lyon (lyon-court.com): Heraldic authority for Scotland, dealing with Scottish heraldry and coats of arms.

Court of Probate: On 12 January 1858, the Court of Probate was established in London to prove all wills throughout England and Wales. (*See also* 'Wills'.)

Court of Wards and Liveries: Dealt with matters of land ownership and inheritance where the deceased person was a tenant in chief of the Crown or the heir to the estate was under age (21 for a boy, 14 for a girl). TNA's guide notes: 'This was a financial institution responsible for collecting feudal dues [and] practical and legal matters relating to the Crown's right of wardship and livery.' The Crown had the right to the income generated by the majority of the estate until the heir reached adulthood. The Court administered the estate and made arrangements for the care and marriage of the young heirs. Wardships were usually sold by the Crown to the next of kin or the highest bidder, or given to individuals as a reward for services. (The most useful set of records can be found in TNA series WARD 9.)

Court records: When delving into court material it is important to find out in which court a trial was heard: police or magistrates' court, quarter sessions or assizes, or Church courts. Generally, TNA has records of the assizes and higher courts, while records of quarter sessions/petty sessions will be at local archives. (There are various TNA guides to court collections. For Criminal trials in the assize courts 1559–1971, for example, go to nationalarchives.gov.uk/help-with-your-research/research-guides/criminal-trials-assize-courts-1559-1971/.)

NLW has its Crime & Punishment Database (www.llgc.org.uk/sesiwn_fawr/index_s.htm), where you can search gaol files of the Court of Great Sessions in Wales from 1730 until its abolition in 1830. The Court could try all types of crimes, from petty thefts to high treason.

NRS's Court & Legal Records guide (nrscotland.gov.uk/research/research-guides/court-and-legal-records) has information on each category of court material – from the A–Z list you can also find guides to Court of Session Records and Crime and Criminals.

Some other interesting online resources include the Cause Papers Database, drawn from the Diocese of York collection (hrionline.ac.uk/causepapers/), which has details of cases heard between 1300 and 1858 in York's Church courts. Similarly, London Lives (londonlives.org) has court records from the City of London, Middlesex and Westminster Sessions.

Cousin: A first cousin is someone who shares the same set of grandparents as you – the children of your aunts or uncles. A second cousin is someone who shares a set of great-grandparents with you (but not grandparents). A third cousin is someone who shares a set of great-great-grandparents as you. A fourth cousin …

Crest: Another common heraldic misconception is that the word 'crest' describes a whole coat of arms. In fact it is the 'specific part of a full achievement of arms: the three-dimensional object placed on top of the helm', see: www.college-of-arms.gov.uk/resources/faqs.

Crew List Index Project (crewlist.org.uk): The Crew List Index Project has gathered a huge database of crew lists held in various archives. It is confined to merchant seafarers on British registered ships for the years 1861–1913 and the name index is also available via Findmypast.

Crew lists or agreements: These formed a contract between a seafarer and employer, recording rank, length of contract and wages. Each agreement lists all members of the crew, with address, pay and dates. This includes officers, seamen, engineering and victualling staff.

Crew Lists of the British Merchant Navy (1915crewlists.rmg.co.uk/): Volunteer led collaboration between TNA and the National Maritime Museum to transcribe all the surviving Merchant Navy crew lists from 1915. These records are of international significance as there are no records for individual merchant seafarers from the period. Approximately 39,000 crew lists featuring over 750,000 names have been photographed and then transcribed by volunteers.

Crime and punishment: Police, court and prison records, and local and national newspapers may all contain traces of black sheep in the family. Where the record survives depends on when the crime occurred, the severity of the crime and the court that heard the case. The Ludlow Borough Collection, for example, has cases heard at Ludlow Castle, and includes a seventeenth-century case of bribery in which the criminal was forced to stand in the pillory in Ludlow market. While Bedfordshire and Luton Archives has Bedfordshire Quarter Sessions Rolls and county gaol records, which detail offence, when tried, marks and previous convictions, often with a photograph of each prisoner.

TNA has research guides to convict transportation, prisoners, civil litigants and bankrupts/debtors. You should also try the Crime and Criminals guide at NRS (nrscotland.gov.uk), and it's allied guide to court records.

One notable resource from the various commercially available datasets is Findmypast's Crime, Prisons & Punishment collection – the third and final tranche of which was launched in the summer of 2016. Spanning the years 1770–1935, it contains more than 5.5 million records digitised from TNA collections. Material includes records from series PCOM 4, featuring details of female felons across England and Wales who were released on licence, including their previous convictions and any misconduct stemming from their time in prison. It also includes records from TNA series HO 26 and HO 27 (also available on Ancestry) providing information about criminal trials across England and Wales.

One particularly interesting free resource is the Proceedings of the Old Bailey (www.oldbaileyonline.org), where you can explore transcribed details of 197,745 criminal trials held at London's central criminal court from 1674–1913. You can search by various fields including punishment, filtering results by imprisonment, hard labour, house of correction, Newgate or penal servitude.

Useful websites

Ancestry (search.ancestry.co.uk/search/db.aspx?dbid=1590)

Ancestry has digitised TNA criminal registers (1791–1892) for England and Wales, which provide dates and locations of court hearings. Other collections include a Bedfordshire Gaol Index (1770–1882), Debtors' Prison Registers (1734–1862), Birmingham prisoners (1880–1913), Prison Hulk Registers (1802–49) and the Australian Transportation series.

Blacksheep Ancestors (blacksheepancestors.com/uk/prisons.shtml)

Website with a range of resources including prison and asylum records from the US and prison records from the UK.

British Newspaper Archive (britishnewspaperarchive.co.uk)

Newspaper reports may represent the only surviving account of some cases and inquests.

Convict Transportation Registers Database (www.slq.qld.gov.au/resources/family-history/convicts)

Findmypast (search.findmypast.co.uk/search-world-records/crime-prisons-and-punishment)

Has a database drawn from TNA material, including the Home Office calendar of prisoners (1869–1929).

NRS (nrscotland.gov.uk/research/research-guides/court-and-legal-records)

Plymouth Prisoners (plymouth.gov.uk/cemeterymortuaryworkhouse)

PRONI (www.proni.gov.uk/index/search_the_archives/proninames/coroners __inquest__papers_-_whats_available.htm)

Scottish Prison Service (sps.gov.uk/Prisons/prisons.aspx)

Victorian Crime & Punishment (vcp.e2bn.org/justice/page11365-debtors. html)

Crimean War: A military conflict between Russian forces and an alliance of Britain, France, Sardinia and the Ottoman Empire (1853–6). It is principally remembered for the Charge of the Light Brigade and the pioneering work of Florence Nightingale. In his 1973 historical novel *Flashman at the Charge*, George MacDonald Fraser places his cowardly anti-hero in the thick of the action at Balaclava, enduring the notable actions of the Thin Red Line, the Charge of the Heavy Brigade and the Charge of the Light Brigade. The TNA research guide (www.nationalarchives.gov.uk/help-with-your-research/research-guides/crimean-war-records/) details some of the main resources held here. It also links to more detailed guides to British Army operations up to 1913, for example.

Crimean War Research Society: cwrs.russianwar.co.uk

Crockford's Clerical Directory: Directory first published in 1858. There's an online version at www.crockford.org.uk, although here you can only explore data going back to 1968. Older editions, from between 1868 and 1932, are currently available via Ancestry. As noted here: 'A typical biographical entry for a clergyman may include where they studied, when they obtained a degree and a work history of where and when they performed their clerical duties. As with many professional directories those listed may have been actively working, or may have retired. Biographies would only be removed when a person died.'

Crofter: A tenant or worker of a small-holding known as a croft.

Cromwell, Thomas: English lawyer and statesman who served as chief minister to King Henry VIII from 1532–40. In 1538 he ordered that parish registers be kept in England and Wales.

Crop returns: These were printed forms originally sent out by the government in 1801 for local clergymen to compile. They noted facts such as acreages and yield devoted to specific crops, and, from 1866, also included summaries of livestock.

The information fed to the gathering clergy should not always be trusted. As W.G. Hoskins notes in *Leicestershire Crop Returns of 1801*: 'The parson was not perhaps the best man to get this information. Farmers suspected that his enquires had something to do with tithes. Or if not that, they saw the shadow of new taxation behind the bland smile of the vicar and the innocent eye of the curate.'

There was space for comments, often far more interesting than the statistics. In Leicestershire alone we can learn that Barlestone is 'bad turnip land', and that bread eaten at Kegworth 'is a mixture of wheat and barley, in proportions varying according to the respective means' of inhabitants. While the community minded farmers at Sapcote refused to sell their good barley to some encroaching maltsters, preferring to sell it to local inhabitants at half the price so they could make bread.

The original documents are held at TNA (HO 67).

Cropper: In agriculture, a person who cultivates or harvests a crop. In textiles, someone who uses shears to remove imperfections from cloth. You'll often hear people explain how the phrase 'to come a cropper' derives from a slew of accidents involving the Minerva printing press sold by H.S. Cropper from 1867 – and popularly known as 'the Cropper'. But it's not true. Most agree that it comes from horses falling 'neck and crop'.

Cross & Cockade International: The First World War Aviation Historical Society (www.crossandcockade.com) website has interesting sections on the history of St Omer aerodrome, first used by the RFC in September 1914, eventually becoming the largest air base on the Western Front.

Culver: A keeper of pigeons.

CUMBRIA:
Cumbria Archives Service (cumbria.gov.uk/archives/)

Has an online catalogue that allows you to trawl material from the four archive branch offices in Barrow, Carlisle, Kendal and Whitehaven. The county is known for boot and shoe manufactures, the woollen industry which flourished particularly around Kendal, and Cumbria was also a major source of bobbins for the cotton industry. Meanwhile, the west coast ports of Workington, Whitehaven and Maryport were shipbuilding centres for the clippers of the West Indian trade. They also have the records of Vickers shipbuilders.

Cumbria FHS (cumbriafhs.com)
Has useful guides detailing the survival and whereabouts of Cumbrian records.

Curia regis: A Latin term meaning 'royal council' or 'king's court'.

Curtilage: Legal term for the land immediately surrounding a house, including associated buildings/structures.

Customs officers: TNA holds 'most surviving records of English Customs officers, as well as many from Ireland. As there is no single index of people or places that can be used to find service records your search for information may require some patience.' Therefore, research will be much easier if you know the county where a family member was posted and the dates of service. You can browse TNA's Discovery catalogue for various CUST record series which include pension records, staff lists and quarterly bills of salaries.

Cymru 1914 (cymru1914.org): Centenary mass-digitisation of sources relating to the First World War in Wales, drawn from libraries, special collections and archives.

Cyndi's List (cyndislist.com): Leading genealogical links site launched by Cyndi Howells in 1996, which provides categorised and cross-referenced lists of websites.

Cynefin (cynefin.archiveswales.org.uk): Crowdsourcing project to digitise approximately 1,200 tithe maps and transcribe the 30,000 pages of associated data held at NLW.

D

Dade registers: These garner a lot of attention considering they only benefit a relatively small, lucky band of genealogists. You'll find them at the Borthwick Institute, which holds parish records for the modern Archdeaconry of York. The Dade registers are a more rigorous and detailed form of record keeping, which was introduced by York clergyman William Dade from the early 1770s, before the practice was adopted across the diocese.

Full Dade baptism registers provide the child's name and seniority, father's name, abode, profession and descent (including the paternal grandparents' names and abode, the grandfather's occupation and details of the paternal great-grandfather), and the mother's name and descent (including the maternal grandfather's name, abode and occupation and the maternal grandmother's name and descent). Dade burial registers are also of particular interest as they include the age and cause of death.

Daguerreotypist: The photographer or person who worked with daguerreotypes – one of the earliest popular forms of photography. Invented by Louis-Jacques-Mandé Daguerre, daguerreotypes were printed on a silvered copper plate. They flourished during the 1850s and 1860s.

Dame schools: Small primary schools run by women – before the setting up of board schools.

Danelaw counties: Danelaw refers to parts of England where the 'laws of the Danes held sway'. The Danelaw counties are Yorkshire, Derbyshire, Leicestershire, Northamptonshire, Nottinghamshire, Rutland and Lincolnshire. These counties were divided into 'wapentakes' instead of hundreds.

Dating photographs: The first step when dating photographs is to pay attention to the type and format of the image. Metal daguerreotypes appeared in the late 1830s, gradually becoming more popular until the 1860s, when they were replaced by ambrotypes, printed on glass, ferrotypes (also called tintypes), printed on thin metal sheets, and the first paper and card prints, such as sepia albumen prints and *cartes de visite*, before portable cameras like the Brownie popularised low-cost photography. If you have studio portraits, the address of the local professional who took the image is often printed on the back, which can lead you to uncover where and when it was taken. Fashion and uniforms are also important clues – wedding dresses and formal attire can often help you date a photograph.

There are some tips about dating photographs, especially a *carte de visite* photograph, available through the Roger Vaughan Picture Library (www.cartes.freeuk.com/time/date.htm). Another useful site is www.

fashion-era.com. There's also *Tracing Your Ancestors Through Family Photographs* by Jayne Shrimpton (Pen & Sword, 2014).

Deacon: Ordained minister, ranked below the priest.

Dead Man's Penny: Popular slang for the Memorial Plaque – bronze plaques issued to the next of kin of all British and Empire service personnel killed during the First World War.

Deanery: A group of parishes forming a district within an archdeaconry, overseen by the dean.

Death certificates: Although not as genealogically useful as the birth and marriage certificates, death certificates still record name, date and place of death, date and place of birth – although before 1969 a death certificate only showed the age of deceased – along with occupation, address, cause of death and the name of the person who provided the information. There are lots of places to search for death registrations, but one example would be FamilySearch, which has the England and Wales Death Registration Index (1837–2007) courtesy of Findmypast. (*See also* 'Civil registration certificates'.)

Death or Estate Duty Wills: Starting in 1796, a tax or death duty was payable on estates with a certain value. Death Duty registers survive at TNA and are an important resource for researching middle-class families. Entries can show what happened to someone's estate after death, their worth, details of the deceased and executors, as well as details of estates, legacies, trustees, legatees, annuities and duty paid. They can also give the date of death, and information about the people who received bequests or who were the next of kin. The records are in series IR 26 and IR 27 at TNA. Records before 1811 are available online and Findmypast has digital copies of the registers.

Debrett's (debretts.com): Specialist publisher of *Debrett's Peerage & Baronetage*, founded by John Debrett in 1769.

Debtors and bankrupts: Charles Dickens' father John owned £40 10s. shillings to local baker John Kerr when he was arrested in February 1824 and held in the infamous Marshalsea Debtors' Prison, which would go on to form the backdrop of much of *Little Dorrit*, while Fleet debtors' prison was described in *The Pickwick Papers*.

The first thing to understand is the difference between 'debtors' and 'bankrupts'. Bankrupts were traders who were legally declared insolvent because of inability to pay debts. In practice many bankrupts were not traders, and bankruptcy was later extended to include craftsmen. Meanwhile, debtors, or more correctly 'insolvent debtors', were individuals unable to pay their debts – and they could not apply for bankruptcy until after 1861. The way the state or local courts dealt with debtors and declared bankrupts changed over time – but the key is that it wasn't illegal to be a bankrupt, but it was illegal to be an insolvent debtor.

You can search the *Gazette* website (www.thegazette.co.uk), the official public record, for the printed notices of bankrupts. These were published by officials to inform creditors about their proceedings. In general newspapers can be an excellent source of information as notices of bankruptcy were printed in the national press, often repeated in local newspapers, and there were specialist titles such as *Perry's Bankrupt & Insolvent Gazette*.

Ancestry has a collection of Debtors' Prison Registers (search.ancestry. co.uk/search/group/uk_debtors_prison) digitised from documents held at TNA. These detail over 700,000 criminals detained in Marshalsea, King's Bench and Fleet Prisons between 1734 and 1862. You can also read about debtors via Victorian Crime & Punishment (vcp.e2bn.org/justice/page11365-debtors.html).

Deceased Online (deceasedonline.com): Leading commercial specialists, providing data from graveyards and municipal cemeteries across the UK. You can search by country, region, county, burial authority or crematorium free of charge, but you will need to register and pay to see digital scans of cremation/burial registers, photographs of graves and memorials, and cemetery maps.

Deeds: Deeds record the transfer of property. The information contained in the documents varies a great deal, but can reveal the conditions in which your ancestor lived, and of course are especially enlightening if the building in question no longer exists. Most deeds should include a fairly detailed description of the type and location of the property, sometimes with an accompanying plan. It should tell you who owns and/or lives in the property, and may also list previous owners and tenants, sometimes going back many years. The occupations of individuals are often recorded, sometimes with former places of residence. If property has been passed down, deeds can give information about many generations of the same family. Finally, if the land was left in a will, then the deed should record the date of death, will and probate.

However, these are problematic sources as collections of deeds are often unindexed. The deeds held at Tower Hamlets Local History Library and Archives in London are popular with researchers precisely because they have been indexed in great detail – the index of owners and tenants includes upwards of 25,000 names.

Another example comes from West Yorkshire, where the Archive Service's Wakefield Headquarters looks after the West Riding Registry of Deeds (www.archives.wyjs.org.uk/archives-wrrd.asp). If your ancestors owned or leased land in the West Riding, it is possible that they will appear in the Deeds Registry, which holds indexes to 14 million deeds registered between 1704 and 1970. The registered copies are summaries of the full original deed and will tell you the names of all the parties and the location of the land involved. A similar Middlesex Deeds Register is at LMA.

DENBIGHSHIRE:
Denbighshire Archives (www.denbighshire.gov.uk/en/resident/libraries-and-archives/denbighshire-archives/denbighshire-archives.aspx)
Clwyd FHS (clwydfhs.org.uk)

Denization: Entitling foreign nationals in the UK certain rights – but not the full rights of British citizenship. You can find out more via TNA's Alien Arrivals research guide (nationalarchives.gov.uk). The last known denization was granted in 1873.

Denizens: Records of immigration often refer to individuals as denizens, permanent residents who were not officially a legal citizen of the parent country.

Deodand: An obsolete term in law for an object forfeited or 'given to God' because it has caused a person's death.

Deponent: Legal term for a person who makes a written or spoken deposition under oath.

DERBYSHIRE:
Derbyshire Record Office (derbyshire.gov.uk/leisure/record_office/)
Some unusual items from the collections include a death mask from the Derbyshire General Infirmary, the earliest known recipe for Bakewell

pudding (written by Clara Palmer-Morewood at Alfreton Hall in 1837) and a fifteenth-century record of courtly dances, known as 'John Banys's Dance Notebook'. It has wills proved at the Derby Probate Registry between 1858 and 1928. There are records of the Ripley engineers Butterley Company, which was heavily involved in the expansion of the railway industry, and contracted for the huge arched roof at St Pancras Station.

Derbyshire FHS (dfhs.org.uk)

Chesterfield & District FHS (cadfhs.org.uk)

Design Collection (design.nationalarchives.gov.uk): Subscription-based portfolio of heritage designs held by TNA (1839–1991).

DEVON:

Devon Archives & Local Studies Service (devon.gov.uk/record_office.htm)

Has records of the Diocese of Exeter, including records of the Bishops of Exeter dating back to the thirteenth century, along with tithe maps for parishes throughout the county. It also holds one of the finest collections of civic records in Britain – the Exeter City Archives, which document the history of the city back to the eleventh century.

Devon FHS (devonfhs.org.uk)

Diamond War Memorial Project (diamondwarmemorial.com): The Diamond War Memorial in the centre of Derry, County Londonderry, Northern Ireland, was erected in 1927. This online project uncovered approximately 400 names that had been overlooked from the memorial. The database includes the full list – those already commemorated and those individuals who were omitted – and there's all sorts of further information, sometimes including family and connections.

Dictionary of National Biography: Known as the *DNB*, this work of reference contains thousands of biographies of notable figures and was first published in 1885, with new editions appearing every decade. Now known as the *Oxford DNB* (oxforddnb.com), the online subscribers' edition boasts biographies of 55,000 people 'who shaped the history of Britain and beyond'. Most local libraries subscribe so you can search for free.

Dictionary of Scottish Architects (scottisharchitects.org.uk): Database providing biographical information about architects known to have worked in Scotland between 1660 and 1980. There's also the 1954 book *A Biographical Dictionary of British architects, 1600–1840* by Howard Colvin.

Diggers: Seventeenth-century Protestant radicals who believed in establishing small communities supported by farming on common land.

Diocese: The diocese or bishopric is an ecclesiastical division above the parish. So parishes would be grouped together under the jurisdiction of a bishop. Some dioceses include one or more archdeaconries administered by an archdeacon. It's important to discover the official diocesan record office for the area. Shropshire Archives, for example, is not the diocesan record office for the county. Historic Shropshire is covered by the Diocese of Lichfield, Hereford and St Asaph. So while Shropshire has parish registers for the county, other diocesan records such as bishops' transcripts, marriage licences and pre-1858 wills are split between the diocesan collections at Herefordshire Archive and Records Centre, Lichfield Record Office and the NLW. The Diocese of Hereford covers 356 parishes including some in South Shropshire. The Lichfield Diocese covers the northern half of Shropshire, and the St Asaph Diocese covers the north-west parishes of Shropshire, and so relevant material may be found at NLW.

Discussion groups: Genuki maintains a database of mailing lists and newsgroups at www.genuki.org.uk/indexes/MailingLists.html. There are also vast networks of message boards (Ancestry's are at boards.ancestry. com) which include specialised topics such as surnames, occupations or areas.

Divorce: Before 1858 a full divorce required a private Act of Parliament – only available to people with means. The Matrimonial Causes Act 1857 enabled couples to obtain a divorce through civil proceedings, while the Herbert Divorce Act 1937 introduced new grounds for divorce that included desertion, cruelty and incurable insanity. No petition for divorce could be made in the first three years of marriage, except under exceptional circumstances. The Legal Assistance Plan of 1949 gave legal aid to the less well-off, which caused an increase in the number of divorces. The Divorce Reform Act (1969) made the irretrievable breakdown of a marriage the sole ground necessary for a divorce.

You can browse lists of private Acts of Parliament to check for divorces before 1858 (www.legislation.gov.uk/changes/chron-tables/private). Divorce case files can contain petitions, certificates and copies of the decrees nisi and absolute. The decrees absolute give the names of the petitioner, respondent and (if applicable) co-respondent and the date and place of the marriage.

The Supreme Court and some county courts grant divorces in England and Wales and records of divorce petitions can be searched at TNA. Bigamous marriages were often tried in assize courts. In Scotland, from 1560, the Court of Session, and then from 1563 the Commissary Court of Edinburgh, oversaw divorce cases. From 1830 the Court of Session had jurisdiction in cases of marriage, divorce and bastardy. From around 1835 (up to 1984) individual divorce cases are listed in the NRS catalogue (nrscotland.gov.uk/research/catalogues-and-indexes). Meanwhile, in Northern Ireland divorces were (rarely) granted at the Royal Courts of Justice in Belfast or at county court.

Divorce case files: TNA's English and Welsh divorce case files (1858–1914) can be accessed through Ancestry. You can also search for divorce cases via Discovery. You can also request copies of a decree absolute in England and Wales (from 1858 to present), via gov.uk/copy-decree-absolute-final-order.

Dr Williams's Library (dwlib.co.uk): 'The pre-eminent research library of English Protestant nonconformity'. Although they hold records about clergymen, they have no records of individual Nonconformists. (*See also* 'Nonconformists'.)

Doctors: *See* 'Hospitals' and 'Medicine'.

Documenting Ireland: Parliament, People & Migration (dippam.ac.uk): Family of websites documenting Irish migration since the eighteenth century.

Doffer: Someone who removes full 'doffs' – bobbins or spindles holding spun cotton or wool – from a spinning machine.

Domesday Book: A survey of much of England and Wales completed in 1086 by order of King William the Conqueror with the aim of determining the value of land and taxes owed. This can be viewed as a county by county stocktake, and loosely functions as an early census (you can explore names recorded in the survey via opendomesday.org/name/). There's also the dated Domesday Book Online (domesdaybook.co.uk).

Domestic service: An occupation that is surprisingly difficult to research considering the fact that there were more than 1 million female servants recorded in the 1851 census alone. There is no centralised source of information about domestic service. There were some highly defined roles – from scullion (scullery maid), tweenie (maid who worked 'between the stairs') to 'necessary woman' (cleaner of chamber pots). Family or estate papers may be your best chance for finding out more about the life and work of a domestic servant.

Dorse: The back of a book or the reverse of a document – from which the word 'endorsement' derives.

DORSET:

Dorset History Centre (dorsetforyou.com/dorsethistorycentre)

The Centre looks after material for the entire county including the boroughs of Bournemouth and Poole. It also has material relating to many local industries such as Poole Pottery. There's also the sixteenth-century Peculiar Court archives of Wimborne Minster – the only complete records of their kind to have survived.

Dorset FHS (dorsetfhs.org.uk)

Somerset & Dorset FHS (sdfhs.org)

Doublet: A man's close-fitting padded jacket.

Dowager: A widow with a title/property derived from her late husband.

D'Oyly Carte Opera Company Archive (doylycarte.org.uk/archive): Information about the company archive which is now housed at the BL.

Dragoon: A mounted infantry soldier.

DUMFRIESSHIRE:

Dumfries & Galloway Libraries & Archives (www.dumgal.gov.uk/lia)

Dumfries & Galloway FHS (dgfhs.org.uk)

DUNBARTONSHIRE:

East Dunbartonshire Archives (www.edlc.co.uk/heritage/archives.aspx)

West Dunbartonshire Council Archives (west-dunbarton.gov.uk/libraries/archives-family-history/archives-collections/)

Glasgow & West of Scotland FHS (gwsfhs.org.uk)

DURHAM:

Durham County Record Office (durhamrecordoffice.org.uk)

Indexes to the Durham Miners' Association trade-union records and 34,500 indexed images from the archive's Durham Light Infantry collection.

Durham University Library (familyrecords.dur.ac.uk)

Holds important genealogical collections such as a catalogue to 150,000-plus probate records (1527–1857) from the Diocese of Durham. Others include bishops' transcripts, marriage licences, tithe records, estates and more.

Tyne & Wear Archives (twmuseums.org.uk/tyne-and-wear-archives.html)

Northumberland & Durham FHS (ndfhs.org.uk)

Cleveland, North Yorkshire & South Durham FHS (clevelandfhs.org.uk)

Durham Records Online (durhamrecordsonline.com)

Includes transcripts from Roman Catholic registers covering County Durham and Northumberland. Uses a credits system to charge for the material.

Durham Mining Museum (dmm.org.uk): Website includes colliery maps, a Who's Who, lists of engineers and transcribed documents.

E

E 179 Database (apps.nationalarchives.gov.uk/e179/): Contains descriptions of every document in series E 179 relating to both lay and clerical taxation in England and Wales (thirteenth century–1689).

East Anglian Film Archive: eafa.org.uk

East India Company: Played a vital role in British expansion and control overseas, employing thousands of traders, administrators, politicians, sailors and soldiers. It established the first British outpost in South Asia in 1619 at Surat. The BL looks after the East India Company archives as part of the India Office collection (indiafamily.bl.uk/ui/home.aspx), and through the BL partnership with Findmypast (findmypast.co.uk) some key resources are available online including BMD material and military/

naval pensions. Other digital resources include the East India Company Ships (eicships.info) database of ships and voyages of the East India Company's mercantile service, and there's lots of useful advice from the Families In British India Society (fibis.org).

East London Theatre Archive (www.elta-project.org): Database of East London theatre ephemera from the V&A, theatre archives and the University East London archives.

EAST LOTHIAN:
John Gray Centre (johngraycentre.org)
Home to East Lothian Council's archive and local history services. Collections include historic newspapers (there are some online indexes), OPRs, census material, MIs, valuation rolls, sasines and newspapers. The photograph and map collections can also be accessed through the online catalogue.
Lothians FHS (lothiansfhs.org)

Ecclesiastical courts: These date back to before the Reformation and existed alongside the network of criminal/civil courts. Until 1858 ecclesiastical or Church courts heard matters relating to wills as well as defamation, divorce, failure to attend church, drunkenness and other types of undesirable behaviour. (*See also* 'Bawdy courts' and 'Court records'.)

Ecclesiastical divisions: Church of England > Province (Canterbury and York) > Archdiocese/archbishopric > Diocese/bishopric > Deanery > Parish.

Edge tool maker: A specialist blacksmith who made specialist tools for other craftsmen.

EDINBURGH:
Edinburgh City Archives (www.edinburgh.gov.uk/info/20249/edinburgh_city_archives)
Lothian Lives (lothianlives.org.uk)

Education Act 1902: Saw county councils take over responsibility for education from school boards. This effectively ended the divide between schools run by school boards and the Church of England voluntary schools.

Education Archives, Institute of (www.ucl.ac.uk/ioe): Based at UCL, the Institute looks after collections relating to the Society of Teachers (which became the College of Preceptors, then the College of Teachers) established in 1846, which includes membership records.

Electoral district: Territorial subdivision for electing local Members of Parliament. It is also known as a constituency, riding, ward, division, electoral area or electorate.

Electoral registers: These list everyone at a particular address who is registered to vote. A surprising amount of information can be extracted from these, including the new surname of a married woman or the existence of other relatives staying with the family. Registers were not compiled during the First and Second World Wars. Some absent voters lists are available which give the names of soldiers in the armed forces along with their army service number. This can be an aid to further research in military records.

Findmypast has Somerset Electoral Registers covering the years 1832–1914, and the BL has a national collection of electoral registers from 1832 to the present day which are also due to appear on Findmypast. FamilySearch also has some unindexed collections of registers from London, Norfolk, Cheshire, West Glamorgan and Kent. Ancestry has Poll Books and Electoral Registers from London, Middlesex, Nottinghamshire, Dorset, Warwickshire, Birmingham and elsewhere. You can explore Dublin Electoral Lists at dublinheritage.ie/burgesses/index.php.

Ellis Island (libertyellisfoundation.org): Explore the vast database of 51 million-plus passenger records as well as the Immigrant Wall of Honor – a permanent exhibit of individual and family names.

Emigration: When researching migrants leaving these shores, the first fact to try to pin down is the name of the ship they sailed on, then the ports of departure and arrival (keep in mind that there are no official registers of departure). This is easier said than done, but there are lots of resources that can help. Both Findmypast and Ancestry, through partnership with TNA, have Outward passenger lists between 1890 and 1960 – these list migrants leaving both UK and Irish ports bound for America, Canada, India, New Zealand and Australia. Findmypast also has an Index to Register of Passport Applications (1851–1903).

Some other key resources at TNA include Correspondence and Entry books (1814–71), which can be explored via Discovery; Land and

Emigration Commission papers (1840–94), which include registers of births and deaths of emigrants at sea from 1854–69; and lists of ships chartered from 1847–75.

The next step is tracking any record of your ancestor's arrival in their new home. For migration to the US, for example, there is the likes of the Ellis Island Foundation, which grants access to vast databases of arriving migrants processed at the famous Ellis Island station (www. libertyellisfoundation.org).

The Families In British India Society (fibis.org) has an immense and very useful wiki, with all kinds of useful advice and data for tracing family members overseas. The Immigrant Ships Transcribers Guild (immigrantships.net) offers transcribed passenger lists that can be searched by port of arrival or departure. Another useful website is Documenting Ireland: Parliament, People & Migration at dippam.ac.uk. This includes Voices of Migration and Return and the Irish Emigration Database, based on roughly 33,000 documents.

Engineers: The records of heavy industry, engineering and manufacturing tend to survive in local record offices. There are also independent bodies, museums and libraries that look after potentially useful collections (although not always aimed at genealogists). These include the likes of the Institution of Structural Engineers' Library (istructe.org/resources-centre/library), the Institute of Mining Engineers (dmm.org.uk/mindex. htm), the Institution of Civil Engineers (www.ice.org.uk/about-us/our-history), whose application forms for all members who joined before 1930 are available through Ancestry, and the Institution of Mechanical Engineers (imeche.org/knowledge/library/archive). The latter includes a catalogue, an interesting archive blog and a virtual archive section. Incidentally, other engineer collections on Ancestry include electrical engineers (1871–1930), Civil and Mechanical Engineer Records (1820–1930) and Civil Engineer Photographs (1829–1923).

Useful websites
Ancestry (ancestry.co.uk/cs/uk/occupations-alta)

Institution of Civil Engineers (ice.org.uk/topics/historicalengineering/Archives)

Institution of Mechanical Engineers (imeche.org/knowledge/library/archive)

Tyne & Wear Archives (twmuseums.org.uk)
Home to an internationally recognised shipbuilding collection.

England's Immigrants Database (englandsimmigrants.com): An interesting resource for researching early recorded migration to England. It contains over 64,000 names of people known to have migrated between 1330 and 1550 – covering the Hundred Years War, the Black Death, the Wars of the Roses and the Reformation.

English language: The divisions are roughly as follows: Old English: 500–1100; Middle English: 1100–1500; Early Modern English: 1500–1800; Late Modern English: 1800 to date. The website www.medievalgenealogy. org.uk has some useful guidance for archaic terms and language.

Ensign: The lowest commissioned rank in an infantry regiment. The calvary equivalent was the cornet.

Entails: Until 1833 real property could be 'Entailed'. This specified how property would be inherited in the future. An entail prevented subsequent inheritors from bequeathing the property to anyone except the heirs specified in the original entail.

Entertainers: These are some useful websites for researching ancestors who worked as actors, musicians or as other performing artistes.

Author Lloyd (arthurlloyd.co.uk)

British Music Hall Society (britishmusichallsociety.com)

East London Theatre Archive (elta-project.org)

Footlight Notes (footlightnotes.tripod.com/index.html)

London Music Hall Database (royalholloway.ac.uk/drama/Music-hall/index.asp)

London Symphony Orchestra Archive (lso.co.uk/about-the-lso-archive)

National Fairground Archive (shef.ac.uk/nfa)

NLS (digital.nls.uk/playbills/)

Royal College of Music Library & Archive (rcm.ac.uk/library/contactus/archivesandrecords/)

Scottish Music Hall & Theatre Society (scottishmusichallsociety.webs.com)

Scottish Theatre Archive (gla.ac.uk/services/specialcollections/collectionsa-z/scottishtheatrearchive/)

Stage Archive (archive.thestage.co.uk)

Theatre Collection, University of Bristol (bris.ac.uk/theatrecollection/

Enumeration district: An enumeration district comprised an area of between 200 and 300 houses (assuming that the enumerator did not have to travel more than around 15 miles visiting each house). Large institutions whose residents numbered more than 100 people counted as its own enumeration district.

Enumerator: From 1841, every census saw a schedule completed by each household, which was then collected by the enumerator who copied the information into enumeration books. It is these books that form the basis of what is now available to explore on and offline.

Epitaph: Inscription on gravestone or monument.

Espousal: Archaic term for a marriage or engagement.

ESSEX:
Essex Record Office (essex.gov.uk/Libraries-Archives/Record-Office/Pages/Record-Office.aspx)

Looks after some fine early parish registers. A page from Chelmsford, dated May 1543, mixes baptisms, marriages and burials together in one sequence, with the note 'C' for christening, 'M' for marriage and 'O' ['obit'] for burials. Another interesting item is a register of mainly female weavers employed at Courtaulds' silk factory in Halstead (1830–84). There are also archive Access Points at Saffron Walden Library, Museum of Harlow, Colchester Library and Southend Central Library, where you can view microfiche copies of parish registers (as well as lots of other documents) alongside local history collections.

Essex Ancestors (seax.essexcc.gov.uk)

Essex Society for FH (esfh.org.uk)

East of London FHS (eolfhs.org.uk)

Waltham Forest FHS (wffhs.org.uk)

Essex Police Museum (essex.police.uk/museum/): You can purchase a complete record of service from the 1880s to present day, including officers who served in Colchester Borough Police (transferred to the Essex County Constabulary in 1947), Southend Borough Police (1914–69) and reserves and female auxiliaries from the Second World War.

Estate and family collections: Estate records can be helpful in researching not only the landed classes but also rural craftsmen, traders and agricultural labourers who lived or worked on the estate. More and more family collections have been catalogued, but detailed indexes and finding aids are still relatively rare. Remember, if a noble family from one area owned land or estates in another county, documents relating to these estates may well remain with the 'parent' archive – the county where they lived. TNA has guides to Estate & Manorial records, while the equivalent NRS guide (nrscotland.gov.uk/research/guides/estate-records) covers rent rolls, leases (tacks) and household accounts.

Useful websites

Arley Hall Archives 1750–90 (arleyhallarchives.co.uk)

Conisbrough Manor (hrionline.ac.uk/conisbrough/)

Estate & Manorial records guide (nationalarchives.gov.uk/records/looking-for-place/landedestates.htm)

Images of England (imagesofengland.org.uk)

National Trust Collections (nationaltrustcollections.org.uk)

Explore items from more than 200 National Trust property collections.

Photographic library of England's listed buildings.

Sutherland Collection (www.sutherlandcollection.org.uk)

Indexed website built around the Leveson-Gower family archive, Marquesses of Stafford and Dukes of Sutherland, which contains many thousands of names – employees, tenants, shopkeepers and suppliers, savers in the Trentham Savings Bank and workers on the building of Trentham Hall.

Estreats: Copies of court records.

European Film Gateway (europeanfilmgateway.eu): Access to hundreds of thousands of films preserved in European film archives, including the likes of IWM and Scottish Screen Archive.

Evacuees: The mass evacuation of Britain's cities at the start of the Second World War was code named Operation Pied Piper. It began on 1 September 1939, the same day that Germany marched into Poland, and it is estimated 1.5 million civilians were on the move within 3 days. During the 'Phoney War' period of the conflict, many returned, only to leave again. There was also a wave of evacuation in the summer of 1944 as a result of to the V1 and V2 flying bombs.

The Research Centre for Evacuee and War Child Studies (reading. ac.uk/merl/collections/Archives_A_to_Z/merl-D_EVAC.aspx) has memoirs and oral history interviews with children evacuated within the UK and those sent overseas. These include those sent by the Children's Overseas Reception Board – the government-sponsored organisation that evacuated 2,664 children.

Remember the 1939 Register (findmypast.co.uk/1939register), which records the 40 million-plus people in England and Wales, was taken on Friday, 29 September 1939 – just weeks after Operation Pied Piper. The house by house data was compiled by enumerators who took down everyone's name (including maiden names), date of birth, occupation and other details. You can access the full household transcript (although keep in mind that some records are officially closed) as well as a scan of the original register page.

Useful websites

BBC People's War (bbc.co.uk/history/ww2peopleswar/)

British Evacuees Association (evacuees.org.uk)

Evacuees research (nationalarchives.gov.uk/help-with-your-research/ research-guides/evacuees/)

Second World War Experience Centre (war-experience.org)

Wartime Memories Project (wartimememories.co.uk/evacuation.html)

Excise men: If you're researching an excise man, you need to attempt to find out the county in which they were posted and the dates of service. You can browse Customs Board minute books (1734–1885) via TNA's Discovery, which may record transfers, suspensions, resignations and pensions for officers.

Executor/executrix: A person or persons named in a will responsible for carrying out the document's instructions.

Eyer: The maker of needle eyes.

F

Factory Acts: The Cotton Mills and Factories Act 1819 decreed that no children under the age of 9 were to be employed. It also limited working hours for children aged under 16. The 1833 Factory Act placed more regulation on working hours and forced factory owners to provide 2 hours of schooling each day for children.

Falling sickness: An archaic term for epilepsy.

Families In British India Society (fibis.org): Society for genealogists researching ancestors who lived in British India, founded in 1998. Parts of FIBIS website are only open to members, but there's useful freely available material here too including a searchable database of more than 1,250,000 names. There's also a very useful wiki at wiki.fibis.org/index. php/Main_Page.

Family History Partnership (www.thefamilyhistorypartnership.com): Specialist genealogical publishers.

Family history society websites: Even if you don't intend to join the genealogical society covering the area that interests you, it is worthwhile visiting society links pages. It takes effort to appear up the Google search list and many a useful index or transcription might not appear in your first hundred pages of search results. So it's good to try the society links pages as this often leads to local bodies, members' websites and other tools that may contain all sorts of valuable and esoteric sources that would otherwise be missed.

Family reconstruction: Collecting all available data relating to a particular surname, within a certain area.

FamilySearch (familysearch.org): The website of the LDS Church, the genealogical portal through which users can search billions of records, including the likes of the IGI, and thousands of individual collections from all over the word. It offers free family tree-building tools, as well as a growing research wiki (familysearch.org/wiki/en) which makes a good starting point for the newbie. It has a complete free index and transcription of the 1881 census and free indexes to the remaining released censuses (1841–1911) for England and Wales – although you will need to consult a subscription website to see the full transcription online. There are free research forms (familysearch.org/learn/wiki/en/Research_Forms) which include pedigree charts and research forms in various formats – helpful for gathering together what you think you know about your family at the start of your research.

The site also administers all kinds of crowdsourcing drives such as FamilySearch Worldwide Indexing, which saw many thousands of volunteers indexing more than 10 million records over a 72-hour event in July 2016.

Farthing: A low value coin (quarter of an old penny) withdrawn from circulation in 1961.

Fatal Accident Inquiries: The Scottish equivalent to a coroner's inquest. These inquiries were processed through the sheriff courts. The NRS guide to the subject is at www.nrscotland.gov.uk/research/guides/fatal-accident-inquiry-records.

Fealty: Oath of allegiance to the Crown or lord sworn by feudal tenant or vassal.

Fear-nothing maker/Fear-naught maker: A weaver of thick, heavy cloth used for overcoats.

Federation of Family History Societies (ffhs.org.uk): International organisation which represents and supports over 220 family history societies and genealogical groups mainly in England and Wales. The website has many useful links and a directory of its member societies.

Fee farm: An annual rent payable to the king by chartered boroughs. Confusingly the word 'fee' here refers to the landholding, while the word 'farm' is an archaic word for rent.

Feet of fines: Useful for tracing land ownership up until 1833, the feet of fines were court copies of agreements over property. Traditionally the document would have the agreement written out three times, with wavy lines between them, which would then be cut along the wavy lines, with two parts given to the buyer and seller, the third filed with the court. Archaic terms you may come across within these records include: querent (purchaser), deforciant (seller) and concord (final agreement). Feet of fines are at TNA series CP 25/2, filed by county, regnal year and legal term. Welsh feet of fines are at the NLW.

Fetterlock: A D-shaped type of padlock often incorporated into heraldic designs.

Fettler: A cleaner and sharpener of machinery in woollen mills.

FIFE:

Fife Archive Centre (fifedirect.org.uk/archives)

Fife FHS (fifefhs.org)

Tay Valley FHS (tayvalleyfhs.org.uk)

Fighter Command: One of the commands of the RAF, which, like Bomber Command, was formed in 1936 and formerly disbanded in 1968 (although in November 1943 it was split into the Air Defence of Great Britain and the RAF Second Tactical Air Force).

Final beneficiaries: In probate these are the 'also rans' – the other individuals named in wills, such as friends of the family or servants. Their relationship to the testator/testatrix is normally recorded in the will.

Find a society: The Federation of Family History Societies website lists member groups (ffhs.org.uk) covering all of the UK, some overseas societies, a handful of one-name studies groups and 'other'. The Scottish Association of FHS's list of members is at safhs.org.uk/members.asp.

Find an archive: TNA's Discovery catalogue (discovery.nationalarchives. gov.uk) now incorporates what was known as 'Archon', an online tool to help you find archives in England, Northern Ireland, Scotland and Wales. You can search by area or by name of the archive.

Fire insurance: A little-known but potentially useful source. You may find your local archive holds indexed fire-insurance registers, which may help identify where a particular person lived as well as giving an indication of the type of property insured. Although it is possible that the person taking out the policy was not actually the resident. Many archives have detailed fire-insurance maps and plans produced by the firm Charles E. Goad Ltd (and the BL holds a comprehensive collection). The Sun Fire Office was founded in London in April 1710 and is now the oldest existing insurance company in the world. There's an index to policy holders at www.londonlives.org/static/AHDSFIR.jsp.

First beneficiary: The first person mentioned in a will, and normally the main beneficiary – usually a husband or wife.

First Fruits and Tenths: A form of taxes placed on clergy. The Court of First Fruits and Tenths (established in 1540) and the proceedings of the court relate to the collection of these dues. You can find details of the records of the Office of First Fruit and Tenths at discovery.nationalarchives.gov. uk/details/r/C568.

First Statute of Highways: An Act of Parliament passed in 1555 which placed the burden of maintenance of highways on individual parishes. Every parish had to elect two people to act as 'Surveyor of Highways' within the parish boundaries, who then had to inspect the roads and organise repairs.

Fish-fag: An alternate name for a fishwife or fishlass – a woman who sells fish.

Fishermen: Maritime collections that might contain records of fishermen or whalers tend to survive in disparate archives and museums – meaning catalogues such as TNA's Discovery and Archives Wales may come in useful. If you know the port or area where your ancestor worked then you can go straight to the appropriate archive – Hull History Centre, for example, looks after material relating to trawlermen, fishermen and shipping companies. Indeed, via the catalogue you can search 25,500 fishing crew lists for fishing vessels operating out of Hull between 1884 and 1914 (hullhistorycentre.org.uk). Meanwhile, North East Lincolnshire Archives (www.nelincs.gov.uk/libraries-and-archives/) has 38,000 Grimsby crew lists and registers of fishing apprentices. You could also try the Scottish Fisheries Museum at scotfishmuseum.org. (*See also* 'Whalers'.)

Fleet Air Arm Archive (fleetairarmarchive.net): Includes a Debt of Honour Register, POW database and biographies of decorated officers.

Fleet Registers: Clandestine marriages were normally performed outside the home parishes of the bride and groom, and originally took place in prison chapels. They were conducted by an ordained clergyman, but without banns or licence. The most notorious venue was around Fleet Prison in London – known as the Liberty of the Fleet. The resulting Fleet Registers record more than 200,000 marriages that took place in the Fleet Liberty, and the likes of the King's Bench Prison, between 1667 and 1754 – the year Hardwicke's Marriage Act made it a legal requirement to be married in the Church of England. According to TNA's guide, it has been estimated that in the 1740s nearly 15 per cent of all marriages in England were celebrated in the Fleet. Because they were clandestine, you always need to treat the information contained within the Fleet Registers with caution. The originals are found in record series RG 7. You can search marriages and baptisms in the Fleet Prison, King's Bench Prison, the Mint and the May Fair Chapel via BMD Registers (bmdregisters.co.uk). There are also indexes available through FamilySearch.

Fleshewer: An archaic term for a slaughter-man or butcher. In Scottish trade directories you will come across the term 'fleshers'.

Flickr.com: Popular with archives and museums who upload all sorts of highlights from their photographic collections, often alongside documents and interesting ephemera. You can search the website by people or groups, and you can follow accounts that interest you. NLI's photostream, for example, can be explored at flickr.com/photos/nlireland/.

FLINTSHIRE:
Flintshire Record Office (flintshire.gov.uk/en/LeisureAndTourism/Records-and-Archives/Home.aspx)
Looks after records of the former Clwyd County Council, as well as hospitals, schools, churches and chapels, clubs, societies, Poor Law unions, records from the quarter sessions and magistrates' courts alongside microfilm copies of parish registers and census material.
Clwyd FHS (clwydfhs.org.uk)

Flycoachman: One-horse carriage driver.

Flying men: An obscure eighteenth-century craze for rope dancing, walking and sliding on the walls of buildings. A Pocklington burial entry from April 1733, held by the Borthwick Institute in York, records the death of Flying Man Thomas Pelling, killed by jumping against the Battlement of the Choir.

Flying stationer: Francis Grose's *The Dictionary of the Vulgar Tongue* defined the flying stationer as 'ballad-singers and hawkers of penny histories'.

Football: Some important museums and bodies for researchers interested in soccer include the National Football Museum (nationalfootballmuseum. com), Scottish Football Museum (scottishfootballmuseum.org.uk), the Football Club History Database (fchd.info) and the Association of Football Statisticians (11v11.co.uk).

Forced migration: Criminals were originally transported to North America from 1615, and later to Australia. Men, women and children were sentenced to transportation, with crimes ranging from petty theft to highway robbery. The American Revolution meant that from 1776 convicts had to be sent elsewhere and the first convict ships, known as the First Fleet, arrived in Australia in January 1788. The flow of convicted transportees slowed from the 1830s and ceased altogether when the system was abolished in 1868. (For more information *see* 'Australia, migration to'.)

Forces War Records (forces-war-records.co.uk): Specialist subscription site with material you can explore by conflict/era. Has data relating to the Royal Naval College in Dartmouth, Royal Marines and RN Officers' Campaign Medal Rolls (1914–20), and a database of RN/Royal Marines recipients of the 1914 Star Medal. Datasets include RAF Formations List 1918, Fighter Command Losses 1940 and Aviators Certificates 1905–26. Also has First World War hospital records and Second World War War Office casualty lists.

Forums: Online forums can be an excellent platform for posing queries or finding out more. Reading queries and replies from other researchers can often resolve your own problem before you even have to ask it. Rootschat is one of the largest UK forums (rootschat.com), with thriving specialist sections. Others include British Genealogy (british-genealogy. com), Family Tree DNA (forums.familytreedna.com/) and the Great War Forum (1914-1918.invisionzone.com/forums/). For a list of forums and mailing lists go to www.genuki.org.uk/indexes/MailingLists.html.

Foundation for Medieval Genealogy: fmg.ac

Foundlings: Abandoned infants. (*See also* 'Workhouses'.)

FRANCE:
Archives Nationales (www.archives-nationales.culture.gouv.fr)

Archives de France, Généalogie (www.archivesdefrance.culture.gouv.fr/ chercher/genealogie/)

Archives départementales (archives.ille-et-vilaine.fr)

France Genealogy, FamilySearch wiki (familysearch.org/wiki/en/France_ Genealogy)

FreeBMD (FreeBMD.org.uk): An important project to transcribe civil registration indexes of births, marriages and deaths for England and

Wales, and to provide free access to the transcribed records. It is part of the Free UK Genealogy family of websites, which also provide transcribed data from parish registers and census material. The transcribing is carried out by teams of volunteers and contains index information for the period 1837–1983. While incomplete, you can explore a regional breakdown of progress by event and year. Early in September 2015 the site contained 249,116,513 'distinct records', and by June 2016 this figure had risen to 254,833,607.

Freeholders' records: PRONI has digitised and indexed its Freeholders' records – lists of freeholders arranged on a county basis. They comprise the registers (those who had registered to vote) and poll books (lists of voters and the candidates for whom they voted). You can search here: apps.proni.gov.uk/freeholders/Default.aspx.

Freemen: Freedom of a corporate city allowed the individual to practise a trade and to vote in elections. Most apprenticeships lasted seven years, after which the person would be admitted to the guild and attain the status of a freeman. The names of freemen were recorded in annual Freeman Rolls – those for the City of London are available at Ancestry.

FreeREG (freereg.org.uk): Volunteer-led drive to provide free online searches of transcribed parish and Nonconformist registers.

Free UK Genealogy (freeukgenealogy.org.uk): Parent website of the above FreeBMD project, its sister initiatives freereg.org.uk (free baptism, marriage and burial records from parish/Nonconformist registers) and freecen.org.uk (free census information from the years 1841, 1851, 1861, 1871 and 1891).

French Hospital: Huguenots were French Protestants who fled persecution during the seventeenth and eighteenth centuries. The French Hospital, founded in London in 1718, would become the seat of the Huguenot Society, which began to record the history of Huguenot migration.

Friendly societies: Any kind of mutual association providing sickness benefits, assurance or pensions to a group of people. Records will normally reside at county record offices.

Friends House (friendshouse.co.uk): Located at 173 Euston Road in London, this is the central offices and archives of British Quakers.

Frith, Francis: A pioneering English photographer born in Chesterfield in 1822 who documented villages and towns across the UK. You can find out more and browse some of his photographs via commercial archive francisfrith.com.

Fundholders: This term often crops up in the occupation field. It indicates that the person supported themselves through their own savings/ investments.

Funerary monuments: Any physical structure that commemorates a deceased person or group of people, usually carved with epitaphs or funerary art. Structures include simple headstones, to cenotaphs, mortuary enclosures, effigies or memorial crosses.

Further reading: Adolph, Anthony. *Collins Tracing Your Family History*, Collins, 2008

Annal, David and Audrey Collins. *Birth, Marriage and Death Records: A Guide for Family Historians*, Pen & Sword, 2012

Barratt, Nick. *Who Do You Think You Are? Encyclopedia of Genealogy*, Harper, 2008

Brooks, Richard and Matthew Little. *Tracing Your Royal Marine Ancestors*, Pen & Sword, 2008

Chater, Kathy. *How to Trace Your Family Tree*, Lorenz Books, 2013

Chater, Kathy. *Tracing Your Huguenot Ancestors*, Pen & Sword, 2012

Christian, Peter and David Annal. *Census: The Family Historian's Guide*, A&C Black, 2014

Clarke, Tristram. *Tracing Your Scottish Ancestors*, Birlinn, 2012

Cox, J. Charles. *Parish Registers of England*, Methuen, 1910

Emm, Adele. *Tracing Your Trade and Craftsmen Ancestors: A Guide for Family Historians*, Pen & Sword, 2015

Evans, Beryl. *Tracing Your Welsh Ancestors*, Pen & Sword, 2015

Few, Janet. *The Family Historian's Enquire Within*, new edn, Family History Partnership, 2014

Fowler, Simon. *Family History: Digging Deeper*, The History Press, 2012

Fowler, Simon. *Tracing Your Army Ancestors*, Pen & Sword, 2013

Fowler, Simon. *Tracing Your First World War Ancestors: A Guide for Family Historians*, Pen & Sword, 2013

Fowler, Simon. *Tracing Your Naval Ancestors*, Pen & Sword, 2011

Gibson, Jeremy and Else Churchill. *Probate Jurisdictions: Where to Look for Wills*, Federation of Family History Societies, 2002

Grannum, Karen and Nigel Taylor. *Wills and Probate Records: A Guide for Family Historians*, The National Archives, 2009

Grenham, John. *Tracing Your Irish Ancestors*, Gill & Macmillan, 2012

Hawkings, David T. *Railway Ancestors*, Sutton Publishing, 2008

Herber, Mark. *Ancestral Trails: The Complete Guide to British Genealogy and Family History*, The History Press, new edn 2005

Heritage, Celia. *Tracing Your Ancestors Through Death Records: A Guide for Family Historians*, Pen & Sword, 2015

Hey, David. *The Oxford Companion to Family and Local History*, new edn, Oxford University Press, 2010

Higginbotham, Peter. *A Grim Almanac of the Workhouse*, The History Press, 2013

Higginbotham, Peter. *The Workhouse Encyclopedia*, The History Press, repr. 2014

Humphery-Smith, Cecil R. *The Phillimore Atlas and Index of Parish Registers*, Phillimore, 2002

Jolly, Emma. *Tracing Your Ancestors Using the Census*, Pen & Sword, 2013

Kershaw, Roger. *Migration Records: A Guide for Family Historians*, The National Archives, 2009

Lumas, Susan and Terrick Fitzhugh. *The Dictionary of Genealogy*, A&C Black, 1998

Osborn, Helen. *Genealogy: Essential Research Methods*, Robert Hale, 2012

Probert, Rebecca. *Divorced, Bigamist, Bereaved?*, Takeaway Publishing, 2015

Probert, Rebecca. *Marriage Law for Genealogists*, Takeaway Publishing, 2012

Raymond, Stuart A. *Tracing Your Ancestors' Parish Records*, Pen & Sword, 2015

Spencer, William. *Medals: the Researcher's Guide*, The National Archives, 2008

Tate, William Edward. *The Parish Chest*, Phillimore, 2011

Tomaselli, Philip. *Air Force Lives*, Pen & Sword, 2013

Tonks, David. *My Ancestor Was A Coalminer*, Society of Genealogists, 2014

Waddell, Dan. *Who Do You Think You Are?: The Genealogy Handbook*, BBC Books, 2014

Waters, Colin. *A Dictionary of Old Trades, Titles and Occupations*, Countryside Books, 2002

G

Gale Digital Collections (gdc.gale.com): Home to vast databases of primary and secondary sources, including newspapers. However subscriptions are only available to institutions, not individuals – so you will need to ask whether your library or archive has an institutional subscription.

Garda Síochána Historical Society (policehistory.com): Society dedicated to the history of Ireland's national police force.

Garter Principal King of Arms: Senior officer of arms of the College of Arms, the heraldic authority with jurisdiction over England, Wales and Northern Ireland.

Gazette, the (thegazette.co.uk): Offers access to the official public record – the London, Edinburgh and Belfast gazettes. The site has been given a makeover in recent years which enables you to search for specific content such as wills and probate, insolvency and civilian awards. Officers' commissions, promotions and appointments were also published in the *London Gazette*. You can search and browse military awards from MiDs to the Victoria Cross. Initially the *London Gazette* contained news stories, including accounts of the Great Fire of London, and classified advertising – most famously King Charles II inserted a small ad seeking the return of a lost dog.

GEDCOM: Acronym for 'Genealogical Data Communication' – a dedicated file format for exchanging genealogical data between software developed by the LDS Church.

TheGenealogist (thegenealogist.co.uk): Commercial family history website run by Genealogy Supplies – part of the S&N Group. It has England and Wales censuses (1841–1911), BMD indexes for England and

Wales back to 1837, parish records, Nonconformist material, directories, military collections, including war memorial records, and tithe maps.

General Register Office: The General Register Office for England and Wales was founded in 1836 by the Births and Deaths Registration Act. Registration started the following year. You can find out more about the GRO's Certificate Ordering Service via: gro.gov.uk/gro/content/certificates/. There are various places where you can access the GRO indexes and once you have the GRO reference number you can order a certificate. You can order a copy without this number, but it will take longer.

GENFair (GENFair.co.uk): Online genealogical shop with thousands of parish records in various formats.

Gentleman's Magazine: Founded in 1731, and printed for almost 200 years, the magazine has long been popular with genealogists and other researchers as it often included lists of births, marriages and deaths, as well as bankruptcies and military promotions and awards. You can explore many volumes via archive.org.

Genuki (genuki.org.uk): GENealogy of the UK and Ireland is a longstanding genealogical web portal run as a charitable trust. Genuki was a trailblazing family history website, with a wiki-style design, that provided a virtual reference library, focused on researchers with UK and Irish roots. Most begin by exploring by the county that interests them, and while many GENUKI pages contain actual transcribed or indexed information, normally it links to external sources of information – with an emphasis on primary sources.

George Cross: The civilian equivalent to the VC, instituted at the height of the Blitz on 24 September 1940 by King George VI. It is awarded to civilians and military personnel showing conspicuous bravery under circumstances of extreme danger – but not in the face of the enemy. The first female winner of the George Cross was Odette Sansom Hallowes, an intelligence officer who endured interrogation and imprisonment during the war. She was also the first woman to be awarded both the George Cross and to be appointed a *Chevalier de la Légion d'honneur*.

German Lutheran Church: Tower Hamlets Local History Library and Archives has material relating to St George's German Lutheran Church (records of which have been comprehensively indexed by the Anglo-

German Family History Society). This is the oldest surviving German Lutheran church in the UK, founded in 1762 by Dietrich Beckman, a wealthy sugar refiner. This area became home to many sugar refiners of German descent and at its height there were an estimated 16,000 German Lutherans in Whitechapel.

Getting started:

1. Start from what you know. Fix and confirm dates of birth, marriage and death, then work backwards.
2. Be wary of erroneous assumptions. Even seemingly obvious things such as a close relative's date of birth or first name can be incorrect – people frequently lie about their age, and people are often known by nicknames or middle names. Simple incorrect assumptions such as a wrong first name or birth date may well mean you're unable to find an individual within civil registration records – likely to be your first port of call.
3. Draw up a rough family tree, with all the names of members of your immediate family, then spreading out to the next generation. Write down all the birth, marriage and death dates that you think you know. (colour coding is useful to keep in mind the information that you're certain about, the facts that you need to double check and the more vague assumptions.)
4. Go to your own family archive and gather together any documentary or printed evidence that you have – certificates, diaries, letters, military records, photographs, etc. Don't discount anything – you never know what might prove relevant further down the line. An unnamed photograph of three austere-looking Victorian ladies might seem useless, but suppose the reverse says 'printed in the Isle of Man'? Could this be evidence of a Manx root in your family tree? Or just a favourite holiday destination?
5. Start interviewing family members. I suggest using some kind of audio recorder (your phone may do the job) as well as taking notes. Alternatively, interview by email – although face to face is preferable because of the unexpected gems that a natural conversation given time can turn up.
6. Check who's been here before. In other words see if anyone else has been researching the same branch of the tree.
7. Write everything down. You need to write not only the information but where it came from – the source. This includes printed, state-created sources and half-remembered 'facts' muttered by a misty-eyed uncle.

8. Record your dead-ends. Despite best intentions, at some point it's likely you will find yourself trawling a website, database or archive, only to be overcome by a creeping dread, a sinking feeling of familiarity. It's not déjà vu. You have been here before. And you're about to come to the same conclusion – that the answer you seek isn't here. Everyone goes through this at some point, and the only way to guard against it is to be methodical – and record both the searches that lead to fruitful information, and those that lead nowhere.

9. Don't try to do too much – start out by focusing on one branch of the family. And if possible, choose the branch with the more unusual surname. A rare surname makes work easier.

10. Focus on identifying where an individual person was living as most records generated about a person will be associated with a place.

There are lots of useful online guides. The best for beginners are: FamilySearch (familysearch.org/ask/gettingstarted); Genuki (genuki.org.uk/gs/); the SoG (sog.org.uk/learn/help-getting-started-with-genealogy/); Cyndi's List (cyndislist.com/free-stuff/getting-started/) and Scotlands People (following Help & Resources > Getting Started).

Gibbeting: Hanging of executed criminals on public display to deter others.

Gilbert's Act: This is the Relief of the Poor Act 1782 proposed by Thomas Gilbert. It aimed to organise poor relief with workhouses for the elderly, sick and orphaned – not able-bodied poor. It led to a number of Gilbert Unions – proto-Poor Law unions.

Girdler: Maker of leather belts and girdles.

GLAMORGAN:
Glamorgan Archives (glamarchives.gov.uk)

West Glamorgan Archive Service (swansea.gov.uk/westglamorgan archives)

Has shipping registers and crew agreements for the port of Swansea. One underused source here are the records of Swansea Hebrew Congregation which apart from minutes, correspondence and financial records contain marriage registers (1840–1986), burial records (1877–1991), photographs and miscellaneous items.

Glamorgan FHS (glamfhs.org.uk)

GLASGOW:

Mitchell Library (glasgowfamilyhistory.org.uk)

Family History resources at the Mitchell Library are made up of records from the Glasgow City Archives, the Registrar's Service, the library's Special Collections and the NHS Greater Glasgow and Clyde Archives. The site details burial records, BMD data, census material and there's a complete A–Z of research guides.

Glasgow & West of Scotland FHS (gwsfhs.org.uk)

Glebe: Area of land within a parish specifically for use by the parish priest.

GLOUCESTERSHIRE:

Gloucestershire Archives (gloucestershire.gov.uk/archives/article/107703/Archives-Homepage)

One highlight from this archive's website and catalogue is its Genealogical Database, which includes names in pre-1834 parish overseers' records – including settlement, apprenticeship and bastardy records. It also includes names from canal boat inspections, gaol registers, inventories, Nonconformist material and wills. (See: ww3.gloucestershire.gov.uk/genealogy/Search.aspx.) Gloucestershire Archives' wills date from 1540, when the diocese of Gloucester was created, to 1941, along with many probate inventories. Remember that since Gloucester is a Reformation diocese, most of the pre-1540 wills for the county are held in the Worcestershire Record Office – most of the county was in the Diocese of Worcester. Some parts of the Forest of Dean fell within the Diocese of Hereford, so the wills for this area are in the Herefordshire Archives.

Gloucestershire FHS (gfhs.org.uk)

Bristol & Avon FHS (bafhs.org.uk)

Forest of Dean FHT (forest-of-dean.net)

Godparent: Someone who formally presents a child at the baptism and also promises to take responsibility for their religious education.

Gordon Highlanders Museum (gordonhighlanders.com): This Aberdeen Museum looks after a postcard sent home from a Japanese POW camp by Lance Corporal Bill Angus, 2nd Battalion The Gordon Highlanders. The entire 2nd Battalion was captured when Singapore fell to Japanese forces in February 1942. Bill was wounded by shrapnel during the battle and sent to work on the 'Death Railway' in Thailand. In addition, it holds the VC awarded to Captain Sir Ernest Beachcroft Beckwith Towse for two separate actions in the Boer War, the second of which blinded him.

GraveMatters (gravematters.org.uk): Gives advice about the best approach to transcribing MIs.

Gravestone Photographic Resource (gravestonephotos.com): An international directory of grave monuments, launched in 1998 and still growing. Coverage is dominated by England and Scotland.

Gray's Inn Archives (graysinn.org.uk/history/archives): Archival highlights include records of the meetings of the Inn's governing body back to the mid-sixteenth century and registers of admissions. (*See also* 'Lawyers'.)

Great Depression of British Agriculture: A depression from *c*. 1873–*c*. 1896 caused by a dramatic fall in grain prices due to increased cheaper competition from the newly cultivated American prairies.

Great Ejection: The Great Ejection created the concept of Nonconformity – the Protestant Christian who did not 'conform'. This followed the new Act of Uniformity 1662, when more than 2,000 clergymen refused to take the oath to abide by new forms of prayers and sacraments and were ejected from their positions by the Church of England.

Great Hunger: The Great Hunger or Great Famine was a period of mass starvation and emigration in Ireland from 1845–52.

Great War Archive (europeana1914-1918.eu): Collects ephemera, artefacts and stories relating to the First World War.

Great War Forum (1914-1918.invisionzone.com): Specialist First World War forum created by Chris Baker, the man behind the Long, Long, Trail website (1914-1918.net).

Green Howards Regimental Museum (greenhowards.org.uk): This North Yorkshire museum has regimental enlistment registers, detailing campaigns, wounds, medals and rewards, as well as rank, 'character' and cause of discharge. And they have the 19th Foot regimental register of marriages and baptisms (1839–50), and a Yorkshire Regiment Punishment Book (1878–89), showing the record of a private sentenced to imprisonment and hard labour for fraudulent enlistment.

Greensmith: Metalworker specialising in copper and copper alloys.

Griffith's Valuation: This was a tax survey of Ireland which saw the detailed valuation of every taxable piece of agricultural or built property, published county by county between the years 1847 and 1864. The valuation books recorded the names of occupiers and landowners, and the amount and value of the property held. Today the Valuation forms an important census substitute resource and is accessible online via a number of platforms including askaboutireland.ie.

GRO Certificate Ordering Service: gro.gov.uk

GRO index tips: Before you start, it's potentially useful to have the names of closest family, as well as the individual you seek.

Knowing the district where the event is likely to have taken place is also very useful.

If you can't find someone, try multiple spelling variations and keep shifting back and forward through the quarters – registrations often took place after the event.

You can order copies of birth, death or marriage certificates from the GRO website (gov.uk/order-copy-birth-death-marriage-certificate). You will need to register and certificates currently cost £9.25.

For Scottish research you can order official via nrscotland.gov.uk/registration/how-to-order-an-official-extract-from-the-registers, and for events in Northern Ireland from www.nidirect.gov.uk/index/do-it-online/government-citizens-and-rights-online/order-a-birth-adoption-death-marriage-or-civil-partnership-certificate.htm.

GRO indexes: Named after the government department the General Register Office, the GRO indexes are quarterly indexes to all births, marriages and deaths.

Groat: A silver coin worth 4 pence in use between 1351 and 1662.

Guardian: The New Poor Law took away the responsibility of poor relief from the parish, and placed it in the lap of newly created Boards of Guardians. Each Board of Guardians had jurisdiction over the poor relief of a new Poor Law union.

Guardian & Observer Archive: theguardian.com/gnm-archive

Guild of One-Name Studies (one-name.org): Umbrella group for one-name study societies, based at the SoG.

Guildhall Library: Now managed by the LMA, some important collections here include the Stock Exchange archives, Lloyd's of London archives (although Lloyd's Captain's Registers are at LMA) and livery company archives.

Guinness Archive (www.guinness-storehouse.com/en/archives): Preserves records of some 20,000 employees of the St James's Gate Brewery in Dublin going back to 1759.

Gunmakers: Stan Cook's Gunmakers & Allied Trades Index (www.genuki.org.uk/big/Gunmakers.html) was first established in 1982. The Index features more than 9,000 surnames, with references to around 25,000 individual workers. It documents people working in the UK gun trade drawing on various sources that include parish records, directories, the census, the Board of Ordnance and patent listings. It also includes 'a complete index of the London Gunmakers' Company apprentice records from 1656 to 1902'. There's an index of gunmakers listed in the Inland Revenue Apprentice Stamp Duty records, 1710–75, and indexes to individuals in census records.

GWENT: *See* 'Monmouthshire'.

H

Habeas corpus: 'Habeas corpus (ad subjiciendum)' – 'You may have the body (subject to examination)'. A writ that requires a person detained by the authorities to be brought before a court of law so that the legality of the detention may be examined.

Hair Powder Tax: The Duty on Hair Powder Act 1795 meant that users had to pay for an annual certificate costing 1 guinea. The use of hair powder gradually dwindled and the tax was repealed in 1869. Few records of this tax survive.

HAMPSHIRE:
Hampshire Archives & Local Studies (hants.gov.uk/archives)
Looks after records of the Winchester Diocese, meaning that alongside parish records it has a county wide index to marriage allegations (1689–1837), bishops' transcripts and, via the catalogue, a searchable

vast collection of wills and inventories from 1398–1941 – that's about 110,000 wills by name. Also looks after the Winchester City Archives, the Wessex Film and Sound Archive and a series of pipe rolls used extensively by medieval historians.

Hampshire Genealogical Society (hgs-online.org.uk)

Portsmouth History Centre & Records Office (portsmouth.gov.uk/ext/events-parks-and-whats-on/libraries/portsmouth-history-centre-and-records-office.aspx)

Southampton Archives (southampton.gov.uk/archives)

(*See also* 'Isle of Wight'.)

Hansard: The traditional name of the official record and transcripts of parliamentary debates in Britain. The name comes from the first official printer to parliament Thomas Curson Hansard (1776–1833).

Hardwicke's Marriage Act: As it was tradition, rather than law, that marriages should take place in the home parish, clandestine marriages were commonplace. This was curtailed by Hardwicke's Marriage Act, passed in 1754. It also laid down a single, compulsory form of entry for marriages – which means lots of parishes acquired a new marriage register in 1754. After the Act marriage registers included signatures of brides, grooms and witnesses, and the clear distinction was made between marriages by banns and by licence. (*See also* 'Clandestine marriages'.)

Harleian Society (harleian.org.uk): Society founded in 1869 to publish heraldic visitations in England and Wales.

Hart of oak: Hampshire's county archives has the parish registers of Winchester St Cross with St Faith. In 1791 chaplain William Rawlins describes the burial of Richard Hart in a coffin made by himself out of a Spanish man-of-war he bought while working as a carpenter at Portsmouth Dock twenty years before. He kept the coffin in his room, drawn up on pulleys to the ceiling, and decorated the side with skulls and images of funeral processions. He writes: 'Brother Hart was a man of a very singular turn and disposition.'

Health and Morals of Apprentices Act 1802: Also known as the 'Factory Act', this imposed new standards of cleanliness and ventilation in cotton mills and factories. Apprentices also had to be provided with some education and attend a weekly religious service. This piece of legislation, introduced by Sir Robert Peel, was in response to a fever outbreak at one of his cotton mills.

Hearth Tax: A useful source for researching householders in the late seventeenth century. This tax was introduced in England and Wales by the government of Charles II in 1662. A tax of a shilling for each fireplace or stove was collected twice a year from 1662–89 (although profoundly poor people were exempt). The original records include the name and number of hearths. The names of those exempt (paupers) were included from 1663. The records are at TNA.

Hearth Tax Online (hearthtax.org.uk): Online database which also provides analysis of the hearth tax. The site covers many counties and also includes maps and background articles.

Heir apparent: Person who is first in line of succession and cannot be displaced from inheriting.

Heir presumptive: An individual who is currently first in line to inherit, but could be displaced by the birth of a more eligible heir.

Henry III Fine Rolls Project (frh3.org.uk): Allows you to search translated versions of the 'fine rolls' – records of money offered to Henry III for various concessions and favours.

Heraldic visitation: County by county tours conducted by heralds during the sixteenth and seventeenth centuries. The purpose was to register coats of arms and regulate those in use – in other words to make sure those who claimed the right to display coats of arms had a valid claim. Records and pedigrees produced by this genealogical policing of the upper classes have been transcribed and published by the Harleian Society (harleian.org.uk).

Heraldry: The design and study of armorial bearings.

Useful websites
College of Arms (college-of-arms.gov.uk)
Governor General of Canada (gg.ca)
Harleian Society (harleian.org.uk)
Heraldry Online (heraldry-online.org.uk)
Heraldry Society (theheraldrysociety.com)

Heraldry Society of Scotland (heraldry-scotland.co.uk)

Institute of Heraldic and Genealogical Studies (ihgs.ac.uk)

Hereditament: An item of property that can be inherited. There's also corporeal hereditament (land/building) or incorporeal hereditament (rent).

HEREFORDSHIRE:

Herefordshire Archives (www.herefordshire.gov.uk/archives)

Herefordshire FHS (herefordshirefhs.org.uk)

Heritage Helpers (heritagehelpers.co.uk): Platform through which you can join crowdsourcing projects – at time of writing this was Waterloo Lives, NAM's digitisation of Napoleonic diaries.

Heritors' records: Under the Old Poor Law system in Scotland (1574–1845), the responsibility for the poor fell on the parish – specifically the heritors (local landowners) and the kirk sessions. The NRS guide explains: 'The heritors often made voluntary contributions to the poor fund in preference to being assessed (a tax on the owners of land or property) ... Heritors' records seldom survive before the late-eighteenth century but their minutes, accounts and other papers can include lists of poor, assessment rolls and discussion of poor relief and related problems (such as crop failures and hardship caused by trade depressions).'

HERTFORDSHIRE:

Hertfordshire Archives & Local Studies (hertsdirect.org/hals)

The Archives' Hertfordshire Names Online website includes indexes to marriage registers, wills and court registers.

Hertfordshire FHS (hertsfhs.org.uk)

Letchworth & District FHG (ldfhg.org.uk)

Royston & District FHS (roystonfhs.org.uk)

Stevenage FHS (stevenagefhs.webspace.virginmedia.com)

Hidden Lives (hiddenlives.org.uk): Website that has details of the history and homes run by the Children's Society (originally known as the Waifs' and Strays' Society) from the late Victorian and early twentieth century period in Britain.

High Court of Justiciary: Supreme criminal court of Scotland.

Highgate Cemetery: Grade I listed place of burial in north London, divided into the East and West cemeteries. Many notable people are buried here – from Karl Marx to Douglas Adams – and there are many fine examples of Victorian Gothic tombs and ostentatious monumental architecture. It is referred to as being one of the 'Magnificent Seven' London cemeteries, the others being Abney Park, Brompton, Kensal Green, Nunhead, West Norwood and Tower Hamlets. The cemetery had fallen into disrepair when, in 1975, the Friends of Highgate Cemetery (highgatecemetery.org) formed to promote its conservation. There are over 170,000 people buried here in 53,000 graves spread over 37 acres and the Friends' website has details of a search service, costing £40. Copies of some of the registers are also held by the Camden Local Studies and Archives Centre.

Highland Clearances: A notoriously brutal period of forced displacement of highland crofters in Scotland after estate owners moved from arable and mixed farming to sheep farming (which was more profitable).

Highlands & Islands Emigration Society: Assisted individuals to leave western Scotland for Australia during the 1850s. Passenger lists for the years 1852–7 survive at NAS. These are organised by ship and by family which record the name, age and residence of each emigrant. You can explore these records via the Scottish Archive Network (www.scan.org. uk/researchrtools/emigration.htm).

Historic Chapels Trust (www.hct.org.uk): Hosts images and information about redundant chapels and places of worship.

Historical Directories of England and Wales (specialcollections.le.ac. uk/cdm/landingpage/collection/p16445coll4/hd/): A free digital library of trade directories printed between 1750 and 1919, part of the University of Leicester's Special Collections Online. Directories can be viewed online or downloaded and are fully searchable by keyword.

History of Advertising Trust (hatads.org.uk): Archives include material relating to trade associations such as the Thirty Club – established in London, *c.* 1905 as a private dining club 'for the betterment of advertising'.

HistoryPin.org: Browse local history photographs and collections, and see old photographs superimposed over Google Streetview.

Hoggard: A pig drover.

Holocaust: The Holocaust, or Shoah, was the systematic mass murder of around 6 million Jews at the hands of Adolf Hitler's Nazi Germany. State-run persecution had begun before the war, but culminated in the 'Final Solution to the Jewish Question' – slave labour and extermination in concentration camp gas chambers. This continued until the end of the conflict in Europe in 1945.

Useful websites

Holocaust Memorial Museum (rememberme.ushmm.org)

Shoah Foundation (sfi.usc.edu)

Voices of the Holocaust (voices.iit.edu)

Wiener Library for the study of Holocaust and Genocide (www. wienerlibrary.co.uk)

Yad Vashem (www.yadvashem.org)

Working to recover the names of the 6 million Jews who perished in the Holocaust.

(*See also* 'Jews'.)

Home Children: Term for 'assisted' migrations which started in the later Victorian period, which saw hundreds of thousands of children sent to Australia, Canada, New Zealand and South Africa. You can search records of more than 100,000 juvenile migrants sent to Canada, for example, via the Library and Archives Canada website (bac-lac.gc.ca). (*See also* 'Child migration'.)

Hospital Records Database (nationalarchives.gov.uk/hospitalrecords): Wellcome Library and TNA collaboration that details records of hospitals across the UK – currently with over 2,800 entries.

Hospitals: Hospital records normally survive at county record offices. And a good starting point to help you track down the correct archives is the Hospital Records Database (at nationalarchives.gov.uk/hospitalrecords). Other useful resources include:

Anaesthesia Heritage Centre (aagbi.org)

Fair Mile Hospital ,1870–2003 (berkshirerecordoffice.org.uk/albums/fair-mile-hospital/)

Tells the story of the former County Lunatic Asylum for Berkshire.

Findmypast (findmypast.co.uk/articles/world-records/search-all-uk-records/institution-and-organisation--records/hospitals)

Includes Prestwich Asylum Admissions (1851–1901) and Salisbury Infirmary Admissions and Discharges (1761–1832).

Great Ormond Street Hospital (gosh.nhs.uk/about-us/our-history/archive-service/)

Great Ormond Street Hospital's archive contains documents, photographs and artefacts spanning its 160-year history.

Historic Hospital Admission Records Project (hharp.org)

Database of patients in 140,000 admission records of hospitals in London and Glasgow between 1852 and 1921. Included is the Royal Hospital for Sick Children in Glasgow, Great Ormond Street Hospital, the Evelina Hospital and the Alexandra Hospital for Children with Hip Disease.

Huguenot Museum (frenchhospital.org.uk/huguenot-museum/)

Lothian Health Services Archives (lhsa.lib.ed.ac.uk)

Alongside records of patients, nurses, doctors and other hospital workers, the Archives, which are part-funded by the Wellcome Trust, preserves clinical and non-clinical records dating back to 1770 and 1594 respectively. There is also a 40,000-strong photographic collection.

Medical Heritage Library (archive.org/details/ukmhl)

Expanding collection of freely available digitised books from the Wellcome Library's historical collections, published between 1800 and 1900.

Medical Museums (medicalmuseums.org)

Old Operating Theatre Museum (thegarret.org.uk)

Oxfordshire Health Archives (oxfordshirehealtharchives.nhs.uk)

Royal College of Nursing Archives (archives.rcn.org.uk)

St Bartholomew's Museum (bartshealth.nhs.uk/bartsmuseum)

Set in the historic North Wing of St Bartholomew's Hospital, the Museum tells the story of this renowned institution, celebrates its achievements and explains its place in history.

Voluntary Hospitals Database (hospitalsdatabase.lshtm.ac.uk)

Wellcome Library (wellcomelibrary.org)

(*See also* 'Medicine' and 'Nursing'.)

Hot presser: A worker who worked the hot press in either textile or paper production.

Housing of the Working Classes Act 1890: Empowered urban authorities to clear slums, placed legal sanitary standards on landlords and began the building of what would become known as council housing.

Hoy: A type of small sloop-rigged ship.

Hudson's Bay Company: Canadian business group originally built on fur trading that was first incorporated by English royal charter in 1670 as The Governor and Company of Adventurers of England trading into Hudson's Bay. For many years it functioned as the de facto government in parts of North America. Useful websites include Hudson's Bay Company Heritage (www.hbcheritage.ca) and Hudson's Bay Company Archives at the Archives of Manitoba (www.gov.mb.ca/chc/archives/hbca/).

Huguenot Library: Formed by the amalgamation of the libraries of the French Hospital (1718) and the Huguenot Society (1885). Important material includes the consistory records of half a dozen London Huguenot churches and records of various relief funds distributed to Huguenot refugees. It also looks after records of the French Hospital, the Westminster French Protestant School, friendly societies and more. The Library is housed within the Special Collections of UCL Library, which is currently at TNA.

Huguenot Museum: In 2014 the Heritage Lottery Fund awarded a grant of £1.2 million to the French Hospital in Rochester to establish the UK's first museum dedicated to Huguenot heritage. The Huguenot Museum was opened in summer 2015. The top two floors of the former French Hospital have exhibitions telling the story of the Huguenots' persecution and fleeing from France. One highlight of the displays is a Bible that had been baked in a bread loaf. There is also an archive and research centre in the building.

Huguenot Society (huguenotsociety.org.uk): Has transcribed, indexed and published all surviving Huguenot church registers.

Huguenots: French Protestants who fled persecution after the Edict of Nantes, which had allowed some religious freedoms in France, was revoked in 1685. They arrived in waves during the seventeenth and eighteenth centuries, establishing communities in England and later Ireland. In 1718 the French Hospital was founded in London, and would become the seat of the Huguenot Society, which began to record the history of Huguenot migration.

Many refugee Huguenots were artisans and craftsmen and they established a major silk-weaving industry in and around Spitalfields. Their legacy can be also found in crafts such as silversmithing and furniture-making, together with banking and insurance.

Many important Huguenot records are at TNA and are available via BMDRegisters/TheGenealogist and FamilySearch. These cover London, Middlesex, Essex, Gloucestershire, Kent, Devon and Norfolk. Remember that until 1754 Huguenots often recorded their marriages in both Huguenot and Church of England registers – none were recorded in Huguenot registers after that date.

Hull's Fishing Heritage (hulltrawler.net): Useful image-rich website with details of Hull's smacks, sterns and sidewinders, as well as genealogy pages with name indexes drawn from sources including the census and newspapers.

Hull History Centre (www.hullhistorycentre.org.uk): Home to the city archives, a local studies library and Hull University Archives. Features important shipping, fishing and other maritime collections. These include records of shipping companies, and 25,500 fishing crew lists (for vessels operating out of Hull between 1884 and 1914). University of Hull Archives include family and estate collections with some manorial records that date back to 1317.

Hundreds: The shire or county was divided into 'hundreds', also known in some areas as wapentakes or wards. Hundred boundaries are often independent of both parish and county boundaries – a hundred could be split between counties, or a parish could be split between hundreds. Until the introduction of districts by the Local Government Act 1894, hundreds were the only widely used descriptive unit between the parish and county. Over time, the principal functions of the hundred became the administration of law and the keeping of the peace – so there would be hundred courts held every few weeks to tackle local disputes or crimes. Their importance gradually declined and most powers shifted to county courts when these were formally established in 1867.

HUNTINGDONSHIRE:

Huntingdonshire Archives (cambridgeshire.gov.uk/info/20011/archives_archaeology_and_museums/177/archives)

Huntingdonshire FHS (huntsfhs.org.uk)

Fenland FHS (fenlandfhs.org.uk)

I

Images of England (imagesofengland.org.uk): English Heritage photo survey of listed buildings.

Immigrant Ships Transcribers Guild (immigrantships.net): Longstanding volunteer led project to transcribe passenger manifests. You can explore the data by departure/arrival point, or there's the Compass section which links to other passenger list sites, libraries and archives.

Immigration: In general surviving records refer to aliens (a non-citizen of the parent country), 'denizens' (a permanent resident, but not a citizen) and the process of naturalisation – when someone from outside the country becomes a legal citizen.

Records of immigration become more commonplace and standardised after the passing of the Aliens Acts (the first in 1793, the second in 1836). After 1836 in particular newly arrived migrants had to sign a certificate of arrival, and these are held at TNA. Through Ancestry, thanks to its partnership with TNA, you can search Alien Arrivals (1810–11 and 1826–69) and Aliens' registration cards (1918–57) covering the London area only. You can also look out for non-parochial registers contained within RG 4 and RG 8 at TNA – as these are records kept by the French, Dutch, German and Swiss churches in London and elsewhere (available through BMDregisters.co.uk).

Naturalisation case papers (1789–1934) can be searched via Discovery and the Ancestry/TNA partnership also means you can search naturalisation certificates and declarations of British nationality (1870–1912) – which will usually list the immigrant's name, residence, birthplace, age, parents' names, name of spouse, occupation and children. Incoming passenger lists (1878–1960) are available on Ancestry/Findmypast. These document people arriving from countries outside Europe and the Mediterranean, and include details such as name, date of birth and age, ports of departure and arrival.

Imperial War Museums (iwm.org.uk/research): The Museum originally opened in Crystal Palace at Sydenham Hill in 1920. Today there are five museum branches, including three in London.

The IWM website has guides to tracing individuals from the army, RFC, RAF, RN and Merchant Navy, POWs and those who had roles on the home front. It also details some of the collections looked after by the Museum and its own research projects. You can also search the catalogue (iwm.org.uk/collections/search) of 600,000 items – 90,000 of which have digitised images, sound or video attached. There's also a memorials register to more than 68,000 UK war memorials.

Improvement commissioners: Local government boards created by private Acts of Parliament during the eighteenth and nineteenth centuries to 'improve' local areas. These boards would be in charge of the likes of street paving and lighting.

In From the Cold (infromthecold.org): Project dedicated to tracking down details of individuals missing from the CWGC Debt of Honour Register.

In-company magazines/journals: These often include details of promotions and appointments, workforce socials and sporting leagues, notices of births, marriages and deaths, and sometimes detailed obituaries. Sheffield Archives holds runs of the *Bombshell*, for example, which was the official employees' journal for workers at Firth Brown steelworks. *Cocoa Works Magazine* records employees on military service during the First World War and survives in archives of confectionery manufacturers Rowntree Mackintosh held at the Borthwick Institute in York. Trade newspapers may also survive at centralised archives and libraries such as the BL.

Inclosure Acts: Now spelt 'enclosure', these Acts enclosed open fields and common land creating legal property rights to land that was previously considered common. It is estimated that between 1604 and 1914 over 5,200 individual Enclosure Acts were put in place, mainly for southern counties. The first was for Radipole in Dorset.

Income tax: There are relatively few records relating to the payment of income tax by individuals. It was first introduced in 1798 (at a rate of 10 per cent on the total income of the taxpayer from all sources above £60, with reductions on income up to £200). Very few people earned £200 per annum so it was paid by relatively few people. It was abolished in 1815 and Parliament had all documents connected with it collected and pulped. It was temporarily reintroduced in 1841, levied on incomes over £150.

Incoming passenger lists (1878–1960): Held at TNA BT 26, this is one of the most important collections that documents people arriving from countries outside Europe and the Mediterranean area, and one that is a available online via Ancestry. It details name, date of birth and age, ports of departure and arrival, and the vessel. Remember, however, that many pre-1890 lists were irregularly destroyed by the Board of Trade, and there are gaps thereafter.

Incumbent: The holder of a benefice (a permanent Church appointment).

Indenture: A legal agreement, contract, or document – for genealogists it is most often associated with apprenticeships.

Indentured servant: Someone bound into service of another person for a specified number of years.

India Office Family Search (indiafamily.bl.uk/UI/): Dated but useful BL website with details of the archives of the East India Company and the India Office. You can search 300,000 births, baptisms, marriages, deaths and burials in the India Office Records, explore a useful dictionary of abbreviations and references, and search East India Company London warehouse labourers (appointed 1801–32). Lots of the material is also available via Findmypast (findmypast.co.uk/articles/world-records/ search-all-uk-records/special-collections/british-india-office-collection). (*See also* 'Families In British India Society'.)

Indian Mutiny Medal Roll (search.fibis.org/frontis/bin/): This is found within the dedicated Families in British India Society database site. Scroll down the Browse Records bar on the left, then choose Military Records > Medal Rolls to find the Indian Mutiny Medal Roll. (*See also* 'Families In British India Society'.)

Inner Temple Admissions Database (innertemple.org.uk/history/the-archives): Details of the Inner Temple archives, including the free Admissions Database (1547–1920). (*See also* 'Lawyers'.)

Inquests: *See* 'Coroner's inquest'.

Institute of Heraldic and Genealogical Studies (ihgs.ac.uk): Charitable organisation founded in 1961 to promote research and education in genealogy and heraldry, running a range of certified courses. The Library is housed in some six rooms of the Institute of Heraldic and Genealogical Studies headquarters in Canterbury. Holdings include the Armorial Index of over 100,000 cards, and the Andrews Newspaper Index Cards to newspaper announcements which is also on Ancestry.

Interment.net: Library of online records drawn from cemeteries and graveyards across the globe.

International Committee of the Red Cross Archives: Via grandeguerre. icrc.org you can search for POWs in Red Cross lists – which record individuals from all sides of the conflict. 'During the First World War, 10 million people, servicemen or civilians, were captured and sent to detention camps. The belligerent countries involved provided lists of prisoners to the ICRC, which created an index card for each prisoner and detainee. Now, you can search through all 5 million of them.' You can also explore accounts, letters sent to the International Committee of the Red Cross, notices of death and other historical records.

International Genealogical Index: A parish-level source first published as a computer file in 1973. The LDS Church holds dizzying hoards of microform copies of parish material at its Family History Library in Salt Lake City, and the IGI includes indexed data mainly from baptisms and marriages. Although very popular, it was also known to have many transcription errors and omissions (partly thanks to the difficulty of reading the originals), and so helpfully illustrated the point that all family historians must take on board – never trust a transcription. You can access the IGI at familysearch.org/search/collection/igi.

Internet archive: If a website you have been using disappears – whether permanently or simply being down for maintenance – you can take the address, enter it into the Internet Archive's Wayback Machine (at archive. org/web/) and it should return dated snapshots of the website which you can then click through and explore.

Interregnum: A period when normal governance is suspended, or between two periods of office. In English history it is the period between the execution of Charles I (January 1649 – the start of the Commonwealth of England) and the arrival of his son Charles II in London (May 1660 – the start of the Restoration).

Interviews: One of the more interesting tasks for a family historian starting a new avenue of research is interviewing family members. Here are some tips:

1. Be suspicious of memories, including your own.
2. Belt and braces: equip yourself with an A5/A4 pad to take notes, as well as an audio recorder – you may find your phone's built-in voice recorder will do the job.

3. If you're using an audio recorder, make sure you check the sound quality at the start, and that it's still working at regular intervals during the interview. This is especially important if you're not making handwritten notes at the same time.

4. Don't rush the interview. People take time to relax into a conversation and being formally interviewed, with a notepad or audio recorder in the room, can feel uncomfortable for both interviewer and interviewee. With time, it should become easier.

5. If it's a long-distance interview you can either use video-call or send questions by email. Again, with video-calls allow time for the conversation to flow, and be prepared for some technical gremlins that may slow things down.

6. Use Push and Pull to guide the conversation. Whether interviewing by email, phone or face to face you need a range of questions: from specific, fact-based questions ('Where were you born?') to more open-ended questions ('Tell me about …'). You could start by drawing up a simple questionnaire – there are lots of ready made templates of genealogical questions available online.

7. Listen carefully and don't force the interview. If an individual seems unwilling to discuss a topic, you need to respect that and take a step back.

8. Take a camera, so you can quickly take photograph copies of any documentary evidence that you might be shown. (Again, you may find that your phone's built-in camera will function perfectly well for this purpose.) And if you're given a group photograph to copy, make a note of the names of those pictured.

Intestate: A person who has died without having made a will.

Inventories: Inventories can provide fascinating insights into ancestors' lives, listing their goods and chattels, and even the tools of their trade. More detailed inventories were drawn up room by room and so can provide a 'virtual tour' through individuals' houses. For more information about wills and inventories and where to find them, see 'Probate'.

INVERNESS-SHIRE:
Highland Archives Service (highlandarchives.org.uk/harc.asp)
Highland FHS (highlandfamilyhistorysociety.org)

IRELAND:

While you can't escape the catastrophic loss of census material in the Four Courts fire of June 1922, lots of surviving census material, and useful census substitute sources have been indexed, transcribed, digitised and placed online.

NLI made microfilm copies of registers from the most Catholic parishes in Ireland and Northern Ireland during the 1950s and 1960s. You can view digital images free of charge via registers.nli.ie.

NAI (nationalarchives.ie) has a specialist genealogy site (at genealogy. nationalarchives.ie) where you can access digital resources that include Soldiers' Wills database, Tithe Applotment Books, census search forms (1841–51), censuses of Ireland (1901 and 1911 censuses, census. nationalarchives.ie) as well as Calendars of Wills and Administrations (1858–1922).

PRONI (proni.gov.uk) has online records that include the Ulster Covenant (containing the signatures of 237,368 men and 234,046 women, September 1912) and records of freeholders (lists of people eligible to vote). There's also an index to Will Calendar entries from the District Probate Registries of Armagh, Belfast and Londonderry. Via streetdirectories. proni.gov.uk you can access digitised street directories covering Belfast and the surrounding area (1819–1900).

The Derry Genealogy Centre (derrycity.gov.uk/Genealogy/Derry-Genealogy) has an index to pre-1922 civil birth and marriage registers, early BMD registers of 85 churches (26 Roman Catholic, 24 Church of Ireland and 35 Presbyterian) and gravestone inscriptions from 117 graveyards. Searches are free via derry.rootsireland.ie, viewing records is on a pay-per-view basis.

Another important free resource is Griffith's Valuation (askaboutireland. ie/griffith-valuation/). This provides access to the full-scale valuation of property in Ireland published county by county between 1847 and 1864. Remember too that FamilySearch offers access to Irish Civil Registration Indexes.

Other useful websites

Association of Professional Genealogists in Ireland (apgi.ie)

Some 360,000 records from Belfast City Cemetery, Roselawn Cemetery and Dundonald Cemetery.

Belfast Central Library (www.librariesni.org.uk)

Belfast City Council Burial Records (belfastcity.gov.uk/community/burialrecords/burialrecords.aspx)

Belfast, the Linen Hall (linenhall.com)

Centre for Migration Studies (qub.ac.uk/cms)

Emerald Ancestors (emeraldancestors.com)

Eneclann (eneclann.ie)

Genealogical Society of Ireland (familyhistory.ie)

Irish Ancestors, Irish Times (irishtimes.com/ancestor)

Irish Ancestors, Townlands Index (irishancestors.ie/?page_id=5392)

Ireland has more than 64,000 townlands, the most basic unit of land division in the country. This index shows which civil parish each townland would have belonged to.

Irish Ancestral Research Association (tiara.ie)

Irish Archives Resource (www.iar.ie)

Irish Family History Foundation (irish-roots.ie)

Irish Family History Society (ifhs.ie)

Irish Genealogical Research Society (igrsoc.org)

Irish Railway Records Society (irrs.ie)

Military Archives (militaryarchives.ie)

National Museums Northern Ireland (nmni.com/home.aspx)

NLI (nli.ie)

North of Ireland Family History Society (nifhs.org)

Presbyterian Historical Society of Ireland (presbyterianhistoryireland.com)

RootsIreland (rootsireland.ie)

Treaty Exhibition (treaty.nationalarchives.ie)

Trinity College, Dublin (tcd.ie)

Ulster Historical Foundation (ancestryireland.com)

Ireland Census 1901/1911 (census.nationalarchives.ie): Search the census of Ireland from 1901 and 1911, and explore surviving fragments (and substitutes) for previous years, all free of charge. All thirty-two counties (for 1901 and 1911) are searchable by all information categories.

Irish Emigration Database: Documenting Ireland: Parliament, People & Migration (at www.dippam.ac.uk) is a family of sites that together document Irish migration since the eighteenth century. It includes the Irish Emigration Database, based on roughly 33,000 documents – including letters, diaries and journals written by migrants, and newspaper material such as advertisements and overseas BMD notices.

Irish Genealogy (irishgenealogy.ie): has online indexes to civil registration that contain quite a lot of information – births after 1900, for example, include child's name, district/registration area, birth date and mother's maiden name.

Irish Genealogy Toolkit (www.irish-genealogy-toolkit.com/Irish-land-divisions.html): This page features a useful guide to the complicated situation of ecclesiastical parishes and land divisions.

Irish land divisions: Modern-day Ireland is split into the Republic of Ireland and Northern Ireland. Across the whole island there are four provinces, each divided into counties. The Republic of Ireland comprises the provinces of Connaught, Leinster and Munster, and three counties within the province of Ulster (Cavan, Donegal, Monaghan). Then Northern Ireland, which is part of the UK, consists of the remaining six counties of the province of Ulster (Antrim, Armagh, Derry, Down, Fermanagh, Tyrone). These four provinces are the oldest subdivisions and broadly follow ancient clan kingdoms, but no longer hold an important administrative purpose.

Irish Mariners (irishmariners.ie): Details of over 23,000 Irish-born (and 1,000 Canadian-born) merchant seamen, contained in the CR10 series of central index cards held in the Southampton Civic Archives.

Irish War Memorials Project: irishwarmemorials.ie

Irish wills: Since 1858 grants of probate and administration in Ireland have been made in the Principal and District Registries of the Probate Court (before 1877) or the High Court (after 1877). These are indexed in the calendars of wills and administrations which are held at NAI. Up to 1917, the calendars cover the whole of Ireland. After 1918 they cover the twenty-six counties in the Republic while indexes covering the six counties of Northern Ireland are at PRONI. NAI testamentary calendars can be searched online (1858–1920 and 1922–82).

Before 1858 grants of probate and administration were made by the courts of the Church of Ireland (the Prerogative Court and the Diocesan or Consistorial Courts). There are separate indexes of wills and administrations for each court and some indexes have been published – such as the Vicar's Index to Prerogative Wills, 1536–1810 and the Indexes to Dublin Grant Books and Wills, 1270–1800.

Via NAI (nationalarchives.ie) you can search Calendars of Wills and Administrations (1858–1922) and there's an online database of Soldiers' Wills (soldierswills.nationalarchives.ie).

Ironbridge Gorge Museum (www.ironbridge.org.uk/about_us/library_ and_archives/): The Museum's research library is based in the Long Warehouse next to the Museum of Iron. Collections cover the history of the iron industry, bridge building, civil engineering, brick and tile manufacture, coal mining, the pottery and porcelain industries, railways, canals, the East Shropshire Coalfield, as well as the Elton Collection of images of industry and the life and work of Thomas Telford.

ISLE OF MAN:
iMuseum (imuseum.im)

Here you can also explore 400,000 pages of digitised newspapers. There's also a general Family History search page, allowing you to trawl through a number of key genealogical sources.

Isle of Man Library & Archives (manxnationalheritage.im)

Isle of Man FHS (iomfhs.im)

ISLE OF WIGHT:
Isle of Wight Record Office (www.iwight.com/Residents/Libraries-Cultural-and-Heritage/Records-Office/)

The website has a useful guide to parish and Nonconformist records. Also all entries in parish registers (1539–1900) have been recorded in the Personal Names Index – a card index accessible in the search room.

Isle of Wight FHS (www.isle-of-wight-fhs.co.uk)

Has a number of useful databases on its website, some only accessible to members. One very useful tool open to all is Isle of Wight BMD – civil registration data from 1837–2010 compiled by society volunteers from the registers held by the Isle of Wight Register Office.

J

Jews: Jewish material is spread across a wide range of archives throughout the UK. One important collection resides at LMA. It doesn't hold any records relating to the medieval Anglo-Jewish community – expelled from the country in 1290 – although there are a small number of references to Jews living illegally in London before the re-admission in 1656 (in the archives of the Middlesex Sessions).

The bulk of the collection is made up of the archive of the United Synagogue, formed by Act of Parliament in 1870, which includes records from the oldest Ashkenazi synagogues in London – the Great, the Hambro, the New, the Bayswater and the Central Synagogues.

It also has school records, including the admission and discharge registers of the Jews' Free School. This was originally opened as a charity school for fifteen orphan boys in 1732. It grew to become the largest Jewish school in Britain and at its peak, between 1880 and 1890, the LMA guide estimates that one-third of all Anglo-Jewish children were educated there. It also holds records of the Jews' Temporary Shelter, opened in 1885 to help migrant Jews, the Nightingale House Home for Aged Jews and many more institutions.

The Scottish Jewish Archives Centre (sjac.org.uk) has synagogue registers of births, marriages and deaths, and copies of some circumcision registers.

Jewish Communities & Records (jewishgen.org/jcr-uk) is a project to record Jewish communities/congregations in the UK, Republic of Ireland and Gibraltar. The All-UK Database search page holds hundreds of thousands of records, including the 1851 Anglo-Jewry Database which covers about 90 per cent of Jews living in the British Isles in 1851.

Via this FamilySearch page (familysearch.org/learn/wiki/en/The_ Knowles_Collection:_the_Jews_of_the_British_Isles) you can find out about the Knowles Collection, a database of Jewish records from the British Isles which has BMD material from the Bevis Marks Synagogue and the Great Synagogue of London, as well as cemetery records from London and Manchester. Via TNA's Discovery you can download aliens' registration cards for the London area (1918–57) and denization and naturalisation case papers (HO 1) for 1801–71.

Some more useful resources, where you can familiarise yourself with the records kept by Jewish communities, include the Jewish Genealogical Society of Great Britain (of which more below), the British-Jewry mailing list (british-jewry.org.uk), which has advice and databases, including a Leeds Database which draws on the census, absent voter's lists, burial/ marriage collections and *Jewish Chronicle* notices. JewishGen (jewishgen. org) has a vast Burial Registry, while Yad Vashem (yadvashem.org) is working to recover the names of the 6 million Jews who perished in the Holocaust.

Useful websites:
Association of Jewish Ex-Servicemen & Women (ajex.org.uk)

Jewish Chronicle (thejc.com)

Jewish Gilroes (jewish-gilroes.org.uk/ancestor-search/)

A 'genealogical and photographic record of the Jewish graves at Gilroes Cemetery, Leicester'.

Jewish Heritage-UK (jewish-heritage-uk.org)

Includes a directory of Listed Synagogues across the UK.

Jewish Museum (jewishmuseum.org.uk)

Manchester Jewish Museum (manchesterjewishmuseum.com)

(*See also* 'Holocaust'.)

Jewish Communities and Records (www.jewishgen.org/JCR-uk/): JCR-UK is a joint project between the Jewish Genealogical Society of Great Britain and JewishGen. It hosts the 1851 Anglo-Jewry Database, and contains more than 7,000 pages and images, covering more than 1,000 Jewish communities and congregations across the UK, as well as the Republic of Ireland and Gibraltar. Other databases include the Bradford Jewish Cemeteries Database and the Caedraw School Register.

Jewish Genealogical Society of Great Britain (jgsgb.org.uk): Founded in 1992, the Society is divided into various special interest (Anglo Jewish, Eastern European, etc.) and UK regional groups (East of London, Leeds, Manchester, etc.). The Society is the driving force behind all kinds of important genealogical projects. One recent collaboration with JCR-UK and the Federation of Synagogues (federationofsynagogues.com) has made available details of burials at the Federation's Edmonton and Rainham cemeteries, for example. The website has a vast amount of useful information, as well as links to important archives, online databases, research tips, news and more. You can also order copies of Marriage Authorisation Certificates.

Jewish Historical Society of England: jhse.org

Jewish Museum London: jewishmuseum.org.uk

JewishGen Family-Finder (www.jewishgen.org/jgff/): 'A compilation of surnames and towns currently being researched by over 100,000 Jewish genealogists worldwide. It contains over 500,000 entries: 125,000 ancestral surnames and 18,000 town names …' There's also the JewishGen Online Worldwide Burial Registry.

John Lewis Memory Store (johnlewismemorystore.org.uk): Memories and photographs of working life at the John Lewis Partnership.

Judaica Europeana (judaica-europeana.eu): Provides access to treasures from libraries, archives and museums across Europe, led by the European Association for Jewish Culture (jewishcultureineurope.org).

Justices of the Peace: Until the introduction of elected county councils, they tried minor crimes, regulated supplies, controlled roads, and had powers to levy local taxes.

Jutland: The Battle of Jutland was the biggest sea battle of the First World War. In total 6,097 UK sailors and 2,551 German sailors died in the 2-day battle. There are various cemeteries and monuments to the battle – including those at South Queensferry and Lyness in Scotland, maintained by the CWGC.

K

KENT:
Kent History & Library Centre (kent.gov.uk/archives)

The Kent History and Library Centre in James Whatman Way, Maidstone, opened in April 2012, boasting some 14km of archival shelves and more than 40,000 books. Kent was known for papermaking, brewing and fishing, and the Centre holds records of the likes of the Whatman Paper Mill in Maidstone and the Whitbread brewery records. They also have registers of shipping crew lists for all of Kent's ports except those in the Medway area.

Canterbury Cathedral Archives (archives.canterbury-cathedral.org)

Medway Archives (cityark.medway.gov.uk/about/medway_archives/)

Friends of Medway Archives (foma-lsc.org)

Kent FHS (kfhs.org.uk)

Folkestone & District FHS (folkfhs.org.uk)

North West Kent FHS (nwkfhs.org.uk)

Tunbridge Wells FHS (tunwells-fhs.co.uk)

Kent Police Museum (kent-police-museum.co.uk): There's a research service offering personnel records of Kent Police Officers (from 1857) held at the Kent History & Library Centre in Maidstone.

KINCARDINESHIRE:
Aberdeen City and Aberdeenshire Archives (aberdeencity.gov.uk/archives)

Aberdeen & North East Scotland FHS (anesfhs.org.uk)

KINROSS-SHIRE:
Perth & Kinross Archives (www.pkc.gov.uk/archives)

Tay Valley FHS (tayvalleyfhs.org.uk)

Kirk session: Congregations of the Church of Scotland and other Presbyterian churches were governed and administered by the kirk session, which consisted of elected members and a minister.

KIRKCUDBRIGHTSHIRE:
Dumfries & Galloway Libraries & Archives (www.dumgal.gov.uk/lia)

Dumfries & Galloway FHS (dgfhs.org.uk)

Knapper: A worker of flint.

Knights register: A register of knights has been kept by the College of Arms since 1662.

Knocknobbler: The person responsible for ejecting unruly dogs from acts of worship.

Knowles Collection (familysearch.org/learn/wiki/en/The_Knowles_Collection:_the_Jews_of_the_British_Isles): Database of Jewish records from the British Isles. Includes BMD material from the Bevis Marks Synagogue and the Great Synagogue of London, as well as cemetery records from London and Manchester.

L

Labour History Archive & Study Centre: phm.org.uk/archive-study-centre/

Lamplighter: Employed to turn on gas street lights.

LANARKSHIRE:
North Lanarkshire Archives (www.northlanarkshire.gov.uk/archives)
South Lanarkshire Archives (www.southlanarkshire.gov.uk/info/200165/local_and_family_history/588/archives_and_records)
Lanarkshire FHS (lanarkshirefhs.org.uk)

LANCASHIRE:
Lancashire Archives (lancashire.gov.uk/libraries-and-archives/archives-and-record-office.aspx)
Lancashire county archives has an online catalogue (LANCAT) that has over 900,000 descriptions, including details of 40,000-plus marriage bonds.

Lancashire Lantern (lanternimages.lancashire.gov.uk)

Manchester Archives & Local History (manchester.gov.uk/info/448/archives_and_local_history)

Liverpool Libraries & Archives (liverpool.gov.uk/libraries/archives-family-history/)

Liverpool Record Office has crew lists, Customs bills of entry, records of merchant families and shipping lines, and a photographic archive for the Liverpool docks. The Mersey Docks and Harbour Board Archive is housed at the Maritime Archives at the Merseyside Maritime Museum.

Lancashire FH & HS (lfhhs.org.uk)

Furness FHS (furnessfhs.co.uk)

Lancaster FHG (lfhg.org)

Liverpool & South West Lancashire FHS (liverpool-genealogy.org.uk)

Ormskirk & District FHS (odfhs.org.uk)

St Helens Townships FHS (sthelenstownshipsfhs.org.uk)

Wigan F & LHS (wiganworld.co.uk/familyhistory/)

Lancashire Infantry Museum (www.lancashireinfantrymuseum.org.uk/research/): Huge regimental archive, 'the premier centre for military historical research in the North of England'. It is based at Fulwood Barracks in Preston, the traditional home of the old county infantry regiments, where it holds archives relating to 120 separate units, including the 59 battalions formed by antecedent Lancashire regiments.

Land Army: Although bodies such as the Women's National Land Service Corps (formed in February 1916) had existed before, the origins of the Land Army can be traced back to the Department for Food Production, and more specifically the Women's Branch, established by the Board of Agriculture in January 1917, led by Meriel Talbot. Gill Clarke's *The Women's Land Army* (Sansom, 2008) describes how in March 1917 Talbot established a women's labour force of civilian mobile workers called the Women's Land Army, to recruit and train women for farm work. Between March 1917 and May 1919, 23,000 women became official full-time members of the Women's Land Army. Useful websites for investigating the Land Army during the Second World War include womenslandarmy.co.uk, www. womenslandarmytribute.co.uk and landarmy.org.uk.

Land Tax: Land Tax Assessments provide an annual list of property owners and occupiers – meaning in theory at least you can track the years in which families or individuals moved in or out of the property. The records can reveal the type of property, and allow you to make deductions about the relative status of the wider community. Although the tax was first introduced in 1692, the survival rate of Land Tax Assessments are patchy at best for most of the first century of their history. The situation improves from the last decades of the eighteenth century. The names recorded are usually male heads of household. The FamilySearch wiki on the subject (familysearch.org/wiki/en/Land_Tax_Assessment_Records) notes that if a widow remarried, her property might be listed in the name of her new husband. Remember too that this was a locally administered system of taxation, meaning originals will normally reside within the appropriate regional record office. From 1780 a copy of the Land Tax Assessment was placed in the quarter session records, so make sure you see what court records have survived from the period.

Larceny: In English law petty larceny (theft) would be tried at the quarter sessions. 'Grand larceny' was the stealing of property worth more than 12 pence.

Latin: The further back you go, the more likely you are to come across Latin terms within English documents, or documents written entirely in

Latin. Google translate can quickly and easily come to the rescue – or at least give you clues to understand meaning. But if not you might try an online glossary of Latin terms. There's a good one at familysearch.org/wiki/en/Latin_Genealogical_Word_List. Here we learn that 'dspml' was an abbreviation for the Latin *'decessit sine prole mascula legitima'*, which means 'died without legitimate male issue (sons)'.

Lawyers: If your ancestor worked as lawyer there are lots of potential sources for finding out more. In the fourteenth century schools of lay common lawyers developed into the four Inns of Court in London: Lincoln's Inn, Gray's Inn and the Inner and Middle Temple.

Law was also the first profession to have a regularly published list of its practitioners. Browne's General Law List was first published in 1775 before becoming the New Law List and finally the Law List.

Useful websites

FamilySearch wiki (familysearch.org/learn/wiki/en/Lawyers_in_England_and_Wales)

Covers law lists, records of attorneys, solicitors, barristers, judges and Justices of the Peace.

Gray's Inn Archives (graysinn.org.uk/history/archives)

Site provides links to external digitised transcriptions of both the Pension Books and Register of Admissions.

Inner Temple Admissions Database (innertemple.org.uk/history/the-archives)

Law Society Corporate Archive (lawsociety.org.uk/support-services/library-services/corporate-archive/)

Law Society's Solicitors Regulation Authority (sra.org.uk)

Maintains a register listing lawyers admitted since 1845.

Lincoln's Inn Archives (lincolnsinn.org.uk/index.php/library/the-inns-archives)

Middle Temple Archives (middletemple.org.uk/about-us/history/

Leavelooker: The municipal inspector of markets in English towns.

Legacies of British Slave-ownership (ucl.ac.uk/lbs): A UCL project that has produced a database containing the identity of slave-owners at the time slavery ended, and the amounts they received in compensation.

Legger: Men employed by canal owners to push boats through narrow tunnels.

LEICESTERSHIRE AND RUTLAND:
Record Office for Leicestershire, Leicester & Rutland (www.leicestershire.gov.uk/leisure-and-community/history-and-heritage/visit-the-record-office/about-the-record-office)

Volunteers have transcribed and indexed records of people in the Leicester Union Workhouse and Countesthorpe Cottage Homes from the late Victorian period. 'Elephant Man' Joseph Merrick is listed in nineteenth-century records of the Leicester Union Workhouse.

Image Leicestershire (imageleicestershire.org.uk)

Leicestershire & Rutland FHS (lrfhs.org.uk)

Levellers: English Civil War-era movement that advocated extended suffrage, religious tolerance and other profound reforms.

Liberty of the Fleet: The area around Fleet Prison in London where clandestine marriages took place. (*See also* 'Clandestine marriages'.)

Libraries: Never rule out your local library as a venue for your research. Many have specialist local studies departments, often with microform copies of census material, parish registers and local newspapers, and many offer free access to Ancestry, Findmypast or the British Newspaper Archive. You may also find some unique local history collection. The Lamb Collection at Dundee Central Library, for example, is a collection of 450 boxes of ephemera, including photographs, maps, prints and books, compiled by Alexander Crawford Lamb (1843–97), owner of a Dundee temperance hotel.

Library & Archives Canada (bac-lac.gc.ca): Bibliothèque et Archives Canada is Canada's national archives, tasked with acquiring, preserving and making Canada's documentary heritage available for study.

Library of the Religious Society of Friends (www.quaker.org.uk/resources/library): The Library is based at Friends House in London and holds one of the largest Quaker collections in the world. This includes books, journals, manuscripts and archives of the organisation of Quakers, such as the archives of Britain Yearly Meeting and its committees, archives of London and Middlesex Quaker meetings, as well as Quaker organisations such as the Friends Ambulance Unit and non-Quaker organisations such as Central Board for Conscientious Objectors.

Lighterman: The operator of a lighter, flat-bottomed type of barge.

Lincoln's Inn Archives (lincolnsinn.org.uk/index.php/library/the-inns-archives): Archive of the Honourable Society of Lincoln's Inn – one of four Inns of Court in London to which barristers of England and Wales belong and where they are called to the Bar. Holds the longest-running record series of any of the four Inns, dating back to 1422. (*See also* 'Lawyers'.)

LINCOLNSHIRE:
Lincolnshire Archives (www.lincolnshire.gov.uk/archives)

Has an internationally recognised collection of Episcopal Rolls and Registers – the core records of the Diocese of Lincoln. The earliest is dated *c.* 1214, and is the earliest example of such a document for any diocese in the whole of Europe.

Lincs to the Past (www.lincstothepast.com)

Lincolnshire FHS (lincolnshirefhs.org.uk)

Isle of Axholme FHS (axholme-fhs.org.uk)

Peterborough & District FHS (peterborofhs.org.uk)

North East Lincolnshire Libraries and Archives (www.nelincs.gov.uk/libraries-and-archives/)

Notable collections include 38,000 Grimsby crew lists which are searchable via the catalogue. Also looks after registers of ships (1824–1988) and registers of fishing apprentices (1879–1937).

Lineage: Direct descent from a specific individual.

List and Index Society (www.listandindexsociety.org.uk): Society founded in 1965 which produces two series of publications. The (yellow) Standard Series focuses on material at TNA, the (red) Special Series focuses on documents held elsewhere.

Livery companies: The livery companies of the City of London are a group of trade associations many of which evolved out of medieval guilds of particular crafts or trades. They controlled training, wages and other standards of trade. They also had religious associations and most maintain original professional roles. Try liverycompanies.com for a database of guilds and livery companies. Archives are usually maintained by the companies themselves, or with the Guildhall Library/LMA.

One important online resource is Records of London's Livery Companies Online (www.londonroll.org), which provides records of apprentices and freemen in City of London livery companies between

1400 and 1900. As the website explains, the database currently includes information for ten livery companies, with more on the way.

Lives of the First World War (livesofthefirstworldwar.org): Centenary crowdsourcing project that aims to record as many individuals who contributed to the war effort as possible – both overseas and on the home front.

Loaves of sugar: A conical measurement of sugar.

Loblolly boy: An assistant to a warship's surgeon. Tobias Smollett's *The Adventures of Roderick Random* was partially based on his naval experience as a surgeon's mate in the mid-eighteenth century.

Local Government Act 1894: Introduced 'districts' as official divisions of land – making the old 'hundred' divisions obsolete.

Locative surnames: More than half of all English surnames are locative – in other words derived from places and place names.

LONDON:
The long-term partnership between Ancestry and LMA (ancestry.co.uk/cs/uk/lma) has seen masses of genealogical material online, including millions of parish registers, Nonconformist registers, workhouse and Poor Law records, school registers, wills, electoral registers, poll books, marriage bonds and transportation papers.

Below are some of the most important websites, borough collections and local archives dotted across the capital. Remember too that historic county collections in Essex, Kent and Surrey will contain material relating to areas that are now part of Greater London. The Middlesex county material is at LMA.

AIM25 (aim25.ac.uk)

Barking & Dagenham, History, Heritage & Archives (www.lbbd.gov.uk/residents/leisure-libraries-and-museums/history-heritage-and-archives/)

Barnet, Local Studies & Archives (www.barnet.gov.uk/info/200111/local_studies_and_archives/702/local_studies_and_archives)

Bexley Borough Photos (boroughphotos.org/bexley/)

Bexley's Local Studies & Archive Centre (www.bexley.gov.uk/index.aspx?articleid=2563#cn2109)

Brent Archives (brent.gov.uk/archives)

Bromley Local Studies Library & Archives (www.bromley.gov.uk/ info/1062/libraries_-_local_collections/377/local_studies_library_and_ archives)

Camden Local Studies & Archives Centre (www.camden.gov.uk/ccm/ navigation/leisure/local-history/)

Croydon Records & Archives (www.croydon.gov.uk/leisure/archives)

Ealing Local History Centre (www.ealing.gov.uk/info/200064/local_ history/1888/local_history_centre)

Enfield Local Studies Library & Archive (www.enfield.gov.uk/ info/200048/museums_and_heritage)

Greenwich Heritage Centre (www.royalgreenwich.gov.uk/info/10053/ heritage_services/251/greenwich_heritage_centre)

Guildhall Library (cityoflondon.gov.uk/things-to-do/visiting-the-city/ archives-and-city-history/guildhall-library/Pages/default.aspx)

Hackney Archives & Local History (www.hackney.gov.uk/ca-archives. htm#.VLRKvFp177V)

Hammersmith & Fulham Archives (www.lbhf.gov.uk/Directory/ Leisure_and_Culture/Libraries/Archives/17430_Archives_and_Local_ History.asp)

Haringey Archive Service (www.haringey.gov.uk/index/community_ and_leisure/time_out_in_haringey/visiting_haringey/archives.htm)

Harrow Local History Centre (www.harrow.gov.uk/info/200070/ museums_and_galleries/183/harrow_local_history_centre)

Havering Local Studies (arena.yourlondonlibrary.net/web/havering)

Hillingdon Local Studies, Archives & Museums (www.hillingdon.gov. uk/article/8976/Local-studies-archives-and-museum-service)

Hounslow Local History & Archives (www.hounslow.info/libraries/ local-history-archives)

Islington Local History Centre (www.islington.gov.uk/islington/history- heritage/heritage_lhc/Pages/default.aspx)

Kensington & Chelsea Local Studies & Archives (www.rbkc.gov.uk/ libraries/localstudiesandarchives.aspx)

Kingston Local History Room & Archives (www.kingston.gov.uk/ info/200239/museum_archives_and_local_history/548/local_history_ room_and_archives)

Lambeth Archives (lambeth.gov.uk/places/lambeth-archives)

Lewisham Local History & Archives Centre (www.lewisham.gov.uk/inmyarea/history/archives/Pages/default.aspx)

Merton Heritage & Local Studies Centre (arena.yourlondonlibrary.net/web/merton/heritage)

Newham Archives & Local Studies Library (www.newham.gov.uk/pages/servicechild/newham-archives-and-local-studies-library.aspx)

Redbridge Heritage (www2.redbridge.gov.uk/cms/contact_pages/i/information_and_heritage_servi.aspx)

Richmond Local Studies Collection (www.richmond.gov.uk/local_studies_collection)

Southwark Local History Library & Archive (www.southwark.gov.uk/info/200161/local_history_library)

Sutton Archives & Local Studies (www.sutton.gov.uk/index.aspx?articleid=15674)

Tower Hamlets Local History Library & Archives (www.towerhamlets.gov.uk/lgsl/1001-1050/1034_local_history__archives.aspx)

Waltham Forest Archives & Local Studies Library (www.walthamforest.gov.uk/archives-local-studies)

Wandsworth History & Heritage (www.wandsworth.gov.uk/homepage/215/local_history_and_heritage)

(City of) Westminster Archives Centre (www.westminster.gov.uk/archives)

East of London FHS (eolfhs.org.uk)

Hillingdon FHS (hfhs.co.uk)

London, Westminster & Middlesex FHS (lwmfhs.org.uk)

Waltham Forest FHS (wffhs.org.uk)

West Middlesex FHS (west-middlesex-fhs.org.uk)

Woolwich & District FHS (woolwichfhs.org.uk)

London Gazette: *See 'Gazette, the'.*

London Lives (londonlives.org): Explores crime and poverty in the Metropolis between 1690 and 1800, part of the Connected Histories family of websites (connectedhistories.org). It's a searchable edition of 240,000 manuscripts from 8 archives – boasting 3.35 million names. The Browse page lists some of the court records available here such as those taken from the City of London, Middlesex and Westminster sessions.

London Metropolitan Archives (search.lma.gov.uk): The principal local government archive for Greater London and the largest county record office in the UK. It holds records of the Corporation of London (City of London), and in 2008 it merged with the Guildhall Library Manuscripts Section and Guildhall Library Prints and Maps. It has vast parish register collections and educational records. Many of its major genealogical sources are available on Ancestry. The Boards of Guardians series of records start in about 1830 and include material from workhouses, asylums and special schools. It also holds records from over 100 hospitals, including the former county lunatic asylums of Hanwell, Colney Hatch and Banstead. It has an important collection relating to the Anglo-Jewish community in Britain. Via Collage (collage.cityoflondon.gov.uk) you can explore more than 250,000 images (*c.* 1860s–*c.* 1980s) from collections at LMA and the Guildhall Art Gallery.

London's Screen Archives (londonsscreenarchives.org.uk): The regional film archive for London. You can also explore highlights via youtube.com/user/LondonsScreenArchive/videos.

London Symphony Orchestra Archive (lso.co.uk/orchestra/history/about-the-lso-archive.html): Archival highlights include programmes dating from 1904 and bound minute books from LSO Board meetings (1905–79).

London Transport Museum: ltmuseum.co.uk

Long, Long Trail (longlongtrail.co.uk): 'A site all about the soldiers, units, regiments and battles of the British Army of the First World War, and how to research and understand them.' This is the best place to get to grips with researching a soldier who fought in the First World War, specifically created with family historians in mind, with information about how regiments, divisions, corps and units functioned.

LOOM: A term that might crop up in the occupation field. This stands for Living Off Own Means – in other words the individual was not in paid employment, self employment or receiving parish relief, but was living off wealth/investments. Remember that it could also indicate an unwillingness to share the means of income.

Lord Lieutenant: First instituted in the 1540s, this was the Crown's direct county representative, responsible for raising and organising county militia.

Lorimer: A maker of small iron objects (bits, stirrups, etc.) for horses' bridles.

Lost Pubs Project (closedpubs.co.uk): Growing database of lost pubs, often with photographs, which you can explore by county.

Lothian Health Services Archives (lhsa.lib.ed.ac.uk): The Family Historians page gives advice for those searching for records of a patient, nurse, doctor or other hospital employee.

Luddites: Textile workers who protested against mechanisation of the trade during the early nineteenth century by smashing labour-saving machines such as stocking frames. It culminated in unrest across Nottinghamshire, Yorkshire and Lancashire. You can find out more at www.luddites200.org.uk.

M

Magic: In 1736 Parliament passed an Act repealing the laws against witchcraft, but imposing fines or imprisonment on people who claimed to be able to use magical powers. According to parliament.uk: 'When it was introduced in the Commons the Bill caused much laughter among MPs. Its promoter was John Conduit whose wife was the niece of Sir Isaac Newton, a father of modern science, although keenly interested in the occult. The Act was repealed in 1951 by the Fraudulent Mediums Act which in turn was repealed in 2008.' The 1824 Vagrancy Act saw fortune-telling, astrology and spiritualism also become punishable offences.

Manchester High School for Girls Archive (www.mhsgarchive.org): Full digital archive of the Manchester school founded in 1874. Here you can explore letters, governors' minutes, newspaper cuttings, programmes, school magazines and reports.

Manchester Jewish Museum (manchesterjewishmuseum.com): Preserves collections that include 'objects, documents, photographs and oral histories charting the many stories and experiences of Manchester Jewish life'.

Mangler: Someone who works a mangle for pressing water out of clothes.

Manorial records: Manorial documents include court rolls, surveys, maps, terriers and documents relating to the boundaries, wastes, customs or courts of a manor – documents generated by the administration of a manor. The 'manor' was essentially an administrative unit of a landed estate, which could vary in size from a few acres to large estates covering several parishes. These records can be useful for researching tenants who would have paid rent and service to the lord of the manor. The payment to and customs within the manor were governed by the manor court, which also acted as the local law court. The manor system also has many terms that may be unfamiliar – 'homagers', for example, was the name given to the twelve jurors of the manor court. What survives where is fairly random. Shropshire, to take one example, has manorial records that span 650 years from the 1270s to the 1920s. These include court rolls and associated court documents, surveys, maps, terriers and other documents relating to boundaries and enfranchisement.

The Manorial Documents Register (discovery.nationalarchives.gov.uk/manor-search) is an online tool to help you find manorial court documents in England and Wales.

Manse: The house provided for ministers of certain faiths, especially associated with the Scottish Presbyterian Church.

Maps: Ordnance Survey and tithe maps in particular can give researchers a vivid picture of the physical environment in which ancestors lived and worked. NLS gives access to many thousands of maps via maps.nls.uk, including military maps, estate maps, town plans, Ordnance Survey maps and trench maps.

British History Online (british-history.ac.uk/catalogue/maps) hosts historic maps of London, and you can explore the original valuation maps produced by Griffith's Valuation of Ireland at askaboutireland.ie/griffith-valuation/index.xml. There's also the Irish OS Historical Mapping at www.osi.ie/products/professional-mapping/historical-mapping/.

Addressing History (addressinghistory.edina.ac.uk) combines data from post office directories with old maps, and Bomb Sight (bombsight.org) is a digital bomb census of the London Blitz.

Useful websites
BL, Maps (bl.uk/onlinegallery/onlineex/maps/)
Bodleian Library's Map Room (bodleian.ox.ac.uk/maps)
Building History (buildinghistory.org/maps.shtml)

Charting the Nation (www.chartingthenation.lib.ed.ac.uk)

Cheshire Tithe Maps (maps.cheshire.gov.uk/tithemaps/)

David Rumsey Map Collection Database (davidrumsey.com)

Map History (maphistory.info)

MAPCO (mapco.net)

NLW (llgc.org.uk/collections/digital-gallery/maps0/)

OldMapsOnline (oldmapsonline.org)

Brings together 'geo-referenced map metadata' from historic maps held at the likes of the BL, Bodleian Library, NLS and more overseas repositories.

Old Maps (old-maps.co.uk)

Ordnance Survey (ordnancesurvey.co.uk)

ScotlandsPlaces (scotlandsplaces.gov.uk)

TNA (nationalarchives.gov.uk/maps/maps-family-local-history.htm)

Details of 12,000 tithe maps held here that are searchable through Discovery.

Vision of Britain (visionofbritain.org.uk)

Type your postcode/place name into the search box, and an historic map of the area appears. You can zoom in to individual buildings, explore surroundings, and choose various other maps of the area going back to 1805.

West Yorkshire Tithe Map Project (tracksintime.wyjs.org.uk)

Your Old Books & Maps (youroldbooksandmaps.co.uk)

Mariners (mariners-l.co.uk): 'Researching the mariners and ships of the merchant marine and the world's navies.'

Maritime: The Registrar General of Shipping and Seamen was responsible for keeping records of merchant seamen and so most material is held in the Board of Trade record series (BT) at TNA (and many records are now available via Findmypast). Important maritime collections survive in disparate archives and museums, covering fishermen, whalers, trawlermen and harbour masters.

Useful websites
Coastguards of Yesteryear (coastguardsofyesteryear.org)

Crew List Index Project (crewlist.org.uk)

Huge database of crew lists held in various archives confined to merchant seafarers on British registered ships (1861–1913).

Crew Lists of the British Merchant Navy (1915crewlists.rmg.co.uk/)

Volunteer-led collaboration between TNA and the National Maritime Museum to transcribe all the surviving Merchant Navy crew lists from 1915.

East India Company (wiki.fibis.org/index.php/East_India_Company)

East India Company Ships (eicships.info/index.html)

Grimsby Fishermen (www.nelincs.gov.uk/faqs/archives-kept-north-east-lincolnshire-archives/)

Searchable catalogue of 38,000 Grimsby crew lists. Also looks after registers of fishing apprentices.

HM Waterguard (hm-waterguard.org.uk)

Dedicated to the history, men and work of the Preventive Service of HM Customs & Excise.

Hull History Centre (hullhistorycentre.org.uk)

Has records of shipping companies, fishing crew lists (1884–1914) and the Sailors' Children's Society.

Irish Mariners (irishmariners.ie)

Details of over 23,000 Irish-born merchant seamen.

Lloyd's Marine Collection, Guildhall Library (www.cityoflondon.gov.uk/things-to-do/guildhall-library/collections/Pages/Maritime-history.aspx)

Maritime History Archive (www.mun.ca/mha/)

Canadian archive that has lots of material relating to British merchant shipping, including Crew Lists and Agreements (1861–1913).

National Maritime Museum (rmg.co.uk/national-maritime-museum)

Register of Merchant Seamen, Southampton Archives (southampton.gov.uk/libraries-museums/local-family-history/southampton-archives/index-merchant-seamen.aspx)

Trinity House Maritime Museum (trinityhouseleith.org.uk)

Welsh Mariners (welshmariners.org.uk)

Includes an index of 23,500 Welsh merchant masters, mates and engineers active from 1800–1945.

Marriage (civil registration): When the new system of civil registration was launched in 1837, registrars dealt with births and deaths, while Church of England clergy would perform and register marriages. Clergy of other denominations could not perform legally valid marriages until 1898 (from when they could apply to become 'Authorised Persons'). Before that date a Registrar of Marriages had to be present.

Two registers had to be completed and signed by the bridge and groom. When a register was full, one copy would be sent to the Superintendent Registrar and the other was kept at the church. In addition, quarterly copies of all marriages were sent to the register office and forwarded to the Registrar General. Quaker and Jewish marriages were performed by Registering Officers and Secretaries of Synagogues, respectively. They were also required to deposit completed registers at the Register Office, and to forward quarterly copies to the Registrar General.

Marriage Act of 1753: Before this act was passed, a formal ceremony of marriage before a clergyman was not a legal requirement – the only requirement for a betrothal was that both parties agreed, and that they had reached the legal age of consent (girls: 12, boys: 14).

Marriage bonds and allegations: Marriage bonds and allegations were drawn up when a couple wished to marry by licence rather than the normal method of banns. The bond was sworn by witnesses, one of whom pledged to forfeit a sum of money should there prove to be any fraud – much like a guarantor of rent. Bonds and allegations survive from c. 1660–1822, after which date only allegations were kept. The Borthwick Institute in York, for example, holds marriage bonds and allegations issued by the authority of the Archbishop of York for the period 1660–1839.

Marriage certificates: These contain the date and place of marriage, the name, age and marital status/condition of the parties, the occupation and address. Most helpfully they also record the name and occupation of each party's father, the names of the witnesses, and the name of the person who solemnised the marriage. They potentially arm you with information to begin your journey back along two branches of the family.

Marriage Duties Act 1694: This was a tax levied on births, marriages, burials, bachelors over 25 and childless widowers to support the war against France. This is a rare but potentially useful source. A collection of marriage duties returns has survived at Shropshire Archives, for example. Here you can find the assessment of the duties payable for Shrewsbury and its liberties (1695–1702), giving the names of people in each household.

Marriage licences: Traditionally, before any ceremony could take place, the banns of marriage would be read – a public announcement in the parish church of the impending marriage – giving people the opportunity to raise any objection. But, there were plenty of reasons why a marriage might have to be carried out quickly. Perhaps secrecy was paramount because of some family objection. Perhaps the bride was already pregnant, and speed was required to guard against scandal. Or perhaps the groom was simply on military leave, and so the marriage had to be carried out within a small window of time.

To circumnavigate the calling of banns on three successive Sundays, the church, for a fee, could provide a licence. And today these are useful to genealogists as they may contain some details not available elsewhere.

A person applying for the licence (usually the groom) had to provide a bond and an allegation (see above), and together licences and bonds can represent a second chance for the genealogist who can't find a marriage in the parish registers. Usually they will survive within the diocesan collections. FamilySearch and all the big commercial sites have collections of banns, licences and bonds. Findmypast's Staffordshire Collection, for example, includes Diocese of Lichfield marriage bonds and allegations.

Useful websites
Borthwick Institute for Archives (york.ac.uk/borthwick/)

One of the oldest diocesan collections in the country, preserving marriage bonds alongside bishops' transcripts back to 1598.

NLW (www.llgc.org.uk)

Search some 90,000 bonds and affidavits relating to marriages held in Wales between 1616 and 1837.

Nottingham Manuscripts and Special Collections (www.nottingham. ac.uk/manuscriptsandspecialcollections/index.aspx)

Houses a collection of bonds and allegations for marriage licences granted by the Archdeaconry Court of Nottingham from 1594–1884.

Matrimonial Causes Act 1857: This transferred jurisdiction over divorce from ecclesiastical to civil courts – although the legal basis for divorce and the cost of the process remained largely unchanged.

Matronymic: A name derived from the name of a mother/female ancestor.

Mayflower Society (www.themayflowersociety.org): The General Society of Mayflower Descendants was founded in 1897. It is an hereditary organisation of individuals who have 'proven lineage' from a pilgrim who sailed on the Mayflower, the ship that transported English Separatists from Plymouth to the New World in 1620. To begin with a second vessel, the *Speedwell*, was to be part of the voyage but it was forced to turn back. The *Mayflower* made its first landing near Provincetown, Massachusetts.

Medal index cards (1914–20): An important First World War source preserved at TNA and available through Ancestry. The index cards were created by the Army Medal Office towards the end of the First World War and record the medals men and women were entitled to claim. There are more than 5 million held in series WO 372, and the majority of the cards record army soldiers and officers (Indian Army personnel and army nurses are recorded too), alongside personnel of the RFC and Royal Naval Division (as well as some RAF).

Medical Directory: First published in 1845, this annual directory lists name, address, qualifications and medical school for each doctor. Remember that this directory was a commercial venture and so, unlike the Medical Register (see below), it was not compulsory. It's always worth seeing if the volume you seek has been digitised and made available through the likes of archive.org, and TheGenealogist also has some.

Medical Museums (medicalmuseums.org): Useful A–Z of medical museums – you can also select 'Family History' and museums with genealogical sources will appear.

Medical Register: First published in 1859, this was a mandatory list of practitioners. Ancestry has UK Medical Registers (1859–1959).

Medicine: Before the National Health Service was established in 1948, health care for those unable to afford private treatment was provided either through charitable institutions such as hospitals and dispensaries or local Poor Law authorities.

TNA has numerous guides to medicine and medical practitioners. You can search and download First World War British Army nurses' service records, for example, which tell you where a nurse trained, as well as references, hospitals, field ambulances or other medical units where they served. There's also the mothballed but still functional section of the website that hosts the Wellcome Library and TNA collaboration Hospital Records Database (nationalarchives.gov.uk/hospitalrecords) which has information about the location of records of UK hospitals – currently over 2,800 entries.

The Wellcome Trust (wellcome.ac.uk) and its Wellcome Library are also full of advice and information, and it is funding all kinds of projects aimed at improving access to medical records. It is also worth visiting the websites of the likes of the Royal College of Physicians, the Royal College of Nursing, the Royal College of General Practitioners and the Royal College of Surgeons of Edinburgh to see what unique collections they preserve.

Useful websites

British Army nurses' service records (nationalarchives.gov.uk/records/army-nurses-service-records.htm)

British Optical Association Museum (college-optometrists.org/en/college/museyeum/)

Hospital Records Database (nationalarchives.gov.uk/hospitalrecords)

Lambeth Palace Library (lambethpalacelibrary.org)

Holds medical licences issued by the Archbishops of Canterbury between 1535 and 1775.

Lothian Health Services Archives (lhsa.lib.ed.ac.uk)

Medical Museums (medicalmuseums.org)

Royal Army Medical Corps (wellcomelibrary.org/collections/digital-collections/royal-army-medical-corps/)

Royal College of Physicians (munksroll.rcplondon.ac.uk)

Wellcome Library (wellcomelibrary.org/collections/digital-collections/mental-healthcare/)

Involved with several mass-digitisation projects including this Mental Healthcare project, drawing on material from the Library's own archives, as well as partner organisation such as Ticehurst House Hospital and the Retreat in York. Other Wellcome Library material scheduled for digitisation includes the Medical Students' Register (1882–1910) and the Dentists' Register (1879–1942). Another important collaboration with the Royal College of Nursing has resulted in nursing registers and application forms being published on Ancestry.

Wellcome Trust (wellcome.ac.uk)

Provides advice aimed at those researching doctors, physicians, surgeons, apothecaries, nurses, midwives and dentists.

(*See also* 'Hospitals' and 'Nursing'.)

Medieval Genealogy (medievalgenealogy.org.uk): Information about potential medieval sources such as manorial records, government enrolments, taxation returns, heraldic visitations and court material.

Medieval Resources Online (www.leeds.ac.uk/ims/med_online/medresource.html): Fascinating annotated list of online resources from the Institute for Medieval Studies, University of Leeds.

Medieval Scotland, People of (www.poms.ac.uk): Consolidated database of about 21,000 individuals recorded in documents written between 1093 and 1314.

Medieval Soldier (medievalsoldier.org): A database of 220,000 soldiers compiled from muster rolls and records of protections held at TNA, as well as records drawn from French repositories.

Mellon Centre for Migration Studies, Ulster American Folk Park: www.qub.ac.uk/cms/

Memorial: In heraldic circles this word refers to an application for a grant of arms.

Memorial Plaque: Issued after the First World War to the next of kin of all British and Empire service personnel killed as a result of the war. The plaques were made of bronze and became popularly known as 'Dead Man's Penny'.

Mentioned in Dispatches: If your ancestor was MiD it means that a superior officer made an official report to high command describing his or her work worthy of merit. The dispatch would then be published in the *London Gazette*. You can search the *Gazette* for commissions, promotions and appointments, and awards including MiDs at thegazette.co.uk. An MiD is indicated by an oak leaf motif. So the Victory Medal 1914–18, for example, would have the MiD oak leaf spray across the ribbon. British VC recipient John Vereker (1886–1946) was MidD nine times. About 2 per cent of soldiers in the First World War were MiD.

Mercement: Archaic term for a punishment or fine.

Merchant Navy: You'll find plenty of guidance for researching members of the Merchant Navy via the likes of the National Maritime Museum and TNA. TNA guides are generally organised by period (searching merchant seamen between 1858 and 1917, for example), and there are links to searchable sources available here and via external websites.

The Registrar General of Shipping and Seamen was responsible for keeping records of merchant seamen and so most material is held in TNA's Board of Trade record series (BT).

One important external source resides at Southampton Archives (www. southampton.gov.uk/archives/). The Central Index Register of Merchant Seamen includes details of those serving on board British-registered vessels from between 1918 and 1941, and all sections of a ship's crew are included – deck crew, engine crew and victualing crew. Indeed, it includes record cards of seafarers born anywhere in the world, providing they worked on board British vessels. One section of the Register, covering 1918–21, even includes a passport-style photograph of the seaman.

Also known as the 4th Register, you can consult it in the reading room of Southampton Archives, or TNA has a copy on microfiche (also on Findmypast). Southampton Archives offer a research service costing £15 per surname for up to three individuals (email: city.archives@ southampton.gov.uk).

Findmypast has more than 2.6 million Merchant Navy records (in partnership with TNA). The two main sections are 1835–57 ('records of individual seamen that the central government created to monitor a potential reserve of sailors for the Royal Navy'); and 1918–41 ('records of index cards that the Registrar General of Shipping and Seaman used between the two world wars to produce a centralised index to merchant seamen serving on British merchant navy vessels').

Another important resource is the Crew Lists of the British Merchant Navy project (1915crewlists.rmg.co.uk/). It's a volunteer-led collaboration between TNA and the National Maritime Museum to transcribe all the surviving Merchant Navy crew lists from 1915. Approximately 39,000 crew lists featuring over 750,000 names have been photographed and then transcribed by volunteers.

Remember that if your relative continued to serve after 1941, the record will usually have been transferred to the next register (the 5th Register of Merchant Seamen) which is held at TNA. Another fantastic resource searchable via Discovery is the 155,000 index cards to the British War Medal, Mercantile Marine Medal and the Silver War Badge (1914–18).

MERIONETHSHIRE:
Gwynedd Archives Service (gwynedd.gov.uk/archives)
Gwynedd FHS (gwyneddfhs.org)

Merseyside Maritime Museum (liverpoolmuseums.org.uk/maritime/): Includes guides to tracing ancestors who worked in HM Customs and Excise.

Methodist Archives and Research Centre (www.library.manchester. ac.uk/searchresources/guidetospecialcollections/methodist/): Manchester University's Methodist Archives and Research Centre houses an enormous collection of material relating to the early days of the denomination and key figures in its foundation and consolidation. It also holds Methodist newspapers and periodicals which can be useful for tracking down ministers' obituaries. In addition, there is material relating to around 4,000 ministers and lay-Methodists from the eighteenth century to the present day. There's also the Oxford Centre for Methodism and Church History at Oxford Brookes University (www.history.brookes.ac.uk/Research/ Centre-for-Methodism-and-Church-History/).

Methodist Central Hall (church.methodist-central-hall.org.uk): Contains their archives. In addition, it preserves the names of over 1 million people who donated a guinea to the Wesleyan Methodist Twentieth Century Fund between 1899 and 1904. The names were published in a booklet by Richard Ratcliffe for the Family History Partnership.

Methodist Historical Society of Ireland (methodisthistoryireland. org): Maintains an extensive archive relating to Methodism in Ireland, including records of individual churches and journals/periodicals. The website has an index of Irish Methodist churches, chapels and preaching houses, as well as guides to, for example, baptismal and marriage records.

Methodists: The Methodist movement covers more than one denomination, which share a common ancestry back to Anglican clergyman John Wesley (1703–91). Methodism is organised by chapels at the centre of large 'circuits' around which particular ministers would preach, perform baptisms and marriages. The North Lancashire District, for example, currently comprises eighteen circuits of town and country churches. Methodism also spread to Ireland – the first Methodist society was formed in Dublin in 1746, and John Wesley came to Ireland for the first time the following year. By the time of his death in 1791 Irish

Methodist membership numbered over 14,000. Via BMDRegisters you can search Wesleyan Methodist Records from the Wesleyan Methodist Registry, set up in 1818 and continued until 1838. It provided registration of births and baptisms of Wesleyan Methodists throughout England and Wales and elsewhere.

Metropolitan Police Heritage Centre (content.met.police.uk/Site/historicalarchives): Research collections include a 54,000-name database from 1829, Central Records of Service from 1911 and pension cards.

Middle Temple Archives (middletemple.org.uk/about-us/history/): Online sources include registers of admissions from the fifteenth century. (*See also* 'Lawyers'.)

MIDLOTHIAN:
Midlothian Local Studies Centre (www.midlothian.gov.uk/info/476/family_history_archives_and_local_history)

Edinburgh City Archives (www.edinburgh.gov.uk/info/20032/access_to_information/600/edinburgh_city_archives)

Lothian Lives (lothianlives.org.uk)

Migration Heritage Australia: migrationheritage.nsw.gov.au

Migration records: The main TNA record series containing information about emigrants and emigration policy are Colonial Office (CO), Home Office (HO), Board of Trade (BT) and Treasury (T). (*See also* 'Immigration' and 'Emigration'.)

Military Archives (militaryarchives.ie): Records of Ireland's Department of Defence, the Defence Forces and the Army Pensions Board.

Military research: Physical evidence of military service in your family's archive may include certificates, photographs, buttons, caps, uniforms or medals. Many of the most important military collections are preserved at TNA. Subscription-based databases online include Ancestry's TNA collections (army service records 1914–20 and Naval Officer and Rating Service Records 1802–1919); Findmypast's Royal Navy & Marine Service records 1899–1919, Royal Navy Officers Medal Roll 1914–20 and pre-1914 army service records; or TheGenealogist has First World War casualty lists – drawn from weekly/daily War Office lists – and a large POW database.

Below are some of the most useful free websites for starting out or taking further your research into a military ancestor:

Age of Nelson (ageofnelson.org)

Anglo-Afghan War (garenewing.co.uk/angloafghanwar/)

Army Museums (armymuseums.org.uk/ancestor.htm)

Australian War Memorial (awm.gov.au)

Battle of Britain Memorial (battleofbritainmemorial.org)

Boer War Roll of Honour (roll-of-honour.com/Boer/)

Britain's Small Forgotten Wars (britainssmallwars.co.uk)

British Battles (britishbattles.com)

British Medals Forum (britishmedalforum.com)

Bomber Command (rafbombercommand.com)

Bomber History (bomberhistory.co.uk)

Cross & Cockade International (www.crossandcockade.com)

CWGC (cwgc.org)

Fleet Air Arm Archive (fleetairarmarchive.net)

The *Gazette* (thegazette.co.uk)

Great War Forum (1914-1918.invisionzone.com/)

History of RAF (rafweb.org)

Indian Mutiny Medal Roll (search.fibis.org/frontis/bin/)

Inventory of War Memorials (ukniwm.org.uk)

IWM (iwm.org.uk/research)

Lives of the First World War (livesofthefirstworldwar.org)

The Long, Long Trail (longlongtrail.co.uk)

Military Archives (Ireland) (militaryarchives.ie)

MoD (www.gov.uk/requests-for-personal-data-and-service-records)

NAM (national-army-museum.ac.uk)

Napoleon Series (napoleon-series.org)

National Maritime Museum (collections.rmg.co.uk)

Naval History (naval-history.net)

Navy Lists (archive.org/details/nlsnavylists)

Operation War Diary (operationwardiary.org)

Peninsular War (peninsularwar.org)

Prisoners of the First World War (grandeguerre.icrc.org)

RAF Museum StoryVault (rafmuseumstoryvault.org.uk)

Red Cross Voluntary Aid Detachments (redcross.org.uk/ww1)

Register of the Anglo-Boer War 1899–1902 (casus-belli.co.uk)

Royal Army Medical Corps, Wellcome Library (wellcomelibrary.org/collections/digital-collections/royal-army-medical-corps/)

Royal Flying Corps 1914-18 (airwar1.org.uk)

Royal Leicestershire Regiment (royalleicestershireregiment.org.uk)

The Sandhurst Collection (archive.sandhurstcollection.co.uk)

Trafalgar Ancestors (apps.nationalarchives.gov.uk/trafalgarancestors/)

Unit Histories (unithistories.com)

Victoria Cross (victoriacross.org.uk)

Victorian Wars Forum (victorianwars.com)

Waterloo Medal (nmarchive.com/our-data)

Welsh Experience of the First World War (cymru1914.org)

Western Front Association (westernfrontassociation.com)

World War 1 Naval Combat (worldwar1.co.uk)

Military Service Bill: Passed in January 1916, this made military service compulsory for all single men in England, Scotland and Wales aged 18–41 – apart from those in reserved occupations. The only other categories for exception were if they were the sole support of dependents, were medically unfit or who could show some kind of 'conscientious objection'. The law was soon amended and tightened to include married men, increase the maximum age and to reduce the net of occupational exemptions.

Militia: There were various systems for mustering local forces before a Militia Act of 1757 established formal militia regiments across England and Wales. These were essentially part-time voluntary forces, organised by county and the records of conscription (between 1758 and 1831) serve as a kind of census as every year each parish was supposed to draw up lists of adult males, before holding a ballot to choose who would serve. To begin with the lists also noted any infirmities, and later occupations, physical descriptions and even the numbers of children.

Once the list was drawn up, a ballot was held and a muster of men selected by lot. Those selected either had to serve, or they could pay for a substitute to take their place – their names were recorded in the militia enrolment lists. These lists are varyingly described as muster lists, rolls or books.

After 1831, the authorities were no longer able to enforce a ballot and henceforth those who served in the militia did so on a voluntary basis. The original lists, where they survive, are often at county or regimental archives and may have been indexed and transcribed.

One important commercially available database is the Findmypast Militia Attestations Index (1860–1915) – attestations were filled in at recruitment and contain lots of personal data – and militia service records (1806–1915) from TNA WO 96.

TNA has some enrolment and casualty books (WO 68), muster rolls and paylists (WO 13) and the Militia Long Service and Good Conduct medal records (WO 102/22).

As militia lists and allied records tend to survive in regimental archives and local archives, it's worth seeing if any indexes have been produced. You can see transcribed Devon militia lists which were originally printed in the weekly paper *Trewman's Exeter Flying Post* at genuki.cs.ncl.ac.uk/ DEV/DevonMisc/MilitiaLists/index.html. Hertfordshire FHS (hertsfhs. org.uk) has produced 112 booklets containing 280,000 militia records (now combined on a single CD-ROM). A transcribed PDF spreadsheet of Royal Lancashire Regiment register of recruits (1779–82) can be downloaded via Manchester Archives. From this we can learn that 5ft 9in, 37-year-old, dark-haired, hazel-eyed, 'fresh'-skinned Bristol-born staymaker William Clegg was discharged at Danbury Camp in August 1781 for bad behaviour after two years of service.

TheGenealogist (thegenealogist.co.uk) also has a growing collection of English and Welsh militia muster lists. Remember too that details of appointments and commissions for militia officers would be published in the *Gazette* (thegazette.co.uk).

Mills Archive (millsarchive.com): The most important archive for millers and millwrights, based at the Library and Research Centre in Watlington House, Reading. The online catalogue includes images and documents from the archives, as well as a Mill People Database.

Mining: Although records of individual miners are hard to track down, you need to start by finding out where they worked. Once you know where, you can try to track down the company or pit and see what information or archival material has survived. Even if you can't find traces of an individual, you may be able to find out more about the history of the company that employed them.

TNA itself has no personnel records at all, but it does have material relating to administration of the industry. Within local collections you may find colliery accounts, reports and photographs, such as those held at the Tyne & Wear Archives Centre, or perhaps letter books, ledgers, dues accounts, setts and cost books, such as those at Cornwall Record Office.

So while the majority of mining records reside at local/county archives, after nationalisation in 1947 you can look for records from the National Coal Board. There are summary descriptions of the archives available via Discovery (discovery.nationalarchives.gov.uk/details/c/F182763).

Useful websites

Coal Mining History Resource Centre (cmhrc.co.uk)

Durham Mining Museum (dmm.org.uk)

National Coal Mining Museum (ncm.org.uk)

North of England Institute of Mining and Mechanical Engineers Library (mininginstitute.org.uk)

Scottish Mining (scottishmining.co.uk)

Scottish Mining Museum (scottishminingmuseum.com)

Tyne & Wear Archives Centre (twmuseums.org.uk/tyne-and-wear-archives/catalogue-amp-user-guides/user-guides.html)

Welsh Coal Mines (welshcoalmines.co.uk)

Database of mines with histories and images.

Welsh Mines Society (welshmines.org)

Ministry of Defence (www.gov.uk/requests-for-personal-data-and-service-records): This is the website through which next of kin can request service records of soldiers who served after 1920 (other ranks) and 1922 (officers).

Minstrels: You can read a fascinating thesis on the subject of minstrels by Professor of Historical Musicology Richard Rastall via townwaits.org. uk. Here's a short excerpt: 'A permanent position at Court was perhaps the best post that a minstrel could hope for. It offered a reasonable wage and a certain amount of security should he be unable to work through illness or old age. It offered, too, plenty of opportunity for independent work, for the royal minstrels were not required to be in Court all the year round ... The royal household ordinances of 1318 made provision for two trumpeters and two other minstrels to be in constant attendance on the king, and to make their minstrelsy to him at his pleasure. A similar nucleus of four minstrels was specified in the ordinances of 1455, with another nine minstrels coming to Court at the principal feasts of the year. The Liber Niger of Edward IV's reign required two minstrels to remain in Court at all times, with the addition of two string-minstrels if the king wished: the other minstrels were required to come to Court for the five principal feasts and to leave Court the day after each feast was finished.'

Minutes: Council minutes are usually of more interest to local historians than genealogists, but personal names do crop up. They normally survive in county record offices. Aberdeen's Town House Charter Room holds the minutes of the council from 1398 to the present day – the oldest council minutes in Scotland.

Miriam Weiner Routes to Roots Foundation (rtrfoundation.org): A guide to Jewish and civil records in Eastern Europe.

Missing from the census: While boycotting Suffragettes went to great pains to duck the enumerator on census night in 1911, there are many more mundane reasons why an ancestor might be absent from a census record. It may be that your ancestor simply gave a different name to the one you were expecting – perhaps because of re-marriage or some petty criminal activity. The most common reason for such subterfuge was simply embarrassment – the unmarried couple who, for respectability's sake, wished to appear married, or the separated couple who preferred to describe themselves as widowed. Another common reason was being out of the country – working overseas or on active service with the army or navy.

If you can't find someone in one online census index, try another. Indexes come from different projects and teams, so a transcription mistake in one may have been avoided in another. Even without an index, if you think you know where an ancestor was living, you can of course go straight to that address in the census. And if you are failing to find an individual make sure you have tried all the spellings variations (also taking into account potential transcription errors).

Remember too that in 1841, what with the practice of rounding down ages and the fact that someone might lie about their age, there may be a huge difference between the age recorded and the age you were expecting.

There are also gaps in the actual census record. So if you think a household is missing from the 1861 census (which has the most gaps), you can confirm missing parishes or districts using the advanced search option in TNA's Discovery catalogue (enter the keyword 'missing' within RG 9). You can also identify pages that are known to be missing within some enumeration districts by using the exact phrase 'missing pages' within RG 9.

Mitchell Library (glasgowfamilyhistory.org.uk): Holds Glasgow City Archives, Special Collections as well as the NHS Greater Glasgow and Clyde Archives. The site includes a complete A–Z of research guides.

Modern Records Centre (www2.warwick.ac.uk/services/library/mrc/): University of Warwick's Modern Records Centre was founded in 1973. It has a useful page aimed at family historians – including a list of commonly searched trades/occupations, adapted from a 1927 dictionary produced by the Ministry of Labour. Collections held here include the Brewers' Society archive, which has bound sets of *Brewing Trade Review* and artwork for advertising campaigns, as well as motor industry records (especially the Rover Group), trade associations and trade-union records.

MONMOUTHSHIRE:
Gwent Archives (gwentarchives.gov.uk)

Gwent comprises most of Monmouthshire and a small part of Breconshire – the rest of Monmouthshire is part of modern Glamorgan.
Gwent FHS (gwentfhs.info)

Monogram: Motif or symbol made by combining two or more letters.

MONTGOMERYSHIRE:
Powys Archives (archives.powys.gov.uk)

Montgomeryshire Genealogical Society (montgomeryshiregs.org.uk)

Powys FHS (powysfhs.org.uk)

Monumental Inscriptions: Gravestones can contain information not found elsewhere and give clues about a family's wealth, status or occupation. Inscriptions will usually confirm dates of birth and death at the very least, and will sometimes mention family relationships, and grander examples may include heraldic devices or designs relating to the source of a family's wealth. Genealogical and antiquarian societies have been plotting, transcribing, photographing and caring for gravestones for years. Resulting publications may sometimes be slim printed booklets relating to a single church right up to county wide indexes on CD. Some societies provide online indexes which then link to MI downloads, and more and more of this data is also coming online through specialist sites such as DeceasedOnline (deceasedonline.com) and through agreements with FamilySearch, Findmypast, Ancestry, TheGenealogist et al.

Moonrakers: The colloquial name for Wiltshire residents, which derives from a folk tale of smugglers who hid contraband brandy in a village pond. When trying to retrieve the items at night, they were caught by revenue men and pretended to be harmless yokels, pointing to the moon's reflection and saying they were trying to rake in a round cheese.

MORAY:
Moray Council Local Heritage Centre (www.moray.gov.uk/moray_standard/page_1537.html)
Moray & Nairn FHS (morayandnairnfhs.co.uk)
Moray Burial Ground Research Group (mbgrg.org)

Mormons: Members of the LDS Church, founded by Joseph Smith in the US in the 1820s.

Mortuary: A payment made to the vicar by a parishioner on the death of someone in the parishioner's household.

Municipal boroughs: Local government districts/towns, formed by the Municipal Corporations Act 1835 and abolished in 1974.

Municipal burial grounds: Partnerships with commercial bodies like DeceasedOnline is leading to more and more data from municipal burial sites coming online. But it's also worth seeing what the relevant local authority website has to offer. Burial records from Kingston and Surbiton cemeteries ranging from 1855 to 2003, for example, are at www.kingston.gov.uk/directory/20/burial_records. And you can search 360,000 Belfast burial records from three cemeteries dating back to 1869, via www.belfastcity.gov.uk/community/burialrecords/burialrecords.aspx. There's also the Manchester Burial Records database at: www.burialrecords.manchester.gov.uk.

Muniments: An umbrella term for a collection of records that prove a person's or institution's rights to an estate.

Museum of English Rural Life (reading.ac.uk/merl/): The Museum in Reading looks after all kinds of collections relating to rural life and craftsmen, as well as special collections such as the Robert Dawson Romany Collection. Several research projects are ongoing, but one completed example is the Digitisation of Countryside Images Project, funded by the Joint Information Systems Committee. It began in 2008, finished the following year and saw some 13,000 glass-plate negatives (mainly from the *Farmers Weekly* and *Farmer and Stockbreeder* photographic collections) digitised and catalogued.

Museum of Scottish Lighthouses (lighthousemuseum.org.uk): This Museum in Fraserburgh has a visitors' book from Hoy Low lighthouse in Stromness, bearing the signatures of Robert Louis Stevenson and his father Thomas Stevenson, who was working for the Northern Lighthouse Board.

My Methodist History (mymethodisthistory.org.uk): Community archive network – there are also the sister websites My Primitive Methodist Ancestors (myprimitivemethodists.org.uk) and My Wesleyan Methodist Ancestors (mywesleyanmethodists.org.uk).

My Slave Ancestors (myslaveancestors.com): American website with advice for tracing slave ancestors.

My Uncle Fred (myunclefred.blogspot.co.uk): Blogged Blitz diary kept by Londoner Fred French. 'Monica called … She recognised the door we now have at the back of the house as coming from her demolished house, it was previously the door of her auntie Winifred's bedroom.'

N

NAIRNSHIRE:

Highland Archive Centre (highlandarchives.org.uk/harc.asp)

Highland FHS (highlandfamilyhistorysociety.org)

Napoleonic Wars: Series of conflicts between Napoleon's France and various European nations (1799–1815). The vast Napoleon Series website (napoleon-series.org) is a collection of online projects relating to the Napoleonic Wars, including the Peninsular Roll Call – an index of officers who served with Wellington's army. This was originally compiled by Captain Lionel Challis, who began working on the project soon after the First World War. NAM has led a volunteer project to transcribe historic diaries penned by soldiers who served during the Napoleonic Wars. You can find out more about the Waterloo Lives project via heritagehelpers.co.uk.

The National Archives (nationalarchives.gov.uk): The official UK government archive based in Kew, formerly known as the Public Record Office. Holdings include records of central government and the legal system of England and Wales. Records relating to the UK as a whole may contain information on Scotland and Ireland – all of Ireland was part of the UK until 1922. Important genealogical resources include military and naval records. All records can be searched through Discovery, TNA's online catalogue (discovery.nationalarchives.gov.uk), which also gives access to catalogued collections from archives across the UK. A good starting point is the A–Z of research guides, which quickly illustrate what you need to know before researching a subject, and what is available at TNA and elsewhere, and what is and isn't available online. The Census research guide, for example (nationalarchives.gov.uk/records/research-guides/census-returns.htm), lists what you can learn from the census returns with links to official partner subscription websites where you can access the material.

National Archives of America: archives.gov

National Archives of Australia: naa.giv.au

National Archives of Ireland (nationalarchives.ie): Preserves records relating to Ireland and there's a specialist genealogy site (genealogy.nationalarchives.ie) where you can access digital resources including surviving censuses of Ireland and Calendars of Wills and Administrations (1858–1922).

National Archives of Scotland: Preserves records of Scottish government and history. It was known as the Scottish Record Office until 1999, and in 2011 it merged with the General Register Office for Scotland to become the National Records of Scotland (nrscotland.gov.uk). Today New Register House is where researchers can order copies of birth, marriage and death certificates. While General Register House (at 2 Princes Street) is home to the ScotlandsPeople Centre and Historical Search Room.

National Army Museum (national-army-museum.ac.uk): London museum that concentrates on Army history from 1485 to date. You can explore sample documents, photographs and prints via Online Collection. The Museum is also leading a crowdsourcing project to digitise and transcribe diaries from its Napoleonic Archive.

National Burial Index: An important national project, overseen by the Federation of Family History Societies, which saw member societies contributing towards a single consolidated index. The first edition was published in 2001 with 5.4 million records taken from registers and bishops' transcripts, mainly between 1813 and 1850. It has gone through several editions and is now available online via Findmypast.

National Coal Mining Museum: ncm.org.uk

National Co-Operative Archive: www.archive.coop

National Fairground Archive (shef.ac.uk/nfa): Part of special collections at the University of Sheffield Library, the NFA has photographic, printed, manuscript and audiovisual material recording the 'culture, business and life of travelling showpeople'.

National Library of Ireland (nli.ie): Ireland's national library is located in Dublin and was opened in 1890. As well as books, maps and manuscripts, the Library houses the National Photographic Archive and Irish newspapers. One important online resource is the digitised microfilm copies of registers from the most Catholic parishes in Ireland and Northern Ireland (registers.nli.ie).

National Library of Scotland (nls.uk): The legal deposit library of Scotland and Scotland's largest library. Based in Edinburgh, it has more than 7 million books and 14 million printed items. Famous rarities here include a Gutenberg Bible and Shakespeare First Folio. The Maps section (maps.nls.uk) gives access to high-resolution images of over 91,000 maps of Scotland from 1580–1919. There's also the Word on the Street (digital. nls.uk/broadsides/) collection of nearly 1,800 broadsides.

National Library of Wales: The national legal deposit library of Wales, based in Aberystwyth. It boasts more than 6.5 million books and periodicals, as well as the principality's largest collections of archives, portraits, maps and photographs. The Library's Crime & Punishment Database is based on gaol files of the Court of Great Sessions in Wales (1730–1830). There's also the wonderful Welsh Newspapers Online (newspapers.library.wales). At time of writing this expanding free resource boasted 15 million articles from 1.1 million pages preserved here. You can search by categories such as family notices and advertisements, browse by exact date, date range or by region/title. The Church in Wales Archive preserves registers of baptisms, marriages and burials, bishops' transcripts, wills and marriage bonds. You can also view wills proved in Welsh ecclesiastical courts before 1858 via cat.llgc.org.uk/probate.

National Maritime Museum (collections.rmg.co.uk): Here you can find out about the Museum's collections and search the Archive/Library catalogue.

National Museum of Rural Life, Scotland: nms.ac.uk/national-museum-of-rural-life

National Railway Museum (nrm.org.uk): The website of the NRM's library and archive includes an online catalogue and family history advice page. There are also PDF indexes to names in various staff magazines.

National Records of Scotland (nrscotland.gov.uk): Responsible for Scottish government records going back to the twelfth century.

National Register of Archives for Scotland (www.nas.gov.uk/nras/): Searchable register of collections held by private individuals and families, landed estates, clubs and societies, businesses and law firms.

National School Registers, 1870–1914: School registers and log books are not only a wonderful source for family history, but also reveal details about the wider community. The registers contain details of pupil's address, occupation of parents and more, and they can also be used to find out more about teachers. They tend to survive either at the schools themselves, or, more usually, in county and borough collections. The Findmypast register project (see findmypast.co.uk/school-registers) draws on school material from a consortium of more than 100 archives and schools. The registers date from 1870–1914 and come from all over England and Wales.

National Screen & Sound Archive of Wales: archif.com

National Society for Promoting Religious Education: The Society was founded in 1811 and ran the so-called 'National Schools' across England and Wales during the nineteenth century. This was the start of elementary education for all in England and Wales and in time the National Schools were mostly absorbed into the state system. There were also at this time the non-denominational 'British Schools' founded by the British and Foreign School Society.

National time: 'Local time' was causing problems with railway timetables. As a consequence, during the 1840s the rail companies lobbied for the creation of a standard 'British Time' throughout the country. By 1847 most were using London Time (Greenwich Mean Time). Daylight Saving was introduced in 1916 to increase productivity.

Naturalisation: A process by which someone from outside a country – often referred to as an 'alien' or 'denizen' – becomes a legal citizen of the parent country.

Naturalisation case papers, 1801–71: This collection of naturalisation and denization papers make up TNA's series HO 1 and are available online via nationalarchives.gov.uk. These documents were completed by those applying to become British citizens, and the series includes applications to the Secretary of State (1844–71), naturalisations by private Act of Parliament (1801–68) and letters applying for denization. (*See also* 'Immigration'.)

Naval-History.net (naval.history.net): Vast website with all kinds of material on RN dispatches, honours and awards, operations, battles and more. These include 350,000 pages of transcribed log books from the First World War.

Navvy: 'Navigator' – a labourer involved in the building of canals, roads and railways.

Navy: RN personnel are either ordinary seaman (ratings) or officers. And how much information was recorded about individual careers varies over time. So an important thing to uncover as you start out your research is when the person joined – the majority of the most useful collections are at TNA. Records of servicemen who joined after 1923 are still held by the navy. Next of kin can request a summary of a service record for an individual who joined after May 1917 from MoD.

Most nineteenth-century service records include officer's name and rank, ships they served in and dates of entry/discharge from each vessel. Records can also include date of death, birth and next of kin. RN officers' service records (1756–1931) are online and include records for commissioned officers joining the navy up to 1917 and warrant officers joining up to 1931. You can search for free via Discovery and download for a fee. You can also search officers' service record cards and files (*c.* 1880–1950s) and Ancestry has a Commissioned Sea Officers of the Royal Navy database.

This TNA site (nationalarchives.gov.uk/records/royal-naval-officers-service-records.htm) is the RN officers' service records (1756–1931) search page. Wills of RN and Royal Marines personnel (1786–1882) can be searched via Discovery. There are also several relevant TNA research guides with details of resources on and offline.

Ancestry has Naval Medal and Award Rolls (1793–1972) and Naval Officer and Rating Service Records (1802–1919), including musters and pay registers. Meanwhile Findmypast has British Royal Navy & Marine Service records (1899–1919), Royal Naval Division Service Records (1914–20) and the Royal Navy Officers Medal Roll (1914–20).

Useful websites

Naval-History.net (naval.history.net)

Navy List (navylist.org)

Nelson's Navy (nelsonsnavy.co.uk)

Royal Navy Research Archives (royalnavyresearcharchive.org.uk)

Ships Pictures (shipspictures.co.uk)

Submarines of the Great War (dropbears.com/w/ww1subs/)

Trafalgar Ancestors (apps.nationalarchives.gov.uk/trafalgarancestors/)

World War 1 Naval Combat (worldwar1.co.uk)

Has sections focusing on the Battle of Heligoland Bight, the loss of HMS *Audacious*, the battles of Dogger Bank and Jutland, and the Scapa Flow Scuttling.

Navy Lists: These were official quarterly lists recording RN officers on active duty. These include rank, seniority and the ship or establishment in which the officer was serving. These are available from a number of websites, including archive.org/details/nlsnavylists – scanned from volumes held at NLS, the earliest dating from 1819 and many dating from the Second World War.

Navy Records Society (navyrecordsonline.co.uk): As the name suggests, this Society publishes rare and original documents relating to naval history – in print and online. Founded in 1893, it has produced over 160 printed volumes.

Nelson, Age of (ageofnelson.org): Has databases of RN officers in the French Revolutionary and Napoleonic wars (1793–1815), and seamen and marines who fought at the Battle of Trafalgar in 1805.

Nelson Society: nelson-society.com

Nephew/niece: These words had a wider meaning in the past. Up to about the seventeenth century they could be used to refer to any younger male or female relative.

NEW ZEALAND:
Archives New Zealand (archives.govt.nz)

Family History Society of New Zealand (www.familyhistorynz.org)

National Library of New Zealand (natlib.govt.nz)

New Zealand Society of Genealogists (www.genealogy.org.nz)

Newspapers: Newspapers can offer all kinds of information not available elsewhere. If your ancestor was involved in some newsworthy event, a local civic celebration, a strike or dispute, sporting event or works outing, a crime, was a witness in a court case or died in circumstances that prompted an inquest you may find some contemporary reports. Indeed, in some cases the report of an incident may be the only evidence that survives. You can also search national and regional newspapers for notices of births, marriages or deaths, or more detailed printed obituaries.

Many current newspapers run their own pay-per-view/subscription archives, but the leading subscription website in the field is the British Newspaper Archive (britishnewspaperarchive.co.uk). It offers access to an expanding database of newspapers held at the BL's newspaper collections. Alongside national British and Irish titles, it has local newspapers from England, Scotland and Wales. Searching is free, but it costs to view the resulting images.

Welsh Newspapers Online (newspapers.library.wales) offers free access to collections of newspapers had at the NLW. You can search by categories such as family notices and advertisements, browse by exact date, date range or by region/title. It currently boasts 15 million articles and 1.1 million pages.

Another free resource is the *Gazette* (www.thegazette.co.uk), offering access to Britain's official public record – the *London*, *Edinburgh* and *Belfast Gazettes*. A great overseas example is Australia's Trove (trove.nla.gov.au), which offers access to books, images and historic newspapers.

There's also the *Spectator* Archive 1828–2008 (archive.spectator.co.uk), *The Times* Archive (thetimes.co.uk/tto/archive/), Last Chance To Read (lastchancetoread.com), Isle of Wight County Press Archive (archive. iwcp.co.uk) and Manx National Heritage (www.imuseum.im).

Nineteenth-Century Serials Edition (www.ncse.ac.uk): Free online edition of six titles including Chartist newspaper the *Northern Star* (1838–52), *Leader* (1950–60) and the *English Woman's Journal* (1858–64).

Nob thatcher: Eighteenth-century slang for a wig maker.

Noble: A coin valued 6s. 8d. which first appeared in the fourteenth century. This was the first English gold coin to be mass-produced – the preceding gold penny and florin were not in wide circulation.

Nonconformists: The term derives from the Great Ejection of 1662, when more than 2,000 clergy were ejected from the Church of England after refusing to swear an oath to the new Act of Uniformity – which set out new forms of prayers and sacraments. This led to the concept of 'Nonconformist' – the Protestant Christian who did not 'conform'.

Nonconformists include Presbyterians (in England and Wales), Congregationalists, Baptists, Quakers and Methodists, among others. And there tend to be regional pockets of Nonconformist churches – Wales was dominated by the Methodist church, while Westmorland, Cumberland, Lancashire, Durham and Yorkshire had larger numbers of Quakers.

Nonconformists would use their local parish church for registration purposes (even after the Toleration Act of 1689 granted some freedom to worship), but they also kept their own registers, particularly for births, baptisms and burials. Between 1754 and 1837 it was illegal to marry anywhere except in a Church of England parish church, unless you were a member of the Society of Friends (Quakers) or Jewish. And after 1837, while people were now allowed to marry in the church of their choice, some organisations still did not keep their own records.

An important digital resource for Nonconformism is the 8 million birth/baptism, marriage and burial records drawn from TNA, including material from Quakers (Society of Friends), Methodists, Wesleyans,

Baptists, Independents, Protestant Dissenters, Congregationalists, Presbyterians and Unitarians. The data is available via TheGenealogist or BMDregisters.co.uk site, and there are free indexes on FamilySearch. Ancestry has the London Nonconformist Registers (1694–1921) collection – drawn from material at LMA.

NORFOLK:

Norfolk Record Office (archives.norfolk.gov.uk)

Has archives of Norwich Cathedral and Norwich Diocese, as well as Nonconformist churches and chapels. The medieval records of the Great Hospital, Norwich, are inscribed on UNESCO's Memory of the World Register. They also have records of several ecclesiastical courts which dealt with probate, including the Consistory Court of Norwich (covering Suffolk and part of Cambridgeshire) and the archdeaconry courts of Norfolk and Norwich.

Norfolk FHS (norfolkfhs.org.uk)

Mid Norfolk FHS (tsites.co.uk/sites/mnfhs/)

North East Inheritance Database (familyrecords.dur.ac.uk/nei/data/): A database of pre-1858 probate records (wills and related documents) covering Northumberland and County Durham. Digital images of the original probate records (including wills and inventories, 1650–1857, copies of wills, 1527–1858, and executors' and administration bonds, 1702–1858) are also available through FamilySearch.

North of England Institute of Mining and Mechanical Engineers Library: mininginstitute.org.uk

NORTHAMPTONSHIRE:

Northamptonshire Archives, Heritage & History (northamptonshire. gov.uk/heritage)

Northamptonshire FHS (northants-fhs.org)

Peterborough & District FHS (peterborofhs.org.uk)

NORTHERN IRELAND: Antrim, Armagh, Down, Fermanagh, Londonderry and Tyrone:

PRONI (proni.gov.uk)

Online records include Will Calendars, Valuation Revision Books, Street Directories, the Ulster Covenant, Freeholders Records, Londonderry Corporation Records.

Derry Genealogy Centre (derrycity.gov.uk/Genealogy/Derry-Genealogy)

Via derry.rootsireland.ie you can access the mass database to pre-1922 civil birth and marriage registers, early BMD registers of 85 churches (26 Roman Catholic, 24 Church of Ireland and 35 Presbyterian) and gravestone inscriptions from 117 graveyards, as well as pre-1910 registers of Derry City Cemetery. There's also the index to 1901 census returns and to Griffith's Valuation of 1858/1859.

Belfast City Council Burials (www.belfastcity.gov.uk/burialrecords/index.asp)

Look up 360,000 burial records from the Belfast City (from 1869), Roselawn (from 1954) and Dundonald (from 1905) cemeteries.

Linen Hall Library (linenhall.com)

NAI (nationalarchives.ie)

North of Ireland FHS (nifhs.org)

Irish Genealogy Research Society (irishancestors.ie)

Northern Ireland Police Museum (www.psni.police.uk/inside-psni/our-history/police-museum)

NORTHUMBERLAND:
Woodhorn Museum & Northumberland Archives (experiencewoodhorn.com)

The main archive is based at Woodhorn, which itself was originally a coal mine – the first shaft dug in 1894, producing its first coal four years later, and at its peak it employed almost 2,000 men. It is the record office for the Diocese of Newcastle, but there were a large number of Nonconformist churches in Northumberland – mainly Methodist and Presbyterian, as well as Roman Catholics. Registers and records of many of these churches survive here.

Museums & Archives Northumberland (manorthumberland.org.uk)

Tyne & Wear Archives (twmuseums.org.uk/tyne-and-wear-archives.html)

Northumberland & Durham FHS (ndfhs.org.uk)

NOTTINGHAMSHIRE:
Nottinghamshire Archives (nottinghamshire.gov.uk/archives)

Nottinghamshire FHS (nottsfhs.org.uk)

University of Nottingham's Collections (nottingham.ac.uk/Manuscripts andSpecialCollections/CollectionsInDepth/Family/Introduction.aspx)

The Manuscripts and Special Collections Department houses a collection of bonds and allegations for marriage licences granted by the Archdeaconry Court of Nottingham from 1594–1884, as well as Family and Estate Collections from important Nottinghamshire landowning families.

Nuncupative will: A will that is dictated rather than written down. The 1627 nuncupative will and inventory of carpenter Nicholas Perry of 'New Sarum' (Salisbury) describes how at a time of plague Perry sought refuge in nearby Coombe Bissett, and took the opportunity to make a will because his son Nicholas had threatened to 'use his wife hardly' and throw her out. Perry decided to give all his property to his younger son Anthony.

Nursing: A key date in the history of nursing is 1846. This is when the first hospital training school for nurses was established in Kaiserwerth, Germany. Florence Nightingale received her training there and she went on to establish the first UK school of nurses at St Thomas' Hospital in London. She then famously oversaw the work of female nurses at military hospitals during the Crimean War.

An important collaboration between the Royal College of Nursing and the Wellcome Library (wellcome.ac.uk) has seen the digitisation of nursing registers and application forms published on Ancestry. To find out more about the Royal College of Nursing Archives go to: archives.rcn. org.uk. Here you can also explore digitised copies of journals including the *Nursing Record*, published from 1888–1956, changing its name in 1902 to the *British Journal of Nursing*.

TNA has British Army nurses' service records (1914–18), and guides to researching patients, doctors and nurses. The website www.scarletfinders. co.uk also has some interesting material relating to nursing during the First World War, and the Hospital Records Database (nationalarchives. gov.uk/hospitalrecords) provides information about the location of the records of UK hospitals. Another of the Wellcome Library's digital collections relates to the RAMC (at wellcomelibrary.org/collections/ digital-collections/royal-army-medical-corps/).

The Royal British Nurses' Association (rbna.org.uk) was founded in December 1887, and its archives are housed at King's College. Highlights include periodicals such as the *Nursing Record* (from 1902), *British journal of Nursing* (1888–1956), *Nurses Journal* (1891–1918), the *International Nursing Review* (1926–39) and the *RBNA Journal* (1947–63).

You can also find out more about Red Cross Voluntary Aid Detachments via redcross.org.uk/ww1.

(*See also* 'Hospitals' and 'Medicine'.)

O

Occupational sources: These can take many forms, from handwritten documents, to staff registers, to in-company magazines, to uniforms and cap badges. If you have found your ancestor in the census, hopefully the enumerator recorded their profession. The highly trained and well paid tended to leave more of a trail than a transient labourer. You may be able to trace lawyers, doctors or architects, for example, through records of further education, examinations or apprenticeships. Meanwhile, for some industries, such as mining or ship building, for example, there are multiple archives and museums dedicated to their study, and yet, finding records of individuals is by no means a certainty.

You need to find out:

1. The company the individual worked for.
2. Their occupation/trade within that company.
3. If an archive of that company survives, and, if so, where is it held – by the parent company? Or is it deposited at the local county archive?
4. Does the archive include staff records – and have the records been catalogued?
5. Is there some centralised source or archive relating to the industry in which they worked? Other records to look for include training or apprenticeship records, or trade association or trade-union material.

If you find an archaic or unfamiliar term in the occupation field, there are several sites with A–Z guides to some old, forgotten occupations:

Dictionary of Old Occupations (www.familyresearcher.co.uk/glossary/Dictionary-of-Old-Occupations-Index.html)

England Occupations (familysearch.org/learn/wiki/en/England_Occupations)

Hall Genealogy (rmhh.co.uk/occup/index.html)

Old Occupations in Scotland (scotsfamily.com/occupations.htm)

ScotlandsPeople (www.scotlandspeople.gov.uk/content/help/index.aspx?r=551&430)

Useful websites
Ancestry (ancestry.co.uk/cs/uk/occupations-alta)

Has the likes of British Postal Service Appointment Books (1737–1969), Civil Engineer Lists (1818–1930) and Electrical Engineer Lists (1871–1930).

Black County Living Museum (www.bclm.co.uk)

British Postal Museum and Archive (www.postalheritage.org.uk)

British Telecom Digital Archives (www.digitalarchives.bt.com)

Business Archives Council of Scotland (www.gla.ac.uk/services/archives/bacs/)

Business/Company Records, TNA guide (nationalarchives.gov.uk/records/looking-for-subject/business.htm)

Findmypast (findmypast.co.uk)

Occupational collections include Thames Watermen and Lightermen (1688–2010) and the Dental Surgeons Directory (1925).

Genuki (genuki.org.uk/big/Occupations.html)

Livery Companies (liverycompanies.com)

New Lanark World Heritage Site (newlanark.org)

NRS (nrscotland.gov.uk/research/visit-us/scotlandspeople-centre/useful-websites-for-family-history-research/occupations)

Scottish Architects (www.scottisharchitects.org.uk).

Tolpuddle Martyrs Museum (tolpuddlemartyrs.org.uk)

Old Age Pensions Act: Passed by the Liberal government in 1908, the Act provided between 1s. and 5s. a week to people over the age of 70 (whose income was below 12s.). The system was administered by local committees whose records are at county record offices. These contain information about applicants for pensions.

Old Bailey Online (www.oldbaileyonline.org): Database of 197,745 criminal trials held at London's central criminal court from 1674–1913.

Old Maps Online (oldmapsonline.org): Gateway to more than 400,000 historic maps online, drawn from institutions and archives across the globe.

Old Occupations in Scotland (scotsfamily.com/occupations.htm): Useful list of unusual occupations drawn from census returns and gravestone inscriptions.

Old Parish Registers: In Scotland parish registers are referred to as Old Parish Registers, or OPRs. Today NRS holds the original registers, which are accessible via the ScotlandsPeople website. The decree that Church of Scotland parishes should keep records was laid down in 1552. As with England and Wales, the system took time to bed in. There was no standardisation, early entries can be spartan and hard to read and indeed many parishes didn't begin keeping the records until much later. The oldest surviving register comes from Errol in Perthshire, and dates from 1553.

Olive Tree Genealogy (olivetreegenealogy.com): Pioneering North American family history website that was launched in February 1996 and provides access to all sorts of free genealogical records.

One-Name Studies, Guild of (one-name.org): While family historians generally focus on researching branches of a family tree, one-name studies research all occurrences of a surname – sometimes restricted to a region, others worldwide. Founded in 1979, the GOONs is a specialist off-shoot of the Federation of Family History Societies, based at the SoG. Via one-name.org you can explore the full list of members' websites.

Online Parish Clerks: Cornwall was the birthplace of the Online Parish Clerks scheme (cornwall-opc.org), and here you can access a free index/transcription database of parish registers. You can explore other examples of regional Online Parish Clerks projects via ukbmd.org.uk/ online_parish_clerk.

Others include:
Devon Online Parish Clerks (genuki.cs.ncl.ac.uk/DEV/OPCproject.html)
Dorset Online Parish Clerks (opcdorset.org)
Essex Online Parish Clerks (essex-opc.org.uk)
Hampshire Online Parish Clerks (knightroots.co.uk)
Kent Online Parish Clerks (kent-opc.org)
Lancashire Online Parish Clerks (lan-opc.org.uk)
Somerset Online Parish Clerks (wsom-opc.org.uk)
Sussex Online Parish Clerks (sussex-opc.org)
Warwickshire Online Parish Clerks (hunimex.com/warwick/opc/opc. html)
Wiltshire Online Parish Clerks (wiltshire-opc.org.uk)

Online searching: Always be wary of narrowing searches too quickly. If you narrow by a parish that turns out later to be incorrect, you may miss the vital reference you have been looking for. Similarly if you go for an exact spelling of a surname, you may miss any misspellings that may have occurred in the original records themselves, or have cropped up in the indexing or transcription. This is sometimes summarised as 'rubbish in, rubbish out'. In other words, if inputted data is incomplete or inaccurate, then the results are likely to be unreliable.

Open Domesday (opendomesday.org): A free online copy of the Domesday Book which allows you to explore entries by county.

Operation War Diary (operationwardiary.org): Crowdsourcing project seeking to unlock the hidden stories contained within 1,500,000 million pages of First World War unit war diaries.

Oral History Society: www.ohs.org.uk

Orders & Medals Research Society: omrs.org.uk

Ordnance Survey (ordnancesurvey.co.uk): The UK's national mapping agency, formed in 1791. In 1841 it moved to a new home in Southampton just days after fire destroyed its former Tower of London headquarters. (*See also* 'Maps'.)

ORKNEY:

Orkney FHS (orkneyfhs.co.uk)

Orkney Library & Archive (www.orkneylibrary.org.uk)

Osbert, William Fitz: A London citizen notable for being the first person to be executed at Tyburn. He was condemned in 1196 for his role in an uprising of the poor. The last to be executed here was highwayman John Austin in 1783.

Our Lady's Day: 25 March, also known simply as Lady Day, which was also New Year's Day between 1155 and 1752 – when 1 January was made the official start of new year. Lady Day was traditionally when year long contracts between owners and tenant farmers would begin and end.

Overseas registrations: TNA has births, marriages and deaths that were registered overseas – including British subjects onboard ships and those on military service. You can search these via specialist website BMDRegisters.co.uk or TheGenealogist.co.uk. Many pre-date the start of civil registration.

Overseers accounts: Like vestry minutes, these record payments made to the poor of the parish, as well as rates charged and received, and are found at county record offices. They tend to record not only the names of individual paupers, but also local tradespeople who were paid to carry out maintenance or other duties.

OXFORDSHIRE:
Oxfordshire FHS (ofhs.org.uk)

Oxfordshire History Centre (oxfordshire.gov.uk/cms/public-site/oxford shire-history-centre)

The Oxfordshire History Centre opened its doors in July 2011. It has lots of material relating to local businesses and firms, such as the archive of Early's Blanket Company of Witney, comprising a large collection from its charter of incorporation in 1711 to its closure in the early twenty-first century. There's also Morrell's Brewery of Oxford, the Morland Brewery of Abingdon and Morris Motors of Cowley.

Oxfordshire Health Archives (oxfordshirehealtharchives.nhs.uk): The archives include those of Oxfordshire hospitals and National Health Service administrative bodies, Leagues of Friends and Nurses' Alumni organisations. It also details records of the training of nurses from 1891 – managed by individual hospitals and later the Oxford School of Nursing.

Oxgang: An archaic unit of land in Scotland and England, also known as a bovate. This is essentially the Danelaw equivalent of the yardland or virgate. It represented the amount of land that could be ploughed using one ox in a single annual season.

P

Palace Green Library (www.dur.ac.uk/palace.green/): The home of Durham University's special collections. Important collections here are the bishops' transcripts of County Durham and Northumberland parish registers from between 1760 and 1840. Images of these transcripts are available through FamilySearch. You can find out more via familyrecords. dur.ac.uk, which gives information and access to marriage licences, tithe records, estates material, consistory court material, land tax records, university material and more.

Palaeography: The study of ancient writing. There are lots of online materials aimed at genealogists to help decipher old handwriting – especially the tricky scripts, Latin terms and abbreviations favoured by document keepers in the sixteenth and seventeenth centuries. On FamilySearch, for example, there are free lessons to reading handwritten documents, a useful Secretary Hand alphabet and a guide to Old English. There's also TNA's Palaeography page (www.nationalarchives.gov.uk/palaeography/), Early modern palaeography (paleo.anglo-norman.org/empfram.html) and Scottish Handwriting (www.scottishhandwriting.com), which gives online tuition to help read and interpret Scottish records.

Pallot's indexes: The original index of marriages and births was begun in the early nineteenth century and compiled on handwritten index slips. Indexing continued regularly over a period of more than 150 years. Each slip identifies the church or chapel in which the event was celebrated, names and some other details. The original slips are owned and held at the Institute of Heraldic and Genealogical Studies. Remember that the index recorded information from some registers that have since been lost. You can access the indexes via Ancestry. It is estimated that the marriage index includes more 1.5 million marriages in England. The birth index was damaged during the London Blitz but still includes around 100,000 entries.

Parish (civil): The lowest tier of local government (below districts and counties). Parishes can vary a great deal in terms of size and population. Civil parishes were established by the Local Government Act 1894, when parishes were grouped into districts and each civil parish had an elected civil parish council. The 1911 census noted that 8,322 parishes in England and Wales were not identical for civil and ecclesiastical purposes.

Parish (ecclesiastical): The jurisdictional unit that governs Church affairs within its boundaries, each keeping its own records. Small villages will often be part of a larger parish whose 'headquarters' are elsewhere. And a parish may consist of one or more chapelries, dependent district churches or 'chapels of ease' – a chapel situated closer to communities who lived a long distance from the parish church. These are particularly common in Northern England.

Parish chest: In 1538 parish priests were ordered to start keeping records of baptisms, marriages and burials. The records were to be kept in a strongbox with two locks – this became known as the parish chest. It was where other records relating to the parish would traditionally be kept, including the likes of churchwardens' accounts or vestry meeting minutes. Today, in genealogical circles, when people discuss 'parish chest' material they are generally referring to these other types of parish-level sources, as opposed to the original parish registers. For further information try W.E. Tate's *The Parish Chest* (third edn, Phillimore, 2009).

Parish Chest (parishchest.com): Long-established online shop selling a wide range of genealogy products often published by family history societies.

Parish register timeline:

1538   Priests ordered to start keeping records of all baptisms, marriages and burials.

1558   By this date, entries had to be in bound books and written on parchment.

1597   An Act of Parliament orders the keeping of bishops' transcripts – contemporary copies of the events recorded in registers.

1754   Hardwicke's Marriage Act, passed in 1752, partially curtails clandestine marriages, and introduces a new standardised form with signatures of brides, grooms and witnesses.

1812   Rose's Act standardises the formats of baptism and burial registers. For the first time, fathers' occupations, where known, were recorded. There was no requirement to record the child's date of birth, although this information is sometimes included.

1837   More information is added to marriage registers – including fathers' names and occupations.

Parish registers: In 1538 priests were ordered to start keeping records of all baptisms, marriages and burials. Like any new system of administration it was viewed with suspicion – perhaps this mechanism would lead to some new taxes.

To begin with all baptisms, marriages and burials during the week were simply recorded together. And the earliest registers were often kept on loose sheets of paper, before a series of later decrees ordered that the records be kept in bound books, and then, in 1558, on parchment. While regional archives do sometimes have examples dating back to the 1530s, survival from the late 1550s is more common, and even more start in 1603 – when priests were reminded to keep the records. (There is often a gap during the Commonwealth period.)

Parish registers are among the most valuable sources for genealogists. They are more complicated to use than the BMD records left behind by the civil registration system, but they can potentially help you research back much further.

Identifying the correct parish, and where that parish material is held is the key to finding registers and there are all sorts of indexes and transcription databases to help you.

Parish registers, some online resources: There are vast parish register materials available from FamilySearch, Ancestry and Findmypast.

Other useful websites include
Essex Ancestors (seax.essexcc.gov.uk/EssexAncestors.aspx)

Essex Record Office digital gateway to various sources including parish registers.

FreeREG (freereg.org.uk)

Volunteer-led drive to provide free online searches of transcribed parish and Nonconformist registers.

London Registers (www.parishregister.com)

Specialises in parish data covering London, particularly from the Docklands.

NLI (nli.ie)

A collection of Catholic parish register microfilms are now freely available via registers.nli.ie.

NLW (llgc.org.uk)

Has parish registers from over 500 parishes on microfilm in the South Reading Room. Findmypast has a significant Wales Collection of parish material.

ScotlandsPeople (scotlandspeople.gov.uk)

Offers access to OPRs and Catholic Registers from across Scotland.

TheGenealogist (thegenealogist.co.uk/parish_records/)

Datasets include the noted Phillimore transcripts of marriages, as well as various regional collections.

UK BMD (ukbmd.org.uk)

Lists of online parish data including Online Parish Clerk websites such as Dorset Online Parish Clerks (opcdorset.org), Cornwall (www.cornwall-opc-database.org) and Kent (kent-opc.org).

Parliamentary Archives (www.parliament.uk/business/publications/parliamentary-archives/): Provides access to the archives of the House of Lords, the House of Commons and other records relating to Parliament. This includes Statute Rolls of all Acts of Parliament. Remember that local, personal and private Acts of Parliament are held with Parliament Rolls at TNA, and local record offices may have copies of Acts that relate to the area.

Passenger lists: Lists of passengers leaving a country by sea. They were sent to the Board of Trade and survive at TNA.

Useful websites
Ancestry (ancestry.co.uk)

Has Alien Arrivals (1810–11, 1826–69), Incoming passenger lists (1878–1960), Outgoing passenger lists (1890–1960) and Aliens Entry Books (1794–1921).

Findmypast (search.findmypast.co.uk/search-world-records/passenger-lists-leaving-uk-1890-1960)

Passenger Lists Leaving UK 1890–1960 in association with TNA. Records can reveal destination, origin, age, occupation and marital status.

TheGenealogist (thegenealogist.co.uk)

Immigration/emigration collections include passenger lists and naturalisation records.

Immigrant Ships Transcribers Guild (immigrantships.net)

Scottish Emigration Database (abdn.ac.uk/emigration/)

Ships List (theshipslist.com)

Passports: Passports were not compulsory for someone travelling abroad until the start of the First World War. Therefore before this time it was mainly merchants and diplomats who carried passports. TNA has registers and indexes of passport applications up to 1916. You can also search indexes of names of passport applicants from between 1851 and 1903 (with gaps) on Findmypast.

Patent rolls: An early source for researching immigration as these Patent rolls are records of parliamentary Acts of naturalisation and grants of denizations. The originals are at TNA, and you can find volumes of calendars/transcriptions via archive.org and British History Online (british-history.ac.uk).

Patronymic: A name derived from the name of a father/male ancestor.

Pauper apprenticeships: Unlike trade apprenticeships, pauper apprenticeships were arranged by the parish so that the child pauper would no longer be a financial burden upon that parish. They were also exempt from the stamp duty that ordinary trade apprenticeships would incur. It meant that under the Old Poor Law parish officials could bind children as young as 7 to a master. The agreements were drawn up between the apprentice and master, overseen by the parish. The indentures themselves often survive, or the agreements may be found within vestry minutes or Overseers of the Poor minutes.

Pedigree: A table/chart recording a line of ancestors.

PEEBLESHIRE:
Scottish Borders archives (www.heartofhawick.co.uk)
Borders FHS (bordersfhs.org.uk)

Peeler: The first slang term for London policemen, named after Home Secretary Sir Robert Peel who passed the Metropolitan Police Act in 1829.

Peerage: The system of hereditary titles and noble ranks bestowed in various European countries – it forms part of the British honours system.
In Britain there are five ranks:
Duke/Duchess
Marquess/Marchioness
Earl/Countess
Viscount/Viscountess
Baron/Baroness

Peerage, the (thepeerage.com): Genealogical survey of the peerage of Britain and royal families of Europe.

PEMBROKESHIRE:
Pembrokeshire Archives (www.pembrokeshire.gov.uk/content.asp?nav= 107,1447)
Dyfed FHS (dyfedfhs.org.uk)

Pentecost: Festival of Whitsuntide, seven weeks after Easter.

People of Medieval Scotland (www.poms.ac.uk): The result of two major academic studies, this website features a consolidated database of about 21,000 individuals recorded in documents written between 1093 and 1314.

People's History Museum (phm.org.uk/archive-study-centre/): 'The National centre for the collection, conservation, interpretation and study of material relating to the history of working people in Britain.' The Museum's archive and study centre houses the Labour Party Archive (including a full run of minutes of the National Executive Committee), the Communist Party of Great Britain Archive, personal papers, 95,000 photographs and Chartist material. There are useful research guides to various subjects including women's suffrage.

People's War (bbc.co.uk/ww2peopleswar/): Archived section of the BBC website where you can access this mass-observation project which collected some 47,000 stories relating to the Second World War.

Pepys, Samuel: Diarist of seventeenth-century London. He started writing the diary in 1660 as a 26-year-old civil servant. You can explore daily entries via pepysdiary.com. At time of writing the entry for Thursday, 9 July 1663 began: 'Up. Making water this morning, which I do every morning as soon as I am awake, with greater plenty and freedom than I used to do, which I think I may impute to last night's drinking of elder spirits. Abroad, it raining, to Blackfriars, and there went into a little alehouse and staid while I sent to the Wardrobe, but Mr. Moore was gone out. Here I kissed three or four times the maid of the house, who is a pretty girl, but very modest, and, God forgive me, had a mind to something more.'

Per diem: For each day.

Periods in British history:

Roman Britain	*c*. 43–410
Anglo-Saxon	*c*. 500–1066
Norman	1066–1154
Plantagenet	1154–1485
Tudor	1485–1603
Elizabethan	1558–1603
Stuart	1603–1714
Jacobean	1603–25
Carolean	1625–49
Interregnum	1649–60

Restoration	1660–88
Georgian	1714–1830
Long Eighteenth Century	**1714–1815**
Regency	1811–37
Victorian	1837–1901
Edwardian	1901–14
Long Nineteenth Century	**1815–1914**
First World War	1914–18
Interwar	1918–39
Second World War/Home Front	1939–45
Post-war	1945–52
Modern/2nd Elizabethan Age	1952–present

PERTHSHIRE:

Perth & Kinross Archive (www.pkc.gov.uk/archives)

University of Dundee Archives (dundee.ac.uk/archives/)

Dundee City Archive & Record Centre (www.dundeecity.gov.uk/archive/)

Tay Valley FHS (tayvalleyfhs.org.uk)

Central Scotland FHS (csfhs.org.uk)

Petty sessions: The lowest tier in the court system developed in the eighteenth century to take some of the workload from the quarter sessions – hearing cases of larceny, drunkenness and bastardy, for example. From 1872 they were responsible for approving licences to sell alcohol. The survival rate of petty sessions material can be very poor, although after 1848 petty session records had to be passed to the quarter sessions. The petty sessions were replaced by magistrates courts in the 1970s.

Photography: The first surviving photograph was taken (over a period of several hours) by Nicéphore Niépce. 'A View from the Window at Le Gras' dates from 1826–7. Daguerreotypes came into widespread use during the 1840s, being gradually superseded by ambrotypes, ferreotypes, albumen prints and the *carte de visite*.

Useful websites

British Photographic History (britishphotohistory.ning.com)

Early Photography (earlyphotography.co.uk)

Flickr (flickr.com)

Countless archives, museums and libraries show off their photographic collections via Flickr.

HistoryPin (historypin.org)

Allows users to attach old photographs/memories and superimpose them onto Google Street View.

Photography & The Archive Research Centre (photographyresearchcentre. co.uk)

Portrait & Studio Photographers (earlyphotographers.org.uk/databases. html)

Information about professional photographers working in the UK. There's also a photo dating tool.

Royal Photographic Society (rps.org/publications/journal-archive)

Victorian & Edwardian Photographs (rogerco.freeserve.co.uk)

Personal collection of *cartes de visite* and portrait postcards.

World of the Victorian Photographer (qvictoria.wordpress.com/victorian-photographers-ad-av/)

Includes a database of UK photographers (1850–1900).

Physicians: The Royal College of Physicians website has a Lives of the Fellows section (munksroll.rcplondon.ac.uk) where you can explore a series of indexes and obituaries first compiled by librarian William Munk and published in 1861.

Playbills/Programmes of the Theatre Royal Edinburgh (digital.nls.uk/playbills/): NLS's website where you can explore digitised playbills to see who performed in a particular play. There's also the sister theatre programmes site at www.nls.uk/collections/british/theatres/index.cfm.

Plea rolls: TNA looks after rolls recording the proceedings of the 'Common Bench', or 'Court of Common Pleas', covering the years 1273–1874. The British History Online (british-history.ac.uk) page on the subject remarks that these are an extremely valuable, but underused resource with all kinds of information relating to people, places and events in later medieval and early modern England, 'However, due to the extremely high volume of material they contain – records of some thousands of cases per year – and the difficulty of their language – highly abbreviated Latin until eighteenth century – they remain a largely untapped resource. Generally speaking, effective finding aids do not exist, and the rolls themselves are large, heavy and unwieldy documents roughly three feet in length, over a foot in width and each formed of hundreds of individual membranes, or "rotulets", bound at the head and written on both front and back sides.' TNA recommends the book *Pedigrees from the Plea Rolls, 1200–1500* by G. Wrottesley (available at archive.org/details/pedigreesfromple00wrotrich) to find out how to locate pedigrees in the plea rolls.

Poldave worker: A maker of poldave – a type of coarse fabric.

Pole: A measure of land: 1 square pole was about 30.25 sq. yd. It was also known as a rod, perch or an even older measure the lug – which was equivalent to around 40 sq. m.

Police Roll of Honour Trust (policememorial.org.uk): Lists all UK Police officers killed in the line of duty. There are various rolls – Annual, English, Scottish, Welsh, Ireland, Ports & Tunnels roll and Islands rolls. The amount of information varies but the information will usually include the force and a description of the incident. Just one example comes from the Cambridge Borough Police: Detective Sergeant Francis James Willis died in June 1930, aged 35, while questioning a student at King's College, Cambridge, about his possession of a firearm. The website also records that a memorial plaque was erected at Cambridge Police Station.

Policing: The origins of policing date back to 1750, when chief magistrate Henry Fielding employed six officers from his offices in Bow Street – becoming known as the Bow Street Runners. This was followed by the formation of the Marine Police (1798), Glasgow Police (1800) and London Metropolitan Police (1829).

Survival and access to police records varies from county to county, and some forces maintain their own museums and archives. Via the Lancashire's county archives, for example, you can search for officers from the Lancashire County Constabulary between 1840 and 1925 (www3.lancashire.gov.uk/education/record_office/records/policesearch. asp). While via Staffordshire Name Indexes (www.staffsnameindexes. org.uk) there's an index to Staffordshire Police Force Registers (1840–1920) and a police disciplinary index (1857–86).

Ancestry has police records from 1833–1914, which detail promotions, disciplinary actions, injuries and even give physical descriptions. Findmypast's holdings include 10,000-plus records in their Manchester Police Index (1812–1941), which also has physical descriptions, religion/ marital status, as well as career history.

Both Essex Police Museum (essex.police.uk/museum/) and Kent Police Museum (kent-police-museum.co.uk) offer online finding aids and research services. In addition, there are special interest groups, such as the British Transport Police History Group (btphg.org.uk), whose website has lists of recipients of various honours, decorations and medals, and the Police History Society (policehistorysociety.co.uk).

TNA's own police holdings relate to the Metropolitan Police, the Royal Irish Constabulary and the Transport Police.

Useful websites

Metropolitan & City Police Orphans Fund: met-cityorphans.org.uk

Metropolitan Women Police Association: metwpa.org.uk

Police Roll of Honour Trust: policememorial.org.uk

Poll tax: There are lots repealed systems of taxation that can sometimes function as an early census of a region. At Aberdeenshire's county and city archives you can find the Aberdeen Poll Book of 1696, from a national poll tax that existed in Scotland between 1693 and 1699. It was levied on individuals (rather than property) and payments were graduated in accordance with the taxpayers' financial status. Poll taxes were levied in England and Wales in the fourteenth century – to finance the war against France – and by Margaret Thatcher in the late twentieth century.

Poor Law: The term 'Poor Law' can be used to describe the various systems that were in place prior to the creation of the modern welfare state. These are grouped into the Old Poor Law (1603–1834), where responsibility was devolved to the parish, and the New Poor Law (1834–1929), when it was managed by elected Boards of Guardians for individual Poor Law unions.

Before 1834 most primary sources for researching the poverty stricken are parish level, such as settlement certificates and examinations, removal orders and other records of the overseers of the poor. After 1834 there are also admission registers and other records relating to the running of workhouses.

Useful websites

Ancestry (search.ancestry.co.uk/search/db.aspx?dbid=1557)

Has vast Poor Law and Board of Guardian records from LMA, as well as collections from Warwickshire, Dorset and Norfolk.

FamilySearch (familysearch.org/learn/wiki/en/England_and_Wales_Poor_Law_Records_1834-1948)

FamilySearch's guide to England and Wales Poor Law records includes links to digital collections from Norfolk, Kent and Cheshire.

Findmypast (findmypast.co.uk/articles/world-records/search-all-uk-records/institution-and-organisation--records)

Has London and Westminster Poor Law Abstracts, and material from Lincolnshire, Cheshire, Derbyshire and Manchester.

London Lives: Crime, Poverty & Social Policy in the Metropolis (londonlives.org)

Poor Law (Scotland): The responsibility for poor relief fell on the parish through heritors (local landowners) and the kirk sessions – the Church courts responsible for each parish. There was a parish poor fund, drawn from donations, fines and services. Heritors' records (where they survive) and kirk session minute books and accounts usually include lists of paupers and relief paid (although often recorded in among all other financial business).

New Poor Law dates from an Act of 1845 when parochial boards were set up in each parish to administer poor relief. The records of parochial boards are generally found in local authority archives. Research becomes a lot easier in 1864 when standardised poor relief registers were introduced. The Scottish Poor Relief System also differed from the English one in that parishes did not have to set up their own poorhouse – they just had to be able to provide 'indoor' or 'out-door' relief.

You can find out more via NRS (nrscotland.gov.uk/research/guides/poor-relief-records), and you can search the online catalogue for heritors' and kirk session records. They also hold records of Destitution Boards, set up in the 1840s to deal with widespread poverty in the Highlands following the failure of the potato crop.

Poor Law Act of 1838 (Ireland): This divided Ireland into 159 Poor Law unions, each with an elected Board of Guardians to administer relief. So, as in England and Wales, the kind of resources you may find are Board of Guardian minutes and workhouse registers, which include names, dates of admission, places of birth or residence, occupations and more.

Poor Law Amendment Act: This Act of 1850 allowed Boards of Guardians to send children under 16 overseas.

Poor Law unions: After the passing of the New Poor Law in 1834, the system of parish-level poor relief was replaced by a system of Poor

Law unions, run by an elected Board of Guardians, which administered workhouses (although workhouses did exist in many areas prior to the creation of the new unions). Records of individual Poor Law unions normally survive at county record offices, while records of the presiding Poor Law Commission survive at TNA.

Poor Law Unions' Gazette: This mainly carried descriptions of men who had left their families. You can access digitised copies (1857–65) held at the BL via the British Newspaper Archive at britishnewspaperarchive.co.uk.

Popish Plot: This was an alleged Catholic plot to assassinate King Charles II fabricated by Titus Oates in 1678. Happily for genealogists, this resulted in the compilation of the Estreat Rolls, held at TNA, which record fines imposed on Catholics and list the person's name, parish and rank/occupation.

Port Cities (www.plimsoll.org): Parts of the Port Cities family of maritime websites are no longer updated, but you can still find some interesting material about trade, travel and migration. This page goes direct to the Southampton section.

Port of London Authority Archive: The archive of the Port of London Authority is part of collections preserved at the Museum of London (museumoflondon.org.uk).

Portsmouth Historic Dockyard (historicdockyard.co.uk): Home to attractions that include HMS *Victory*, *Mary Rose* and the National Museum of the Royal Navy. Off-site there's also the Royal Navy Submarine Museum.

Post Office: Traces its origins back to the reign of James I who created the office of Postmaster of England. The website of the British Postal Museum & Archive in Camden (postalheritage.org.uk) has details of collections and exhibitions, an online catalogue and educational resources.

Post Office directories: There's a free searchable hub to more than 700 digitised directories from NLS, covering most of Scotland between the years 1773 and 1911, at www.nls.uk/family-history/directories/post-office.

Potato badger: A potato seller. 'Badger' was a term used for all kinds of sellers and tradesmen.

Prerogative Courts: Before 1858 Church of England courts handled probate. These ranged from the lowest peculiar courts, to archdeaconry courts to the prerogative courts of York and Canterbury – the latter being the highest of all. You can search TNA's Discovery for records of the PCC wills in series PROB 11 (1384–1858). The wills are downloadable from TNA website, and an index is also on Ancestry.

Presbyterian Church of Scotland: Recognised as the national church of Scotland since 1690. In Scotland, before 1834 Nonconformist ministers could not legally perform marriages as clergymen. After 1834 they could, but only if the banns had first been read in the parish church. Total authority was granted in 1855.

Presbyterian Historical Society: www.history.pcusa.org

Presbyterian Historical Society of Ireland: presbyterianhistoryireland.com

Presbyterians: A Christian denomination with origins in Calvinism. You can search the Protestant Dissenters' Registry via BMDRegisters.co,uk/TheGenealogist. This served the congregations of Baptist, Independents and Presbyterians in London and within a 12-mile radius of the capital.

Preventive Water Guard: One of three services that were amalgamated to form the Coastguard in 1822.

Primary sources: Original documents or objects created at the time. These are distinct from secondary sources which are created by someone without first-hand experience. Primary sources remain problematic and may be fragmentary or hard to interpret. When being taught how to interpret primary sources historians are encouraged to consider who was the intended audience of the source, and what was the purpose of the publication of the source.

Principal Probate Registry: From January 1858 the Principal Probate Registry, a network of civil courts called probate registries, replaced the ecclesiastical probate courts. And you can search the official government index to wills and administrations in England and Wales via the Probate Search (probatesearch.service.gov.uk/#wills) website. This includes wills/administrations between 1858 and 1995 (and 1996 to present), as well as an index to soldiers' wills (1850–1986) and there's the National Probate Calendar (1858–1966) available via Ancestry.

Printer's devil: Boy serving as an apprentice for a printers.

Prisoners of War: During the First World War some 7,000-plus officers and 174,000-plus other ranks of the British Army were detained. By the end of the Second World War, in the Far East alone, more than 190,000 Allied servicemen were prisoners of the Japanese. TNA's website has research guides, as well as downloadable POW interviews/reports (1914–20), or via Discovery you can search Foreign Office reports (1915–19) and a 1943 list of army POWs in Germany and occupied territories.

One wonderful resource comes from the International Committee of the Red Cross. The Prisoners of the First World War website (grandeguerre. icrc.org) allows you to search Red Cross lists of POWs from both sides of the conflict.

Aside from the TNA, the IWM preserves personal papers/diaries, camp journals, photographs, artworks and recorded interviews (iwm.org.uk/collections-research). There's also a useful guide to finding records of First World War British POWs via the Long, Long Trail (1914-1918.net/soldiers/powrecords.html).

Findmypast has its large Prisoners Of War 1715–1945 collection (search. findmypast.co.uk/search-world-records/prisoners-of-war-1715-1945). Ancestry has British POWs 1939–45, TheGenealogist has a collection of First World War prisoners (www.thegenealogist.co.uk/prisoner-of-war/) and the Naval & Military Archives (nmarchive.com) has three Second World War POW datasets, as well as British Officers Taken POW August 1914–November 1918.

There are lots of places where you can find out more about specific camps. Examples include Stalag VIIIb (stalag-viiib.com), Stalag VIIIB (lamsdorf.com), Children & Families of Far East POW (cofepowdb.org. uk) and Stalag Luft I Online (merkki.com).

Prison hulks: Decommissioned ships that were used as floating prisons in the eighteenth and nineteenth centuries. There's a list of British prison ships at en.wikipedia.org/wiki/List_of_British_prison_hulks, and Ancestry has Prison Hulk Registers (1802–49).

Prisons: Prison or jail registers often survive within local collections and it's always worth seeing if anything has been produced by local archives, societies or museums. The Lancaster Castle Archives (lancastercastle. com/Archives), for example, has information about the Castle's famous history as a place of punishment, as well as a convict database, listing inmates who were tried and sentenced at Lancaster Assizes. The Centre for Buckinghamshire's Studies has an online database of prisoners from Aylesbury Gaol. Inveraray Jail (www.inverarayjail.co.uk/the-jails-story/prison-records.aspx) has records for over 4,000 former prisoners.

There are national collections of prison records, many of which have been digitised.

In mid-2016 Findmypast released the final instalment of its Crime, Prisons and Punishment collaboration with TNA, which now boasts more than 5.5 million records. These include Home Office and Prison Commission Female Licences – notes of licences to female convicts and, in some cases, transfer papers. Each file can include a photograph (from 1871 onward), letters or notes from the prisoner, a Medical History sheet, reports of misconduct while in prison, the court of conviction, details of crime and of previous crimes. There's also Criminal Registers of 'all persons in England and Wales charged with indictable offences showing the results of the trials, the sentences in case of conviction, and dates of execution of persons sentence to death; some of the registers contain personal information respecting the prisoners'.

Ancestry also has digitised TNA criminal registers for England and Wales, 1791–1892, which provide dates and locations of court hearings. It also has a Bedfordshire Gaol Index (1770–1882), Debtors' Prison Registers (1734–1862), Birmingham prisoners (1880–1913) and Prison Hulk Registers (1802–49).

Probate clause: In a will, this is the final section where the document is officially proven.

Probate courts: Broadly speaking, prior to 1858, the situation in England and Wales was similar to pre-1824 Scotland – in that the Church courts handled probate. There were more than 300 Church probate courts in England and Wales, set within a hierarchy – the higher court would handle the probate if the testator owned property in two or more areas. The lowest were the peculiar courts, which had jurisdiction over small areas. Next came archdeaconry courts (divisions within dioceses), bishops' courts (the highest diocesan courts), prerogative courts and the PCC – the highest court of all, used for wills of testators who died or owned property outside of England, foreigners who owned property in England, military personnel, persons having property in more than one probate jurisdiction and wealthier individuals.

To track down probate records you need to try to confirm the parish and year in which your ancestor died, then confirm which court (or courts) had jurisdiction. Then you can look for any surviving indexes and records.

Probate tips:

1. The eldest son in family wills may not actually be mentioned, because he automatically inherited property of the deceased father.
2. Technically, a will conveys immovable property to heirs and a testament conveys personal moveable property. But in general the term 'will' usually refers to both.
3. A 'codicil' is a signed addition to a will.
4. If someone dies 'intestate' (without leaving a will), then you may find 'Letters of Administration'. This a document that appoints someone to preside over the distribution of the estate. There may also be a letter of administration attached to a will, if the named executor is deceased, unwilling or unable to act.
5. Other potential probate sources you may come across include 'act books' (accounts of court actions) and 'bonds' (written guarantees that a person will perform tasks set by the probate court).
6. Very few wills and probate documents survive before about 1400.
7. Before 1882 a wife who died before her husband could not make a will except with her husband's consent or under a marriage settlement created before her marriage.
8. Until 1858 the courts of the Church of England proved wills but after this a simpler system of civil probate was introduced.

Probate websites:

Ancestry (search.ancestry.co.uk/search/db.aspx?dbid=1904)

Collections include important National Probate Calendars.

Findmypast (findmypast.co.uk)

Has Cheshire Wills and Probate (1492–1911), Kent Probate Index (1750–1858), London Probate Index (1750–1858), Northamptonshire and Rutland Probate Index (1462–1857), Prerogative Court of Canterbury Wills Index (1750–1800) and Suffolk Testator Index (1847–57).

Gazette (www.thegazette.co.uk/wills-and-probate)

Includes wills and probate notices printed in the *London, Edinburgh* and *Belfast Gazettes*.

TheGenealogist (thegenealogist.co.uk)

Diamond subscribers can enjoy probate collections that include county wills indexes covering Yorkshire, Staffordshire, London, Leicestershire and more, as well as the PCC indexes and indexes to some Irish and Scottish wills.

NLW (llgc.org.uk)

Explore 193,000 records of wills proved in the Welsh ecclesiastical courts prior to the introduction of Civil Probate in 1858. You can either search the entire index, or narrow down by individual courts.

North East Inheritance Database (familyrecords.dur.ac.uk/nei/data/)

A database of pre-1858 probate records (wills and related documents) covering Northumberland and County Durham. Digital images of the original probate records (including wills and inventories, 1650–1857; copies of wills, 1527–1858; executors' and administration bonds, 1702–1858) are also available through FamilySearch.

PRONI (www.proni.gov.uk/index/search_the_archives.htm)

Details of all PRONI's online probate collections, including Will Calendars – a free index of wills from the District Probate registries of Armagh, Belfast and Londonderry (1858–1943).

ScotlandsPeople (scotlandspeople.gov.uk)

Trawl the index to Scottish wills and testaments dating from 1513–1901 (listing surname, forename, title, occupation and place of residence), as well as the associated database of soldiers' wills.

Proceedings of the Old Bailey (www.oldbaileyonline.org): Free database of 197,745 criminal trials held at London's central criminal court from 1674–1913. You can search by various fields including punishment, filtering results by imprisonment, hard labour, house of correction, Newgate or penal servitude.

Proctor: A disciplinary officer or supervisor appointed at university.

Professional genealogists: Most record offices and many museums offer look-up or copying services or have a list of recommended professional researchers who may have specialist knowledge in the area. Having selected a professional you need to approach them with all the relevant details of your research and what you want from them. Most charge on a basis of an hourly rate. Once their work is complete they normally produce reports which include pedigrees, typed up transcriptions, copies and details of everything that was searched. Try the Association of Genealogists and Researchers in Archives (www.agra.org.uk) to find out more. There's also the Association of Scottish Genealogists & Researchers in Archives (asgra. co.uk) and Accredited Genealogists Ireland (accreditedgenealogists.ie).

PRONI Street Directories: Specialist PRONI site reproducing directories from Belfast and environs dating from 1819–1900 (streetdirectories.proni. gov.uk).

Prosopography: An investigation of common characteristics of an historical group.

Prosopography of Anglo-Saxon England (pase.ac.uk): An attempt to record the names of all inhabitants of England from the late sixth to the end of the eleventh centuries.

Protestant Dissenters' Registry: This served the congregations of Baptist, Independents and Presbyterians in London and within a 12- mile radius of the capital. However, parents from most parts of the British Isles and even abroad also used the registry. It was started in 1742, with retrospective entries going back to 1716, and continued until 1837. You can search the registry via BMDRegisters.co,uk/TheGenealogist and FamilySearch.

Protestation Returns: By order of the House of Commons (in 1642), all adult men were asked to swear an oath of allegiance to the Protestant religion. Often described as the nearest thing to a national census of the era, names were inscribed in lists produced at the parish level, which were then returned to Parliament. These returns survive for about a third of English counties. You can search the Parliamentary Archives' online catalogue Portcullis (www.portcullis.parliament.uk/calmview/) to see if any lists survive for the area that interests you. It's also worth checking with the local county record office to see if any copies survive.

Proto-census sources: A census is a statistical count of the population of a country. Before and after the establishment of a country wide census system there are sources that are sometimes described as 'proto-census' for family historians, such as tax material, town surveys and militia lists.

Pub History Society (pubhistorysociety.co.uk): Has guidance for people researching publican ancestors.

Public Health Act 1848: Edwin Chadwick, one of the architects of the 1834 Poor Law, published *The Sanitary Condition of the Labouring Population of Great Britain* in 1842. He argued that if public health was improved, money would be saved on poor relief. The central aims were to improve drainage/sewers, remove refuse from houses, streets and roads, provide clean drinking water and appoint a medical officer for each town. You can browse medical officer health reports from London between 1848 and 1972 via the Wellcome Library project London's Pulse (wellcomelibrary. org/moh/). Or, to take another random example:

Southampton's Local Studies department at the city's central library has a copy of the Medical Officer of Health report into an outbreak of typhoid following the outgoing Mayor's banquet, 10 November 1902. And the 1892 report of unhealthy areas and dilapidated housing describes Lansdowne Place: 'The houses are very old and dilapidated; most of them are damp dark and unhealthy. The water supply for 61 inhabitants is obtained from a common tap in the Court.'

Public Record Office of Northern Ireland (proni.gov.uk): The official archive for Northern Ireland, universally known as PRONI. It moved to new offices at Titanic Boulevard in 2011, offering vastly improved facilities for researchers. It houses Church registers, landed estates records, maps, valuation records, workhouse records, court records, wills and more.

Pubs History (pubshistory.com): Database of pubs across England.

Pursuivant: An attendant. In heraldic circles the term means a College of Arms officer ranked just below a herald. The four ordinary pursuivants are Rouge Croix, Bluemantle, Rouge Dragon and Portcullis.

Q

Quakers: Quaker history begins with George Fox who established the Religious Society of Friends in the mid-seventeenth century. Members of the society became known as 'Quakers' because they trembled during religious experiences. Quakers faced persecution and many emigrated to North America.

There were four hierarchical levels of Quaker meetings and registers were originally kept by local or monthly meetings. From 1776 copies were also sent to the quarterly meeting (and these are now held at TNA – although the holdings end in 1837). The registers were also recorded in 'digests', which contain much of the detail of the originals, and are often housed at local record offices and at Friends' House – the Quaker headquarters in London. An important online source available through TheGenealogist and FamilySearch are the Quaker BMD registers held by TNA (series RG 6). These include registers, notes and certificates of births, marriages and burials from between the years 1578 and 1841.

Quakers kept meticulous registers of births (Quakers did not practise baptism), marriages and deaths, as well as other records related to congregations. Register books began to be kept by Quaker meetings from the late 1650s, but in 1776 their whole registration system was overhauled. Post-1776 birth entries, for example, contain the date of birth, place of birth (locality, parish and county), parents' names (often with the father's occupation), the child's name and names of the witnesses.

Quakers' refusal to pay tithes led to them being subject to fines and even imprisonment. They were anxious to record these persecutions so books of sufferings were kept by monthly or quarterly meetings, and then recorded in the 'great book of sufferings' in London.

Useful websites
Library of the Religious Society of Friends (quaker.org.uk)

Quaker Archives, Leeds University Library (library.leeds.ac.uk/special-collections-quaker-collection)

Comprises the Carlton Hill collection (broadly covering Leeds, Bradford, Settle and Knaresborough) and the Clifford Street collection (York and Thirsk areas, as well as Yorkshire-wide material).

Quaker FHS (qfhs.co.uk)

Useful for getting to grips with unique Quaker records. Explains types of records such as minute books, membership lists and digests.

Yorkshire Quaker Heritage Project (www.hull.ac.uk/oldlib/archives/quaker/)

Quarter sessions: The courts of quarter sessions, or quarter sessions, were local courts traditionally held at four set times each year from the thirteenth century right up to 1971. These were the county level courts, above the petty sessions, and below the assize courts. (*See also* 'Assizes', 'Court records' and 'Petty sessions'.)

Quarter sessions rolls: These can include jury lists, recognisances (bonds to appear), statements, names of prisoners in the House of Correction, bastardy and settlement orders, examinations of vagrants and coroner's inquisitions.

Quo warrant: A legal document that requires someone to prove their rights to a claim of office or franchise.

R

RADNORSHIRE:
Powys Archives (archives.powys.gov.uk)
Powys FHS (powysfhs.org.uk)

RAF Museum StoryVault (rafmuseumstoryvault.org.uk): Repository for stories of ordinary service men and women, as well as digitised archives of conflict casualty cards, the 1918 muster roll and 1918 Air Force List. You can find out more about the RAF Museums at Cosford and London via rafmuseum.org.uk.

Rag cutter: A worker who cut up rags for paper making.

Railway & Canal Historical Society: rchs.org.uk

Railway workers: If your ancestor was a rail worker you need to find out when, where and exactly what they were doing. Employment with a rail company could mean as an engineer, driver, fireman, signalman, or perhaps a manager or clerk, guard or porter. There was a huge number of railway companies that sprang up all over the UK. These amalgamated into larger, regional companies in 1923, before nationalisation brought a little more order in 1947.

Company records will often be held at the appropriate local record office and might include staff registers, or there may be in-company magazines or journals, or perhaps employee associations or trade unions.

Ancestry's Railway Employment Records collection includes details of employees on the payroll of the London and North Eastern Railway Company between 1897 and 1947, for example, ranging from porters to drivers. The records have been digitised from material held in series RAIL 397 at TNA. The wider rail collection covers employment records between 1833 and 1956. The most common record type in this collection is the staff register, but there are also station transfers, pension and accident records and apprentice records. Ancestry also has material drawn from the *Great Western Railway Magazine* (1838–1943) and *Southern Railway Magazine* (1840–1942).

NRS holds the largest written and pictorial archive of Scottish railway history – mainly made up of the records formerly held by the British Transport Records Historical Records Department in Edinburgh. Cheshire Archives has an online Railway Staff Database (archives.cheshire.gov. uk), drawn from seventeen staff registers from four railway companies, and the National Railway Museum's research and archive pages (nrm. org.uk) include the online catalogue Search Engine and advice aimed at family historians.

The Modern Records Centre (www2.warwick.ac.uk/services/library/ mrc/) has some useful information about trade unions that train workers tended to join – from the Associated Society of Locomotive Engineers and Firemen to the National Union of Railwaymen.

Useful websites
ASLEF, The Train Driver's Union (www.aslef.org.uk/information/ 100011/102822/history_of_aslef/)

British Steam (britishsteam.com)

GWR's Steam Museum (steam-museum.org.uk)

Irish Railway Record Society (irrs.ie)

London Transport Museum (ltmuseum.co.uk)

Midland Railway Society (midlandrailway.org.uk)

Mike's Railway History (mikes.railhistory.railfan.net)

Rail Map Online (railmaponline.com)

Signal Box (signalbox.org)

Transport Archives Register (trap.org.uk)

Warwickshire Railways (warwickshirerailways.com)

Railways Archive (railwaysarchive.co.uk): Includes data drawn from the Beeching reports and an Accidents Archive of nearly 9,000 incidents. Flanders and Swann's song 'Slow Train' was inspired by the Beeching station closures. 'No churns, no porter, no cat on a seat / At Chorlton-cum-Hardy or Chester-le-Street.' (Chester-le-Street actually survived the Beeching cuts.)

Raleigh, I Worked at (iworkedatraleigh.com): Home to video clips, stories, photographs and more relating to working life at the bicycle factory in Nottingham.

Rate books: Rates were a kind of property tax. Rate books list the owners/occupiers of properties on which rates were paid. Parish rate books were normally kept by the church vestry, or within overseer's or churchwarden's accounts. Rates were levied to raise money for poor relief, local services and maintenance, and county rates would fund gaols or hospitals. The always reliable GenGuide (genguide.co.uk) has a useful page on the subject which notes: 'Most rates were introduced following Parliamentary Acts of 1598 (Act for the Relief of the Poor) and 1601 (Poor Law Act) which formalised the rating system and specified the compulsory setting of a local rate. The Acts made the parish responsible for poor relief and required the registration of all property. Other rates collected at parish level included County or Borough rates and national rates. Rates were usually levied in June (Midsummer), October (Michaelmas) and January (Christmas).' Digitised collections are available through a number of website, both free and subscription-based. So Findmypast, for example, has rate book collections from Plymouth, West Devon, Westminster and Manchester.

Ratings: The RN term for an ordinary seaman. Tracing ratings before 1853 can be difficult. Ships' muster and pay books (1667–1878) were essentially crew lists, and are the likeliest place to find references to ratings before 1853. You can search TNA's Discovery catalogue for muster/pay books from a particular ship. Ratings records after 1853 become more detailed. The RN ratings' service records (1853–1928) collection is available online via the TNA website. This comprises more than 700,000 RN service records for ratings, drawn from continuous service engagement books, registers of seamen's services and continuous record cards.

Really Useful Websites: These are some of the most important and useful websites for genealogical research.

General
British Genealogy Network: britishgenealogy.net
British History Online: www.british-history.ac.uk
Connected Histories: connectedhistories.org
Cyndi's List: cyndislist.com

FamilySearch: familysearch.org

FreeBMD: freebmd.org.uk

Free UK Genealogy: freeukgenealogy.org.uk

GenGuide: genguide.co.uk

Genuki: genuki.org.uk

Rootsweb: rootsweb.ancestry.com

ScotlandsPeople: scotlandspeople.gov.uk

UK BMD: ukbmd.org.uk

UK GDL: ukgdl.org.uk

1911 Census: 1911census.co.uk

National
BL: bl.uk

Federation of Family History Societies: ffhs.org.uk

NAI: nationalarchives.ie

NLI: nli.ie

NLS: nls.uk

NLW: llgc.org.uk

NRS: nrscotland.gov.uk

PRONI: proni.gov.uk

Scottish Association of FHSs: safhs.org.uk

SoG: sog.org.uk

TNA: nationalarchives.gov.uk

Wellcome Library: wellcomelibrary.org

Finding aids
AIM25: aim25.ac.uk

Archives Hub: archiveshub.ac.uk

Archives Wales: archiveswales.org.uk

Discovery, TNA: discovery.nationalarchives.gov.uk

Scottish Archive Network: scan.org.uk

Subscription/pay-per-view
Ancestry: ancestry.co.uk

AncestryDNA: dna.ancestry.co.uk

BMD Registers: bmdregisters.co.uk

British Newspaper Archive: britishnewspaperarchive.co.uk

DeceasedOnline: deceasedonline.com

FamilyRelatives: familyrelatives.com

Findmypast: findmypast.co.uk

Forces War Records: forces-war-records.co.uk

TheGenealogist: thegenealogist.co.uk

GenesReunited: genesreunited.co.uk

MyHeritage: myheritage.com

England

Cause Papers Database, Diocese of York: hrionline.ac.uk/causepapers/

City of Westminster Archives Centre: www.westminster.gov.uk/archives

Electoral Registers: electoralregisters.org.uk

Guildhall Library: cityoflondon.gov.uk

Hearth Tax Online: hearthtax.org.uk

Historical Directories: specialcollections.le.ac.uk/cdm/landingpage/collection/p16445coll4

Lancashire Lantern: lanternimages.lancashire.gov.uk

Lincs to the Past: www.lincstothepast.com

LMA: cityoflondon.gov.uk

London Lives: londonlives.org

North East Inheritance Database: familyrecords.dur.ac.uk/nei/data/intro.php

Sheffield Indexers: sheffieldindexers.com

Staffordshire Name Indexes: www.staffsnameindexes.org.uk

Warwickshire's Past Unlocked: archivesunlocked.warwickshire.gov.uk/calmview/

West Yorkshire Tithe Maps Project: tracksintime.wyjs.org.uk

Windows on Warwickshire: www.windowsonwarwickshire.org.uk

Ireland

Association of Professional Genealogists in Ireland: apgi.ie

Catholic parish registers: registers.nli.ie

Census of Ireland 1901/1911: census.nationalarchives.ie

Documenting Ireland: Parliament, People & Migration: dippam.ac.uk

Dublin City Archives: www.dublincity.ie

Genealogical Society of Ireland: familyhistory.ie

Griffith's Valuation: askaboutireland.ie

Ireland: ireland.ie

Irish Ancestors: irishancestors.ie

Irish Ancestral Research Association: tiara.ie

Irish Family History Foundation: irish-roots.ie

Irish Family History Society: ifhs.ie

Irish Genealogical Research Society: igrsoc.org

Irish Genealogy: irishgenealogy.ie

Irish Times: irishtimes.com/ancestor

RootsIreland: rootsireland.ie

Tithe Applotment Books: titheapplotmentbooks.nationalarchives.ie/search/tab/home.jsp

Northern Ireland

Armagh Ancestry: www.armagh.co.uk/place/armagh-ancestry/

Belfast, the Linen Hall: linenhall.com

Belfast Street Directories: lennonwylie.co.uk

Derry Genealogy Centre: derry.brsgenealogy.com

General Register Office Northern Ireland: nidirect.gov.uk/family-history

Irish World: www.irish-world.com

Street Directories, PRONI: streetdirectories.proni.gov.uk

Ulster Historical Foundation: www.ancestryireland.com

Scotland

Aberdeen City and Aberdeenshire Archives: aberdeencity.gov.uk/archives

Addressing History: addressinghistory.edina.ac.uk

Am Baile, Highland History & Culture: ambaile.org.uk

Edinburgh City Archives: www.edinburgh.gov.uk/info/20032/access_to_information/600/edinburgh_city_archives

Glasgow Family History, Mitchell Library: glasgowfamilyhistory.org.uk

Glasgow & West of Scotland FHS: gwsfhs.org.uk

Highland FHS: highlandfamilyhistorysociety.org

John Gray Centre – Library, Museum & Archive: johngraycentre.org

Lothians FHS: lothiansfhs.org

Lothian Lives: lothianlives.org.uk.

National Register of Archives for Scotland: www.nas.gov.uk/nras/

Scotland BDM Exchange: sctbdm.com

ScotlandsPeople Centre: scotlandspeoplehub.gov.uk

ScotlandsPlaces: scotlandsplaces.gov.uk

Scotsman Archive: archive.scotsman.com

Scottish Catholic Archives: scottishcatholicarchives.org.uk

Scottish Indexes: scottishindexes.com

Scottish Post Office Directories: digital.nls.uk/directories/

Scottish Screen Archive: ssa.nls.uk

Wales

Cymru 1914: cymru1914.org

Cynefin: cynefin.archiveswales.org.uk

Digging up the Past: diggingupthepast.org.uk

NLW, Crime & Punishment Database: www.llgc.org.uk/sesiwn_fawr/index_s.htm

North Wales BMD: northwalesbmd.org.uk

Welsh Coal Mines: welshcoalmines.co.uk

Welsh Mariners: welshmariners.org.uk

Welsh Newspapers Online: newspapers.library.wales

General

Archive.org: archive.org

Archives New Zealand: archives.govt.nz

Britain on Film: player.bfi.org.uk/britain-on-film/

Building History: buildinghistory.org

Chartist Ancestors: chartists.net

Ellis Island: ellisisland.org

Gazettes Online: www.thegazette.co.uk

GENFair: GENFair.co.uk

HistoryPin: historypin.org

Immigrant Ships Transcribers Guild: immigrantships.net

Isle of Man Museum: imuseum.im

Library & Archives Canada: bac-lac.gc.ca/eng

Mayflower 400: mayflower400uk.co.uk

National Archives, America: archives.gov

National Archives of Australia: naa.gov.au

Parish Chest: parishchest.com

Probate Search, GOV.uk: probatesearch.service.gov.uk/#wills

Proceedings of the Old Bailey: www.oldbaileyonline.org

Ships List: theshipslist.com

US Immigrant Ancestors Project: immigrants.byu.edu

Waifs & Strays Society: hiddenlives.org.uk

The Workhouse: workhouses.org.uk

Military

Age of Nelson: ageofnelson.org

Anglo-Afghan War: garenewing.co.uk/angloafghanwar/

Anglo Boer War: angloboerwar.com

Army Service Numbers blog: armyservicenumbers.blogspot.co.uk

Battle of Britain Memorial: battleofbritainmemorial.org

British Medals Forum: britishmedalforum.com

Cross & Cockade International: www.crossandcockade.com

CWGC: cwgc.org

Fleet Air Arm Archive: fleetairarmarchive.net

Great War Staffordshire: staffordshiregreatwar.com

IWM: iwm.org.uk

Lives of the First World War: livesofthefirstworldwar.org

The Long, Long Trail: www.longlongtrail.co.uk

Medals of the World: medals.org.uk

NAM: national-army-museum.ac.uk

Naval History: naval-history.net

Operation War Diary: operationwardiary.org

RAF Museum StoryVault: rafmuseumstoryvault.org.uk

Royal Flying Corps 1914-18: airwar1.org.uk

Sandhurst Collection: archive.sandhurstcollection.co.uk

Trafalgar Ancestors: www.nationalarchives.gov.uk/trafalgarancestors/

UK MFH: ukmfh.org.uk

Unit Histories: unithistories.com

Victorian Wars Forum: victorianwars.com

Overseas/special interest groups
Anglo German FHS: agfhs.org

Anglo-Italian FHS: anglo-italianfhs.org.uk

Association of Genealogists and Researchers in Archives: agra.org.uk

Australasian Federation of Family History Organisations: affho.org

British Association for Local History: balh.co.uk

Catholic FHS: catholic-history.org.uk/cfhs

Families In British India Society: fibis.org

Federation of Family History Societies: ffhs.org.uk

Federation of Genealogical Societies, US: fgs.org

Guild of One-Name Studies: one-name.org

Heraldry Society: theheraldrysociety.com

Huguenot Society of Great Britain and Ireland: huguenotsociety.org.uk

Institute of Heraldic and Genealogical Studies: ihgs.ac.uk

Jewish Genealogical Society of Great Britain: jgsgb.org.uk

New Zealand Society of Genealogists: genealogy.org.nz

Quaker FHS: qfhs.co.uk

Romany and Traveller FHS: rtfhs.org.uk

Society of Australian Genealogists: sag.org.au

Recognisance: A bond to appear before a court.

Rector: Tithes were a local tax levied on the parish – divided into the 'greater' and 'lesser' tithes. Historically the difference between a vicar and a rector was that the vicar received only the lesser tithes, the rector received greater and lesser tithes.

Recusant: The word means any person who refuses to submit to authority, but it was most commonly used to describe Catholics who did not attend Anglican services. 'Recusant Rolls' listed people, mainly Roman Catholics, who refused to conform and were compiled from between 1592 and 1691. The Catholic Record Society (catholicrecordsociety.co.uk) has transcribed and republished Recusant Rolls.

Red Cross: You can search Red Cross lists of First World War POWs from both sides of the conflict via grandeguerre.icrc.org. You can also find out more about Red Cross Voluntary Aid Detachments – units providing field nursing services, mainly in hospitals – via redcross.org.uk/ww1.

1939 Register: The vital census replacement source for researching home-front ancestors at the outbreak of war. The National Register (its formal title) was compiled by the British government to issue identity cards, organise rationing and was later used to set up the National Health Service. It has been digitised by Findmypast, in association with TNA, and records 40-plus million Britons alive on 29 September 1939 (1939register.co.uk).

Register of the Anglo-Boer War 1899–1902 (casus-belli.co.uk): Includes the Anglo-Boer War Memorials Project, currently with nearly 300,000 names.

Registration of Merchant Seamen: The Merchant Shipping Act 1835 required all men serving in the Merchant Navy to register – essentially so that they could be called up for the RN if required. Although the system was abandoned in 1857, it was re-established in 1913, creating a central indexed register. A new registration system was also introduced in 1941.

Religious Society of Friends: *See* 'Quakers'.

Removal orders: If someone applied for poor relief, a settlement examination might be carried out to determine if that person had a legitimate right to parish residency – and therefore the right to poor relief from the parish coffers. Often, the examination would find that some other parish should be responsible, and therefore they would serve a removal order – basically an order to clear off, and head to the parish that should be looking after them.

Removed: When describing a family relationship, this word is used to indicate that a person is in a different generation to another person. A first cousin 'once removed' would mean your father or mother's first cousin. Twice removed would mean a difference of two generations and so on.

RENFREWSHIRE:

East Renfrewshire Archives (eastrenfrewshire.gov.uk/archives)

East Renfrewshire local history (portaltothepast.co.uk)

Renfrewshire Heritage Services (www.renfrewshire.gov.uk/webcontent/home/Services/Libraries/Heritage_Services/)

Renfrewshire FHS (renfrewshirefhs.co.uk)

Glasgow & West of Scotland FHS (gwsfhs.org.uk)

Research forms (familysearch.org/learn/wiki/en/Research_Forms): Handy printed forms for noting down information from FamilySearch.

Residenter: A term you will sometimes come across in trade directories and other sources. It is an obsolete or colloquial word meaning simply 'a resident', often in terms of someone who lives and works in the same place, such as a minister or teacher.

Retours of Services of Heirs: Scottish probate records generated through inquests heard by a jury to establish the right of an heir to inherit property. 'Special Retours' dealt with property subject to inheritance. 'General Retours' provide details of the chain of inheritance, but not the property involved.

Revenue Cruisers: One of three services that were amalgamated to form the Coastguard in 1822. The others were Riding Officers and the Preventive Water Guard.

Rifles, The (www.thewardrobe.org.uk/home): This is the website of the Rifles Berkshire and Wiltshire Museum. It contains a Soldier Search database where you can trawl discharge records and militia material, as well as transcriptions of the battalion war diaries of both Berkshire and Wiltshire regiments for both world wars – totalling almost 16,500 records. Thanks to a very detailed catalogue you can also search for named references in photographs and other artefacts held here. The Soldier Search incorporates the Militia Directory, which will sometimes give details of birthplace, as well as place, date and age on enlistment.

Roman Catholic Relief Act 1829: The culmination of the process of Catholic emancipation in Britain – the gradual removal of restrictions placed on Roman Catholics by the Act of Uniformity.

Rootschat (rootschat.com): The UK's largest free family history forum.

RootsWeb (rootsweb.ancestry.com): Immense genealogical co-operative first launched in the 1990s and acquired by Ancestry in 2000. Users can upload GEDCOM files to the WorldConnect portion of the site which are then searchable via RootsWeb and Ancestry. (*See also* 'GEDCOM'.)

Rose's Act 1812: Standardised the formats of baptism and burial registers. From this date baptisms recorded the fathers' occupations for the first time.

ROSS & CROMARTY:
Highland Archives Service (highlandarchives.org.uk/genealogy.asp)

Glasgow & West of Scotland FHS (gwsfhs.org.uk)

Highland FHS (highlandfamilyhistorysociety.org)

Rough music/Charivari/Skimmington: A custom where a community would parade around making a discordant cacophony to demonstrate disapproval to a person or at a situation – perhaps an adulterous relationship or domestic violence.

ROXBURGHSHIRE:
Scottish Borders Archives (heartofhawick.co.uk/info/1/about_us/12/heritage_hub)

Borders FHS (bordersfhs.org.uk)

Royal Air Force: The RAF was formed in April 1918 when the RFC and RNAS were amalgamated. TNA's guide to RAF personnel notes that 'someone who served in the RFC or RNAS as well as the RAF may have service records in more than one place'. There are also research guides dedicated to both RFC officers/airmen and RNAS officers/ratings, and the WRAF.

Just as the RN has ratings and officers, and the army has soldiers and officers, so RAF personnel are made up of airmen and officers. Again, the records of RAF men and women will reside in different places depending on when they served.

You can search some RAF service records (officers only) via TNA's Discovery catalogue for free (individual image downloads cost £3.30). RAF airmen service records between 1912 and 1939 are available on Findmypast. These include details of date/place of birth, physical description, next of kin, promotions, units and medals. The record set contains records of almost 343,000 airmen. It also has officer service records (1912–20), containing records of 101,266 officers, and the RAF 1918 Muster Roll.

Useful websites

Air Historical Branch (www.raf.mod.uk/ahb/)

Battle of Britain Memorial (battleofbritainmemorial.org)

History of RAF (rafweb.org)

RAF Museum Navigator (navigator.rafmuseum.org)

RAF Museum StoryVault (rafmuseumstoryvault.org.uk)

Royal Air Forces Association (rafa.org.uk)

Royal Flying Corps 1914-18 (airwar1.org.uk)

Royal Army Medical Corps: To begin with Medical Officers or Regimental Surgeons were appointed to each regiment. Then by the mid-Victorian period a medical service existed within the British Army, although medical officers at this time did not have military rank, which caused much unrest among army physicians. This changed in 1898 with the formation of the RAMC. Via the Wellcome Library website (wellcomelibrary.org/collections/digital-collections/royal-army-medical-corps/) you can explore a digitised archive covering more than 150 years of military medicine and the RAMC. It includes more than 130,000 digitised pages of correspondence, reports, field diaries, memoirs, photographs and memorabilia.

Royal charters: These are formal document issued by a monarch granting some kind of power to individuals or institutions. For an annual rent to the Crown, towns could earn themselves charters that officially granted privileges such as the exemption from feudal payments, rights to hold markets and the rights to levy certain types of taxes. The oldest item held at LMA, for example, is a charter from William the Conqueror, dated 1067.

Royal College of General Practitioners (www.rcgp.org.uk/about-us/history-heritage-and-archive/researching-a-medical-ancestor.aspx): As the Royal College of General Practitioners was founded in 1952, it holds only limited biographical information about members. For most ancestors prior to 1952 you will have to seek out sources elsewhere. However this page does have a brief and useful guide to key sources, including medical school records, publications and common abbreviations. (*See also* 'Medicine'.)

Royal College of Music Library & Archive: rcm.ac.uk/library/contactus/archivesandrecords/

Royal College of Nursing (archives.rcn.org.uk): An important collaboration between the Royal College of Nursing and the Wellcome Library has seen the digestion of nursing registers and application forms published on Ancestry. (*See also* 'Nursing'.)

Royal College of Physicians (munksroll.rcplondon.ac.uk): This particular section of the Royal College of Physicians website takes you to the Lives of the Fellows, a series of indexes and obituaries first compiled by librarian William Munk and published in 1861. (*See also* 'Medicine'.)

Royal College of Surgeons of Edinburgh, Library & Special Collections: library.rcsed.ac.uk/content/content.aspx

Royal Commission on the Ancient and Historical Monuments of Wales: rcahmw.gov.uk

Royal Engineers Museum, Library & Archive (re-museum.co.uk): Military engineering museum and library in Gillingham, Medway. It preserves the history of the Corps of Royal Engineers and the wider story of British military engineering. The website has details of research facilities and collections, as well as an online catalogue. Collections include diaries, letters and official war diaries from both world wars.

Royal Flying Corps: The RAF was formed in April 1918 by the merger of the RFC and the RNAS. Some individuals who served in the RFC/RNAS as well as the RAF may have service records in more than one place. The TNA website includes research guides dedicated to both RFC officers/airmen and RNAS officers/ratings, and the WRAF. The Royal Flying Corps 1914-18 website is at airwar1.org.uk, and there's also www.airhistory.org.uk/rfc/.

Royal Hospital Chelsea: Founded in 1682 by King Charles II as a home for soldiers who were unfit for further duty because of injury or old age. Records are at TNA. See: www.chelsea-pensioners.co.uk.

Royal Irish Rifles (www.royal-irish.com/research): The Trace a Relative page contains names and details of over 15,000 soldiers who served in the Royal Irish Rifles up to 1922. Eventually this will contain details of soldiers who served in the Royal Inniskilling Fusiliers, Royal Ulster Rifles, Royal Irish Fusiliers, Royal Irish Rangers, Ulster Defence Regiment and Royal Irish Regiment.

Royal Leicestershire Regiment (royalleicestershireregiment.org.uk): Has a wonderful digitised regimental archive, where you can search through over 65,000 soldier records dating back to 1688, read associated medals, awards and citations, and explore digital copies of regimental journals back to 1904.

Royal Military Academy Sandhurst: Sandhurst is where all British Army officers are trained. Via the Sandhurst Collection website (archive. sandhurstcollection.co.uk) you can search cadet/staff registers, containing details of almost every officer cadet that attended the Royal Military Academy Woolwich and Royal Military College Sandhurst, recording name, age, date of entry, commissioning date and corps or regiment joined. Searches are free, downloading an image costs £2.99.

Royal Naval Air Service: The RAF was formed in April 1918 when the RNAS was amalgamated with the army's RFC. The RNAS was formed in 1914. You can search and download records of men who served between 1914 and 1918 via the nationalarchives.gov.uk.

Royal warrant: Issued to tradespeople and companies who supply goods or services to a royal court or certain royal personages. TNA has various record sets relating to royal warrants including bill books (1800–37) containing the original bills presented by tradesmen to the Lord Chamberlain's department, as well as annual lists of warrant holders that were published in the *London Gazette* (www.thegazette.co.uk). You can also visit the website of the Royal Warrant Holders Association (royalwarrant.org), established in 1840 and 'representing individuals and companies holding Royal Warrants of Appointment'.

Royal Welsh Archives (royalwelsh.org.uk/research/archives.htm): Looks after material relating to the 24th South Wales Borderers, 41st and 69th Welch Regiment, Monmouthshire Regiment and the Royal Regiment of Wales.

Ruhleben Civilian Internment Camp (ruhleben.tripod.com): Website that explores the history and life of British internees at Ruhleben in Germany.

Rump Parliament: The original 1648 Rump Parliament was made up of leftovers – after those opposed to the trying of King Charles I for high treason had been kicked out.

Rural craftsmen: The kind of evidence that survives relating to ag labs, smiths, millers and rural craftsmen varies from place to place and industry to industry.

Useful websites

Blacksmiths Index (blacksmiths.mygenwebs.com)

Irish Agricultural Museum (www.irishagrimuseum.ie)

Mills Archive (millsarchive.org)

Museum of English Rural Life (reading.ac.uk/merl/)

National Museum of Rural Life, Scotland (nms.ac.uk/national-museum-of-rural-life)

National Wool Museum (www.museumwales.ac.uk/wool/)

Rural Life Centre, Surrey (rural-life.org.uk)

RUTLAND:

Record Office for Leicestershire, Leicester & Rutland (www.leics.gov.uk/recordoffice)

Image Leicestershire (imageleicestershire.org.uk)

Leicestershire & Rutland FHS (lrfhs.org.uk)

S

S&N Genealogy (genealogysupplies.com): Genealogical publisher, supplier and the team behind TheGenealogist website.

Sainsbury Archive(archive.museumoflondon.org.uk/sainsburyarchive/): Home to more than 16,000 documents, photographs and objects tracing the history of the supermarket since the first shop opened in 1869.

Saint Helena Medal (stehelene.org): Database of the medal awarded to soldiers still living in 1857 who had fought with Napoleon between 1792 and 1815.

Sandhurst Collection (archive.sandhurstcollection.co.uk): Royal Military Academy's archives go back to the eighteenth century, and here you can search cadet/staff registers, containing details of almost every officer cadet, recording name, age, date of entry, commissioning date and corps or regiment joined. Searches are free, downloading an image costs £2.99.

Sardinian Chapel in Lincoln's Inn Fields: Known as 'the Mother Church of the Catholic faith in the Archdiocese of Westminster'. The Catholic FHS has transcribed the registers of the Sardinian Chapel (1772–1841), and the indexes contain over 60,000 names.

Sasines: A legal document in Scottish law that records the transfer of ownership of land or building. The national register of sasines stretches back to 1617 (there was an earlier register but it is very incomplete). You can read more about the creation, range and coverage of the register in this NRS guide: nrscotland.gov.uk/research/guides/sasines.

Scarlet Finders (scarletfinders.co.uk): Explores 'administrative and organisational aspects of the British military nursing services in France and Flanders' during the First World War. This includes details of pay and contracts, the mechanics of mobilisation and demobilisation, marriage, off-duty time, sickness, discipline and more.

School records: School records not only document your ancestor's education, but also reveal a great deal about the wider community in which they lived.

Admission registers include names, addresses and dates of pupils, and sometimes other genealogically useful details. Essex Record Office has the admission register of Maldon National School, which besides being a remarkably early example (it starts in 1817) is also unusual in giving the father's occupation. Aberdeenshire archives looks after an example from Alford Academy, which records child's date of admission to the school, date of birth, name, name of parent/guardian and address. Meanwhile, log books can contain enlightening references to individual children, as well as details of bouts of sickness, civil celebrations, parents and more.

Findmypast has been leading a multi-archive project to digitise school admission registers and log books between 1870 and 1914 (search. findmypast.co.uk/search-world-records/national-school-admission-registers-and-log-books-1870-1914). Findmypast also has some teacher registration records. Ancestry, meanwhile, has London School Admissions & Discharges (1840–1911), digitised from LMA's school collections – containing more than 1 million students from 843 different schools.

Some schools have produced their own online archives. Good examples include Manchester High School for Girls Archive (www.mhsgarchive.org) and Radley College Archives (radleyarchives.co.uk). The latter includes registers, staff records, photographs, newsletters and manuscript collections. There are also photograph albums showing alumni who served and lost their lives in both world wars.

Other informative websites include Hidden Lives (hiddenlives.org.uk), which explores the schooling of children in the care of the Children's Society (formerly the Waifs and Strays' Society) from 1881, and the Workhouse website (workhouses.org.uk) is useful for finding out more about reform schools, as is the sister website childrenshomes.org.uk.

(*See also* 'University archives'.)

SCOTLAND:
Familiarity with Scotland's legal structure, Church hierarchy and governmental history can all be helpful when you start to dig deeper into your Scottish roots. There are differences in the mechanics of civil registration and the keeping of parish registers, but thankfully there's also lots of guidance online not only for bread and butter sources such as these, but also for the more complicated areas of court records, probate law, local government and Poor Law material.

Some of the key bodies and institutions include:

NRS (nrscotland.gov.uk)

The General Register Office for Scotland merged with the National Archives of Scotland in 2011 to become the National Records of Scotland. It is responsible for Scottish government records back to the twelfth century, law, Church, business and estate records, statutory registers and the census.

ScotlandsPeople (scotlandspeople.gov.uk)

The most important web resource for Scottish research. There's a credits system for accessing the material, which includes statutory BMD registers, OPRs, Catholic registers, census records, valuation rolls and soldiers' wills and testaments. There's also the ScotlandsPeople Centre, located in central Edinburgh with search rooms in historic General Register House and New Register House.

NLS (nls.uk)

Preserves newspapers, electoral registers, maps, military listings to emigration passenger lists dating from the mid-sixteenth century.

Other useful websites

Addressing History (addressinghistory.edina.ac.uk)

Anglo-Scottish FHS (anglo-scots.mlfhs.org.uk)

Edinburgh City Libraries (www.capitalcollections.org.uk)

Glasgow City Archives (glasgowlife.org.uk/libraries/the-mitchell-library/archives/Pages/home.aspx)

Glasgow Story (www.theglasgowstory.co.uk)

Historic Hospital Admission Records Project (hharp.org)

Mitchell Library (glasgowfamilyhistory.org.uk)

NAS (nas.gov.uk)

National Register of Archives for Scotland (nas.gov.uk/nras/)

Old Occupations in Scotland (scotsfamily.com/occupations.htm)

Scottish Archive Network (scan.org.uk)

Scottish Association of Family History Societies (safhs.org.uk)

Has compiled a useful Inventory of published pre-1841 population listings, which include poll tax and hearth tax records.

Scottish Genealogy Society (scotsgenealogy.com)

Scottish Handwriting (www.scottishhandwriting.com)

Scottish Indexes (scottishindexes.com)

Scottish Maritime Museum (scottishmaritimemuseum.org)

Scottish Printing Archival Trust (scottishprintarchive.org)

Scottish Screen Archive (ssa.nls.uk)

(*See also* Ian Maxwell's *Tracing Your Scottish Ancestors* (Pen & Sword, 2014))

ScotlandsPeople (scotlandspeople.gov.uk): Click the Help & Resources tab and choose Getting Started to read a tailored guide to Scottish research. The site hosts statutory BMD indexes, old parish records, valuation records as well as other material held by NAS. It has census returns for Scotland (from 1841–1911). It costs £7 to search the census indexes, which includes thirty page credits for viewing images of the original enumerator's pages. (*See also* 'Census in Scotland'.)

ScotlandsPlaces (scotlandsplaces.gov.uk): Website designed to help document, preserve and research Scotland's physical heritage. You can explore collections by geographical location, and it's particularly useful for finding out more about forgotten and obscure forms of taxation.

Scotland's East Coast Fisheries (historyshelf.org/secf/): Project that brought together 6,600 digitised photographs, documents, audio recordings and other artefacts, various East coast archives, Scottish Fisheries Museum, University of Aberdeen and NAS.

Scotsman Digital Archive (archive.scotsman.com): Explore issues of the liberal weekly back to its launch in 1817 (for a fee).

Scottish Archive Network (scan.org.uk): Catalogue to records in fifty-two Scottish archives.

Scottish Book Trade Index (www.nls.uk/catalogues/scottish-book-trade-index): NLS index with names, trades and addresses of people involved in printing in Scotland up to 1850, including printers, publishers, booksellers, bookbinders, printmakers, stationers and papermakers. There's also the Scottish Archive of Print & Publishing History Records at sapphire.ac.uk.

Scottish Catholics: After the Reformation Scottish Catholics were mainly concentrated in Dumfries-shire and Kirkcudbright, Moray and Aberdeenshire, Inverness-shire and the Western Isles. ScotlandsPeople has Catholic records from all Scottish parishes in existence by 1855 (the start of civil registration), as well as records of the Catholic cemeteries in Edinburgh and Glasgow. Baptismal registers, for example, often record dates of birth as well as baptism, as well as name, parents' names (including the mother's maiden surname), place/parish of residence, father's occupation, witnesses (occasionally with relationship to the child) and name of the priest. See Scottish Catholic Archives (scottishcatholicarchives.org.uk).

Scottish Emigration Database (abdn.ac.uk/emigration/): Records of passengers who embarked from Scottish ports between 1890 and 1960.

Scottish Handwriting (www.scottishhandwriting.com): Online tuition to help researchers read and interpret Scottish records dating as far back as the sixteenth century.

Scottish Jewish Archives Centre (sjac.org.uk): Founded in 1987 and based in Scotland's oldest Synagogue – the Garnethill Synagogue in Glasgow. Has synagogue minute books and registers, membership lists, personal papers and photographs. The Archive maintains a collection of Jewish newspapers, which often contain personal announcements.

Scottish Mining (scottishmining.co.uk): Website includes a database of more than 22,000 names of those involved in coal, iron and shale mining.

Scottish Record Society (scottishrecordsociety.org.uk): One of the oldest historical societies, which has been publishing volumes since 1897. Follow the links to Old Series, then scroll down the various volumes and choose Read Online to see digitised copies on archive.org.

Scottish Register of Tartans (www.tartanregister.gov.uk): Here you can find out more about the history of tartans and explore the database of tartan designs, maintained by NRS. The website also has a useful set of FAQs: 'Historically tartan was the everyday wear of Highlanders, spun, dyed, woven and fashioned locally. Wealthy families were able to afford brighter fabrics coloured with imported dyes and fashionably tailored. In the eighteenth century the association of tartan with the Jacobites (considered outlaws and rebels by the British government) led to its proscription in the Highlands from 1747 to 1782. During this period tartan was worn in the lowlands of Scotland, often as a political statement. It was also popularised across the world as the uniform of the Highland regiments.'

Scottish testaments: This is the collective term for documents relating to wills and inventories. After a person died, if there was a will it would be taken to the sheriff courts to be confirmed, producing a document called a 'testament testamentar' (a grant of probate). If there was no will a 'testament dative' would be drawn up (a letter of administration) which would give power to executors to deal with the estate.

Testaments from between 1514 and 1925 have been digitised and copies are available through ScotlandsPeople, which also contains an index, each entry listing surname, forename, title, occupation and place of residence (where known) of the deceased person, the court in which the testament was recorded, and the date. Index entries do not include names of executors, trustees, heirs to the estate, date of death or value of the estate.

Before 1823 testaments were recorded in the Commissary Court with jurisdiction over the parish in which the person died. And just as England's diocesan boundaries won't match ancient county boundaries, so these court boundaries, which roughly corresponded to medieval dioceses that existed before the Reformation in Scotland, bear no relation to county boundaries. Remember that the Edinburgh Commissary Court confirmed testaments for those who owned property in more than one area and for Scots who died outside Scotland. From 1824 Sheriff Courts took over responsibility for confirmation of testaments.

Scottish Theatre Archive, University of Glasgow: gla.ac.uk/services/specialcollections/collectionsa-z/scottishtheatrearchive/

Scout Association: Scouting traces its roots back to the original Brownsea Island Scout event in Poole Harbour in 1907, organised by Robert Baden-Powell. The following year he published *Scouting for Boys*. In 1909 he decided girls should not be in the same organisation, and Girl Guides were founded the following year. The Scout Association Archive is at www.scoutsrecords.org. For information about Girl Guides go to girlguiding.org.uk.

Scrivener: A clerk who wrote or copied legal documents.

Search tools and commands: Here are some useful tools for weeding out unwanted results. Remember that many of these commands and shortcuts are transferable to other search engines (Bing, Yahoo) and websites (from FamilySearch to eBay).

1. The quickest way to avoid irrelevant hits is simply to put your search term in 'double quotes'. This ensures the search engine will return matches to that exact term.
2. You can remove unwanted results by placing the 'minus' symbol (-) before the word that you want excluded from the search. This can be really helpful if your surname research keeps being swamped by a famous person. So if you're researching the surname Blair, for example, and you want to avoid the former prime minister, you would search '-Tony Blair'. This is also a good way of removing unwanted spelling variants, or any other keyword that appears to be clouding your results.
3. There are all kinds of useful time-saving keyboard shortcuts, most of which are transferrable between operating systems and browsers.

When working through text-heavy web pages, indexes or other long lists, for example, use spacebar-scroll tool. You simply press the spacebar to scroll down, and shift and spacebar to scroll up.

4. Another keyboard shortcut is quick zoom. This is really useful if you're working with any images – deciphering digitised documents, poring over maps or inspecting photographs – especially if the website in question doesn't have its own built-in zoom function, or if the zoom function is fiddly to use. You simply press the Ctrl key (Command key on Macs) and then use the + and – keys to zoom in and out.

5. While some sites have built-in search functions, many don't. To overcome this problem use the site command and URL to trawl for names/keywords within. So to find references to probate in FamilySearch you would type 'probate site:https://familysearch.org' into your search engine. You can also use the minus symbol if you want to exclude a website. So if you want to find probate material but don't want the results to be cluttered by FamilySearch you'd type 'probate -site:https://familysearch.org'.

6. If you return to a useful website and it appears to have disappeared, you can enter the URL into the Internet Archive's Wayback Machine at archive.org/web/. Alternatively you can search with the command cache (e.g. 'cache:www.pen-and-sword.co.uk') which should display cached copies of pages from the last three months.

7. If you find a website that's useful for researching a subject, you can quickly find out what other websites link to it (so websites that might have allied content) by searching with the link command (e.g. 'link:www.pen-and-sword.co.uk').

8. The allinurl command allows you to search for websites that have a keyword within the web address (e.g. 'allinurl:genealogy'). You can use the allintitle command to look for a word contained within the website's title (e.g. 'allintitle:genealogy'). Both could be useful for tracking down one-name studies.

9. Using 'Or' between two search terms combines the search into one – returning results relating to both words individually.

10. Using the ~ symbol leads to additional synonyms and related words.

11. Filetype search is another handy online command that can help you track down specific content through your search engine. So 'Scott filetype:xls' would search for the word 'Scott' within online Excel spreadsheets. 'Scott filetype:jpeg' would turn up jpeg image files, or,

you could try subject keywords and PDF to look for indexes, guides or digital resources relating to subject (e.g. 'Probate family history filetype:pdf').

12. Search tip: To quickly scan a text-heavy web page for a surname or subject, use your browser's built-in search tool. Just press Ctrl F (or Command F on Macs) and a search bar should appear towards the top-right corner. Type in a surname or keyword and it should jump to any reference it finds, with the ability to scroll back and forth between matches using the arrow key. This can be a great way to quickly scan an online index, transcription or digitised source such as a trade directory.

Seax (seax.essexcc.gov.uk): The Essex Record Office catalogue boasts indexes and many free images of a large number of documents, as well as linking through to the ERO's own subscription service, Essex Ancestors, where you can download images of parish registers and wills for a fee.

Secretary hand: A style of handwriting common in documents from the sixteenth and seventeenth centuries. The SoG has a useful guide to reading secretary hand in the Learn > Hints and Tips section of the website (www.sog.org.uk).

SELKIRKSHIRE:
Scottish Borders Archives (heartofhawick.co.uk/info/1/about_us/12/heritage_hub)
Borders FHS (bordersfhs.org.uk)

Senior Service: The name for the Royal Navy as it is the oldest part of the British armed forces having been founded during the reign of Henry VIII.

Session, Court of: Highest civil court in Scotland. It sits in Parliament House in Edinburgh.

Settlement certificates: An act of 1662 established the need to prove entitlement to parish-level poor relief by issuing settlement certificates. The certificates proved which parish a family belonged to and therefore which parish had the legal responsibility to provide relief.

Settlement examinations: If a person had become a burden on the parish, a settlement examination would be carried out to determine whether the person had a legitimate right to residency and relief. If it was found they did not, they would be served a removal order – basically meaning that it was some other parish's responsibility to pay for their relief. The examinations can be incredibly enlightening for family historians as they often give potted biographies of those applying for relief. And of course they can also point in the direction your family may have moved next.

Shepster: An obsolete term for a seamstress.

Sheriff: A legal official with responsibility maintaining law and order within the 'shire'.

Sheriffdoms: Just as English counties derive from ancient shires, so Scottish counties can trace their lineage back to sheriffdoms – areas of land over which local sheriffs held jurisdiction.

SHETLAND:
Shetland Museum & Archives (shetland-museum.org.uk)

Shetland FHS (shetland-fhs.org.uk)

Shetland Museum & Archives Photo Library (photos.shetland-museum.org.uk)

Great example of a regional archive/museum photo library, with more than 65,000 images online documenting Shetland Life. You can use the index to narrow results by parish or subjects such as 'wrecks' or 'Roll of Honour'.

Ships List (theshipslist.com): Mainly hosts transcribed passenger lists but does also include material that could be helpful researching merchant shipping.

Ships' muster and pay books: Muster and pay books were essentially crew lists, and are the likeliest place to find references to RN ratings before 1853. You can search TNA's Discovery catalogue for muster/pay books (1667–1878) from a particular ship.

Ships Pictures (shipspictures.co.uk): Exhaustive database of images with details of each vessel including type, launch date, actions and fate. Has images of some 10,000-plus warships.

Shires: A traditional term for a large division of land – the reason why so many British counties have 'shire' within their names. The Anglo-Saxon Kingdom of England was divided into shires, and these were further divided into 'hundreds', 'wapentakes' or 'wards'.

Shoah Foundation (sfi.usc.edu): 'Dedicated to making audio-visual interviews with survivors and witnesses of the Holocaust and other genocides ...'.

Shops and retail: The vast majority of shop keepers worked in small family run businesses and as there's no single centralised source covering the retail industry, you may struggle to track down sources beyond the census and local trade directories. There are some excellent tips in the hour-long podcast on the subject, recorded in 2009 by TNA's Family History Records Specialist Audrey Collins (www.nationalarchives.gov. uk/podcasts/shop-workers.htm).

If your ancestors sold unfamiliar sounding products, you could try the *Dictionary of Traded Goods and Commodities 1550–1820*. It contains nearly 4,000 terms drawn from all kinds of documents relating to trade and retail. You can search it at British History Online (www.british-history. ac.uk).

If your ancestor supplied goods to a royal court, they may have been issued with royal warrants and annual lists of warrant holders were published in the *London Gazette* (www.thegazette.co.uk).

The *Chemist & Druggist*, a weekly trade magazine for UK pharmacists first published in 1859, has now been digitised and placed online by the Wellcome Library (wellcomelibrary.org).

Useful websites
John Lewis Memory Store (johnlewismemorystore.org.uk)

Marks & Spencer Company Archive (marksintime.marksandspencer. com)

National Co-Operative Archive (www.archive.coop)

Sainsbury Archive (archive.museumoflondon.org.uk/sainsburyarchive/)

Woolworths Museum (woolworthsmuseum.co.uk)

SHROPSHIRE:
Shropshire Archives (shropshire.gov.uk/archives/)

Shropshire FHS (sfhs.org.uk)

Remember that parish boundaries have changed over the years and that many 'lost' Shropshire ancestors may be found just over the border in Wales. This is not a diocesan record office, meaning most pre-1858 wills, bishops' transcripts and marriage licences for Shropshire are split between Herefordshire Archive Service, Lichfield Diocesan Record Office and NLW.

Signalman/signaller: Rail employee who operates points and signals to control the movement of trains. If your ancestor was a signalman, try the website Signal Box (signalbox.org). It includes descriptions and illustrations, rules and regulations, photographs, articles, reminiscences and lists of museums and books.

Signature books: Books of signatures will often survive in your family archive and may contain the handwriting of long-lost forebears. My own, given to me in the early 1980s, has my signature, my sisters' and … that's it. But another example that survives in the family papers dates from the early 1900s and includes almost every attendee at a birthday ball held in 1907. The names there include two relations who lost their lives during the First World War.

Slavery: While there are relatively few records of individual slaves, there is a lot of online information about voyages, vessels, crews and the men and women who profited from slavery, as well as the abolition movements in Britain, Europe and America.

Useful websites
Centre for the Study of International Slavery (liv.ac.uk/csis/)

Global Slavery Index (globalslaveryindex.org)

International Slavery Museum (liverpoolmuseums.org.uk/ism/)

Information on the trade triangle – from European ports towards Africa's west coast, the voyage across the Atlantic known as the Middle Passage and the return to Europe with goods produced by slave labour.

Legacies of British Slave-ownership (ucl.ac.uk/lbs)

When Parliament abolished slavery in the British Caribbean, Mauritius and the Cape, an apprenticeship scheme was introduced for freed individuals, and compensation was paid to former owners. The resulting records form the core of this UCL database, where you can find owners, see how much they were awarded and the number of slaves at each property.

My Slave Ancestors (myslaveancestors.com)

Parliament and the British Slave Trade (www.parliament.uk/slavetrade)

Explore Parliament's relationship with both transatlantic slavery and the public campaign against it.

Recovered Histories (recoveredhistories.org)

Digitised eighteenth- and nineteenth-century literature on the transatlantic slave trade.

Slavery, Abolition & Emancipation (brycchancarey.com/slavery/index.htm)

Includes biographies of various British Abolitionists including Ignatius Sancho, the first known African to vote in a British election.

Slave Genealogy (slavegenealogy.com)

TNA (nationalarchives.gov.uk/slavery/)

Has samples of slave-ship logs and abolitionists' wills. TNA also has slave registers (1812–34), which are available on Ancestry – most registers have indexes to slave owners and estates and give the name of the parish or district where they lived.

Trans-Atlantic Slave Trade Database (slavevoyages.org)

Slavers tended to keep careful records and this website hosts a database of more than 35,000 slave-trading voyages, detailing owners, captains and crew. There's also a database of 91,491 Africans taken from captured slave ships or from African trading sites, giving name, age, gender, origin, country and places of embarkation/disembarkation.

Understanding Slavery Initiative (understandingslavery.com)

Draws on collections from six UK museums including the International Slavery Museum and the National Maritime Museum.

Wilberforce Institute for the study of Slavery and Emancipation (www2. hull.ac.uk/fass/wise/about_us.aspx)

Society of Genealogists (sog.org.uk): Educational charity founded in 1911 to foster the study of genealogy. The SoG library in Clerkenwell is the largest specialist genealogical library outside North America. Holdings include parish/Nonconformist registers on microfilm/fiche and other formats, along with MIs, wills, marriage licences, census transcripts, directories, poll books, as well as all kinds of pedigrees and family histories. The library catalogue is available on the Society's website and many SoG datasets are available via Findmypast – with a separate free service to members run by the Society itself. Membership is by annual subscription and the website has useful guides to various common sources and records.

Soldiers of Gloucestershire Museum (soldiersofglos.com): Alongside details of the museum itself, you can use the Soldier Search page to trawl for individuals who served in the 28th North Gloucestershire Regiment during the nineteenth century, or with the Gloucestershire Regiment during the First World War. Currently the nineteenth-century database contains nearly 10,000 entries, the First World War equivalent over 40,000.

Soldiers of Oxfordshire (www.sofo.org.uk): Military museum in Woodstock, Oxfordshire, opened in 2014. The website includes sections on county regiments, VC winners and a useful Soldier Search tool where you can trawl names of just over 120,000 Oxfordshire and Buckinghamshire Light Infantry soldiers'/officers' names, nearly 3,000 Queens Own Oxfordshire Hussars' names and names of those that served with the RAF, Home Guard and Royal Garrison Artillery.

SOMERSET:
Somerset Record Office (www1.somerset.gov.uk/archives/)

Catalogue has 480,000 entries, online indexes include Somerset Wills (1812–57), Bridgwater Shipping Crew Lists and prisoners in Ilchester Gaol. Important collections here include the archive of the Somerset Light Infantry, which has First World War Diaries and a complete roll of the 1st Battalion, and the recently catalogued Quarter Session rolls for Somerset. These begin in 1607 and run in a complete unbroken series until 1971.

Bath Archives (batharchives.co.uk)

Bath Ancestors Database covers 1603–1990 and contains information taken from a wide variety of records.

Somerset & Dorset FHS (sdfhs.org)

Bristol & Avon FHS (bafhs.org.uk)

Weston-Super-Mare & District FHS (wsmfhs.org.uk)

SOUTH AFRICA:
Genealogical Society of South Africa (www.genza.org.za)

National Archives and Records Service of South Africa (www.national.archives.gov.za)

South Africa War Graves Project (southafricawargraves.org)

South Sea Bubble: A financial crash caused by the collapse of a joint stock company called the South Sea Company which dealt in national debt.

Southampton Archives (www.southampton.gov.uk/archives/): An important national source held here is the Central Index Register of Merchant Seamen, also known as the 4th register. This is a collection of over 1¼ million Merchant Navy service record cards, with details of those serving on board British-registered vessels between 1918 and 1941. Other maritime material here includes crew lists for Southampton-registered vessels (from 1863–1913). Some other maritime records include disaster funds, such as the Southampton branch of the Titanic Relief Fund, and staffing records from some shipping lines – including the Prince Line (late nineteenthth century–1960s), Royal Mail Line (mid-nineteenth century–1960s), and Shaw, Savill and Albion deck officers (1909–60s).

Special interest groups:
Anglo German FHS (agfhs.org)

Anglo-Italian FHS (anglo-italianfhs.org.uk)

Association of Genealogists and Researchers in Archives (agra.org.uk)

Australasian Federation of Family History Organisations (affho.org)

British Association for Local History (balh.co.uk)

Catholic FHS (catholic-history.org.uk/cfhs)

Families In British India Society (fibis.org)

Federation of Family History Societies (ffhs.org.uk)

Federation of Genealogical Societies, US (fgs.org)

Guild of One-Name Studies (one-name.org)

Heraldry Society (theheraldrysociety.com)

Institute of Heraldic & Genealogical Studies (ihgs.ac.uk)

Jewish Genealogical Society of Great Britain (jgsgb.org.uk)

New Zealand Society of Genealogists (genealogy.org.nz)

Quaker FHS (qfhs.co.uk)

Romany and Traveller FHS (rtfhs.org.uk)

Society of Australian Genealogists (sag.org.au)

Spinning the Web (spinningtheweb.org.uk): Resource that draws on images, sound files and documents from collections across North-West England to 'tell the story of the Lancashire Cotton Industry'. *See also* 'cottontown.org'.

Sports and pastimes: If your ancestor was talented enough to play for club or country, there are plenty of museums, archives and websites where you may be able to find out more about their careers. The club itself may keep an archive, or there may be a more general national collection relating to the sport. Even if their skills were more modest, you may still be able to find evidence through your own family archive, through school magazines, club archives, local newspapers, regimental or occupational journals or in-company magazines. So the likes of the British Newspaper Archive (britishnewspaperarchive.co.uk), for example, could be useful for tracking down match reports printed in local newspapers. It also has specialist titles such as the *Sports Argos* (1914–18).

Football
Association of Football Statisticians (11v11.co.uk)
Football Club History Database (fchd.info)
National Football Museum (nationalfootballmuseum.com/collections/family-history/)
The National Football Museum in Manchester is working to digitise FA and Football League records.
Scottish Football Museum (scottishfootballmuseum.org.uk)
Soccer Data (soccerdata.co.uk)

Cricket
Association of Cricket Statisticians & Historians (acscricket.com)
Cric Info (espncricinfo.com)
Search *Wisden Cricketers' Almanac* back catalogue to 1864, with lots of reproduced essays and obituaries.
Cricket Archive (cricketarchive.co.uk)
Home to a growing database of scorecards and players.
Lord's (lords.org/history/mcc-museum-library-and-collections/mcc-museum/)

Rugby (League and Union)
Rugby Football History (rugbyfootballhistory.com)
Rugby League Heritage (rugbyleaguecares.org/heritage)
Talk Rugby Union (talkrugbyunion.co.uk)
World Rugby Museum (www.englandrugby.com/twickenham/world-rugby-museum/)

Others
Bicycle Racing (theracingbicycle.com)
British Golf Museum (britishgolfmuseum.co.uk)
Olympic Studies Centre (olympic.org/olympic-games)
Wimbledon Heritage (wimbledon.com/heritage)

Squire: The main landowner within the parish.

STAFFORDSHIRE:
Staffordshire & Stoke-on-Trent Archive Service (staffordshire.gov.uk/leisure/archives/homepage.aspx)

The Archive Service runs its own dedicated indexes website at www. staffsnameindexes.org.uk, where you can trawl through the likes of 'Calendar of Prisoners at Staffordshire Quarter Sessions, 1779–1900', 'Staffordshire Police Force Registers Index, 1842–1920' and 'Diocese of Lichfield Wills, 1640–1760'. More recent additions include 'Staffordshire Police Disciplinary Index' and 'Canal Boat Register Index'. The Gateway to the Past catalogue is at www.archives.staffordshire.gov.uk.

Sutherland Papers collection (www.sutherlandcollection.org.uk)

Staffordshire Views (www.views.staffspasttrack.org.uk)

Great War Staffordshire (staffordshiregreatwar.com)

Birmingham Archives & Heritage (birmingham.gov.uk/archives)

Wolverhampton City Archives (wolverhamptonart.org.uk/about-wolver hampton-archives/)

Birmingham & Midland Society for Genealogy & Heraldry (bmsgh.org)

Burntwood FHG (bfhg.org.uk)

Staffordshire Collection: Another Findmypast project, which on completion boasts around 6 million searchable transcripts/images, covering all Anglican parish registers up to 1900, and including Stoke-on-Trent and parishes now within Wolverhampton, Dudley, Sandwell and Walsall.

Stage Archive, The (archive.thestage.co.uk): Subscription-based online archive of more than 6,500 issues of the *Stage*, founded by Maurice Comerford and Lionel Carson in February 1880.

Statute of Apprentices: Passed in 1563, this statute meant that by law to enter certain trades a worker had to serve an apprenticeship. The earliest centralised records of apprentices do not appear in England and Wales until 1710, when stamp duty was payable on indentures of apprenticeship.

Statute of Artificers: A sixteenth-century Act of Parliament which sought to regulate prices, wages and training of workers.

Steam Engine Makers Society (www.geog.port.ac.uk/lifeline/sem_db/ sem_history.html): History and database relating to this early British trade union which in 1835 had 442 members across 10 branches, and by 1919 had nearly 30,000 members across 225 branches.

Stephenson's *Rocket*: Pioneering locomotive designed and built for the Liverpool & Manchester Railway's Rainhill Trials, held in 1829. Built at the Forth Street Works in Newcastle upon Tyne, the *Rocket* triumphed, leading to a contract to provide locomotives for the first passenger line. The official opening of the L&MR line took place in September the next year, with a procession of trains. This event was marred by the death of MP for Liverpool William Huskisson who was struck and killed by *Rocket*.

STIRLINGSHIRE:

Stirling Archives (stirling.gov.uk/archives)

Falkirk Archives (falkirkcommunitytrust.org/heritage/archives/)

Central Scotland FHS (csfhs.org.uk)

Straw plaiter: A maker of straw braids for hats.

Strays: Records of ancestors that appear in unexpected places. Many genealogical groups compile databases and indexes of county individuals who have appeared in records elsewhere.

Strict Baptist Historical Society (www.strictbaptisthistory.org.uk): Includes a Pastor and Chapels database, library catalogue and a personal names database – comprising a biographical index to Strict Baptist members mentioned in *Christian's Pathway*, *Gospel Standard*, *Earthen Vessel* and the *Gospel Herald* magazines. Many of the entries relate to service records and obits in connection with the First World War.

SUFFOLK:

Suffolk Record Office (www.suffolkarchives.co.uk)

Has branches in Bury St Edmunds, Ipswich and Lowestoft. As a general guide, Bury holds material for West Suffolk, Ipswich covers East Suffolk and Lowestoft looks after material for the north-eastern parishes. The much improved website has sections on Suffolk people and places.

Suffolk Heritage Direct (suffolkheritagedirect.org.uk)

Suffolk FHS (suffolkfhs.org.uk)

Alde Valley Suffolk FHG (aldevalleyfamilyhistorygroup.onesuffolk.net)

Felixstowe FHS (itgen.co.uk/ffhs/)

Suffrage: Election records become more useful and complete as more people became eligible to vote.

1832	Only men with property could vote.
1867	Men with property worth £5 per annum, or tenants paying £12 per annum.
1884	Male householders/tenants paying £10 per annum could vote.
1918	Men over 21 and married women over 30 could vote.
1928	All women over 21 could vote.
1969	Men and women over 18 could vote.

Sugar: A large database of sugar refiners and bakers is at www.mawer. clara.net/intro.html, compiled Bryan Mawer. It includes information about refineries, a glossary, details of the German influence on the trade, the manufacturing process and a 40,000-plus database of names, with details of the source – from parish registers to shipping lists.

Supremacy, Act of: The Act of Supremacy of 1558 re-established the Church of England's independence from Rome.

Surname: Surname customs evolved during the medieval period when a second name (based on an individual's occupation or area of residence) would be used when two people shared first names. Hereditary surnames were first adopted from the thirteenth century by the aristocracy. Many Welsh people did not adopt surnames until the seventeenth century or later.

SURREY:

Surrey History Centre (surreycc.gov.uk/recreation-heritage-and-culture/ archives-and-history/surrey-history-centre)

Looks after the diaries of English antiquary William Bray, featuring what is believed to be the earliest known manuscript reference to baseball. On the day after Easter in 1755, the then 18-year-old William wrote: 'After Dinner Went to Miss Seale's to play at Base Ball, with her, the 3 Miss Whiteheads, Miss Billinghurst, Miss Molly Flutter, Mr. Chandler, Mr. Ford, H. Parsons & Jolly. Drank tea and stayed till 8.' Also holds the Queen's Royal Surrey Regiment archive, spanning four centuries and 45m of shelving, comprising battalion war diaries, private journals, official photograph albums and even recordings of veterans' reminiscences.

Exploring Surrey's Past (exploringsurreyspast.org.uk)

Chertsey Poor Law Union admission and discharge books and Godstone Poor Law Union application and report books.

East Surrey FHS (eastsurreyfhs.org.uk)

Surrey in the Great War (www.surreyinthegreatwar.org.uk)

West Surrey FHS (wsfhs.org)

SUSSEX:

East Sussex Record Office, The Keep (thekeep.info)

East Sussex collections include a large number of hospital records, including the mental hospitals at Hellingly and St Francis, Haywards Heath. Patient records are not generally accessible if they are less than 100 years old but some of the hospital records go back much further than that — those of the Royal Sussex County Hospital's predecessor, the Voluntary Hospital in Brighton, start in 1828. Friends of East Sussex Record Office (fesro.org) have produced an index to 'East Sussex Sentences of Transportation at Quarter Sessions 1790—1854'. The Keep also has Brighton & Hove collections and the Sussex University collections, including Mass Observation archive.

West Sussex Record Office & Archives (www.westsussex.gov.uk/leisure/record_office_and_archives.aspx)

Brighton Pavilion, Museums & Libraries (brightonmuseums.org.uk)

Sussex FHG (sfhg.org.uk)

Eastbourne & District FHS (eastbournefhs.org.uk)

Hastings & Rother FHS (hrfhs.org.uk)

SUTHERLAND:

Highland Archives Service (highlandarchives.org.uk/genealogy.asp)

Highland FHS (highlandfamilyhistorysociety.org)

Sutherland Collection (www.sutherlandcollection.org.uk): A Staffordshire and Stoke-on-Trent Archive Service website where you can explore a fully indexed database of the Leveson-Gower family archive, Marquesses of Stafford and Dukes of Sutherland, which contains many thousands of names – employees, tenants, shopkeepers and suppliers, savers in the Trentham Savings Bank and workers on the building of Trentham Hall.

Swansea Mariners (swanseamariners.org.uk): Transcribed information about merchant seaman on Swansea and Cardiff-registered ships.

Sweetapple, Revd W.: A clergyman who peddled clandestine marriages from his Nottinghamshire parish of Fledborough, until his trade was curtailed by Hardwicke's Marriage Act, passed in 1754.

Swing Riots, 1830: A widespread uprising by rural workers which began with the destruction of threshing machines in the Elham Valley area of East Kent. The website black-sheep-search.co.uk has some interesting material relating to the Swing Riots. This includes a transcribed list of individuals aboard *Eliza* – the first of the ships transporting Swing Rioters to leave England. 'She sailed from Portsmouth on the 6th February 1831, on board were 224 male convicts, all of them Swing Rioters and arrived at Hobart Town, Tasmania (or Van Diemen's Land as it was called then) on the 29th May 1831, after a voyage of 112 days.'

T

Tally: A method of keeping records. A tally was a narrow piece of wood, scored across with notches and then split into halves – each party keeping one half.

Tapster: Archaic term for someone who sells beer/ale.

Taxation records: There are all kinds of obsolete forms of taxation, from the hair powder tax to the hearth tax. Not all left behind genealogically useful records, and the coverage of those that did can often be patchy.

It's always important to remember the purpose behind a series of records. The seventeenth-century hearth tax, for example, saw householders paying tax within bands decided by the number of hearths in the dwelling. Therefore it can represent a kind of census, recording the head of household of each property. There's also the window tax, which took a similar approach. Remember that our forbears would often sign up to the tax-avoidance schemes of the day: sealing up windows to avoid the window tax, hearths to avoid the hearth tax or using bigger (and thus fewer) bricks to avoid the brick tax.

Significant categories include land tax, building tax, stamp duties, rates, income tax or taxes levied on luxury items. Remember, some taxation (and its non-payment) would lead to paperwork going through the quester Sessions, which generally survive at county record offices.

For example, there's a set of Land Tax Assessments from about 1780–1832 covering all Wiltshire parishes among the quarter sessions material held at the Wiltshire & Swindon History Centre (wshc.eu).

Findmypast has Northamptonshire hearth tax material, Cheshire land tax assessments (1786–1832) and 19 million rate book records from Devon, London and Manchester. Ancestry also has collections of rate books from London, West Yorkshire and Birmingham.

A useful site for finding out more is ScotlandsPlaces (scotlandsplaces. gov.uk) which has an army of volunteers transcribing all sorts of data, including various tax rolls, such as servant tax rolls, the farm horse tax and poll tax records from the 1690s. Ancestry's collections include London Land Tax Records (1692–1932). The website Building History has a useful page focusing on the kinds of taxation levied on properties (buildinghistory.org/taxation.shtml).

Some useful websites
Centre for Hearth Tax Research (www.roehampton.ac.uk/Research-Centres/Centre-for-Hearth-Tax-Research/)

E 179 Database of Records relating to lay and clerical taxation (national archives.gov.uk/e179/search.asp)

Glasgow Valuation Rolls (theglasgowstory.com/valuation-rolls/)

Hearth Tax Online (hearthtax.org.uk)

NRS (nrscotland.gov.uk/research/guides/taxation-records)

Taxation Database (hrionline.ac.uk/taxatio/)

Teachers: Registers and log books that usually survive in school archives and at local record offices can be a goldmine for finding out about your ancestor's schooling, but also useful for researching the careers of teachers. In addition, more and more universities offer online access to their digitised archives. Teachers' Registration Council records are with the SoG (sog.org.uk), which you can search via Findmypast. The records include details of just under 100,000 teachers registered with the Council back to its formation in 1914. The register also recorded teachers already working in 1914, so in effect the records stretch back much further. The information includes name, registration date, address, training and more.

Findmypast is also home to the National School Registers collection (1870–1914) drawn from registers and log books from more than 100-plus archives.

Teachers, Society of: Established in 1846 as the Society of Teachers. It later became the College of Preceptors, then the College of Teachers. Membership records are looked after by the Institute of Education Archives Based at UCL (www.ucl.ac.uk/ioe).

Teaser: A worker that opens up matted wool for carding.

***Teesdale Mercury* Archive** (teesdalemercuryarchive.org.uk): Explore the archives of County Durham's *Teesdale Mercury*, 1854–2005.

Testament dative: In Scottish probate law, if there was no will a 'testament dative' would be drawn up (a letter of administration), giving power to executors to deal with the estate.

Testament testamentar: A Scottish grant of probate.

Testator/testatrix: These are the legal, gender-specifc terms given to individuals making a will.

Textile workers: The textile industry was the powerhouse of the Industrial Revolution, feeding a global demand for high-quality materials from three main districts – the Midlands, the North-West and the Clyde Valley of Scotland. Remember to see what material survives at local repositories – although tracking down records of workers may be problematic, you can at least find out more about the subject. The University of Manchester Library's Special Collections, for example, looks after the Oldham and Ashton Textile Employers' Association Archives and has the *Cotton Factory Times*, printed between 1885 and 1937. See also Vivien Teasdale's *Tracing Your Textile Ancestors* (Pen & Sword, 2009).

Useful websites
Cotton Town (cottontown.org)
Derwent Valley Mills (www.derwentvalleymills.org)
Scottish Textile Heritage Online (scottishtextileheritage.org.uk)
Spinning the Web (spinningtheweb.org.uk)
Weaver's Triangle (www.weaverstriangle.co.uk)

Theatre Collection (bris.ac.uk/theatrecollection/): 'One of the world's largest archives of British theatre history and live art', looked after by the University of Bristol.

Tithes: These were a kind of local tax which resulted in a pre-census snapshot of landholders, tenants and farmers. Tithes meant literally 'tenths', and were usually a tenth of a landholding's produce which was payable to the Church. Enclosure Acts of the seventeenth and eighteenth centuries formalised the system and the 1836 Tithe Act extended the system to all of England and Wales. Commissioners were sent to each parish to establish which tithes were due to the Church. These tithes, which had previously been paid in goods and produce and stored in so-called tithe barns, were now translated into money, and apportioned to landholders throughout the parish as a kind of rent. The system produced maps and accompanying apportionment data, recording all kinds of details about ancestors' landholdings, noting use, rentable value and the names of owners and occupiers.

Of commercial bodies, thegenealogist.co.uk has been digitising maps and record books, but there are also a number of free resources online. There's the crowdsourcing project Cynefin (cynefin.archiveswales. org.uk), which is transcribing digitised tithe material at NLW – about 1,200 tithe maps and more than 30,000 pages of index documents. Other sites include the West Yorkshire Tithe Maps Project (tracksintime.wyjs. org.uk), Historic Maps of Norfolk (historicmaps.norfolk.gov.uk) and the NAI's Tithe Applotment Books (1823–37) (titheapplotmentbooks. nationalarchives.ie/search/tab/home.jsp).

Toleration Act of 1689: Granted Nonconformists the freedom to worship.

Tolpuddle Martyrs Museum (tolpuddlemartyrs.org.uk): Celebrates the foundation of modern trade unionism through the story of the Tolpuddle Martyrs. These were six Dorset agricultural labourers who were put on trial and ultimately deported in 1834 for forming the Friendly Society of Agricultural Labourers in response to the lowering of agricultural wages.

Tonnage and poundage: Refers to duties and taxes levied on every tun (cask) of imported wine, and on every pound of exported or imported merchandise. Disputes about tonnage and poundage were one of the many factors that led to the English Civil War.

Tool helver: A maker of handles for tools.

Town surveys: It's always worth seeing what census-like sources exist in a city's borough collections. West Glamorgan Archive Service, for example, has two unique town surveys of Swansea from the late

1830s. Like the census, these were organised by household and record the surname, occupier, proprietor, description of the property, rental/ rateable value and address. The more detailed 1839 survey includes details of profession and/or business, the number of families/individuals at each property and their religion.

Townland: The smallest official division of land in Ireland – not to be confused with 'town'. Originally this unit of land was based on an area deemed sufficient to sustain a cow.

Trade directories: These can sometimes be the only potential source left to you of an ancestor's working life. If they ran a small shop, firm or school, if they were working craftsmen or artisans, their details may appear here. The most established publishers of trade directories were Kelly's and Pigot's, and both became ever more detailed over time. Most commercial sites have digitised directories, and several firms offer them on CD-ROM or as PDF downloads. You can also access free digitised directories from several online sources:

Historical Directories of England & Wales (specialcollections.le.ac.uk/ cdm/landingpage/collection/p16445coll4)

Digitised trade directories covering England and Wales from the 1760s to the 1910s.

Library Ireland (libraryireland.com)

PRONI Street Directories (streetdirectories.proni.gov.uk)

Reproduces directories from Belfast and environs dating from 1819–1900.

Scottish Post Office Directories (digital.nls.uk/directories/)

More than 700 digitised directories from NLS.

Sheffield Directories (sheffieldindexers.com/DirectoriesIndex.html)

Trade unions: The website Trade Union Ancestors (www.unionancestors. co.uk) estimates that around 5,000 trade unions have existed at one time or another, and that tens of millions of people have been members. It has an A–Z of trade unions, information about membership, a trade-union timeline, a list of major strikes and histories of many individual unions. A large number of records relating to trade unions reside at the Modern Records Centre at the University of Warwick (www2.warwick. ac.uk/services/library/mrc/) and the site has a list of commonly searched trades/occupations. Findmypast also has Trade Union Membership

Registers – over 3 million British trade-union records from the Modern Records Centre, including digitised images of the original record books from 26 unions. For a history of the TUC try: unionhistory.info, and Mark Crail (creator of the Trade Union Ancestors website) has written the very useful *Tracing Your Labour Movement Ancestors* (Pen & Sword, 2009). (*See also* 'Occupational sources'.)

Trafalgar Ancestors (nationalarchives.gov.uk/trafalgarancestors/): Lists all those who fought in Nelson's fleet at the Battle of Trafalgar on 21 October 1805. More than 18,000 individuals are recorded in the database, along with service histories (including ships) and various biographical details.

Trans-Atlantic Slave Trade Database (slavevoyages.org): Has information on almost 36,000 slaving voyages between the sixteenth and nineteenth centuries.

Transport Archive (www.transportarchive.org.uk): Website telling 'the story of Britain's transport system since the eighteenth century'.

Treasury in-letters: Another useful TNA source for researching early immigration to the UK. They contain references to refugees and other foreign people who received annuities, pensions and other payments in return for services rendered to the Crown. You can search indexes to the Calendar of Treasury papers between 1556 and 1745 – indeed free digitised editions of this are available through archive.org.

Trench maps: You can access images of First World War trench maps held by NLS via maps.nls.uk/ww1/trenches. There are also First World War trench maps and aerial photographs available via the McMaster University library website at library.mcmaster.ca/maps/ww1/home.

Trinity House, London (trinityhouse.co.uk): Charity dedicated to safeguarding shipping and seafarers, with a statutory duty as a General Lighthouse Authority to deliver aids to navigation. The Corporation of Trinity House was incorporated by Royal Charter in 1514 to regulate pilotage on the River Thames and provide for aged mariners. LMA holds the archives of Trinity House (reference CLC/526).

Trinity House Maritime Museum (trinityhouseleith.org.uk): A charitable foundation that traces its history back to the fourteenth century, when

Leith shipowners and masters set up Trinity House to assist destitute sailors and their families.

Truck Acts: A series of Acts passed to outlaw the truck system – payment of wages in commodities or other currency substitute.

Turnpike trusts: Set up to collect road tolls for maintaining important roads. Trusts were formed by individual Acts of Parliament. The system began in 1663, when a trust was established specifically to repair part of the Great North Road, and peaked in the early decades of the nineteenth century. It is estimated that in the 1830s there were more than 1,000 trusts maintaining around 30,000 miles of roads, with 8,000 toll-gates and side-bars.

Your local archives may well hold records relating to former trusts. Hertfordshire Archives and Local Studies, for example, has minute books, extracts of orders, trustees' appointments, oath books and rolls, lists of trustees, officers' bonds, ledgers of income and expenditure and toll receipts. Turnpikes declined with the coming of the railways, before the Local Government Act of 1888 gave responsibility for maintaining main roads to county/borough councils.

Twitter: Joining Twitter and following your local archives, museums and societies, or those covering the area or subject relevant to your research, is an easy way of keeping abreast of developments. You can also find me @thejonoscott.

Tyburn: The Tyburn (Marble Arch) was the principal place for execution of London criminals and traitors. The earliest known execution here took place in the twelfth century, the last in 1783. On 21 January 1664 Samuel Pepys described going to see the hanging of Colonel James Turner, at Tyburn. 'A comely-looked man he was, and kept his countenance to the end: I was sorry to see him.' Pepys estimated there were in the region of twelve to fourteen thousand people there. You can read the account at pepysdiary.com.

Tyne & Wear Archives (twmuseums.org.uk): Looks after an internationally recognised shipbuilding collection, as well as catalogued mining records.

U

UK BMD (ukbmd.org.uk/local_bmd): Provides useful links to county websites offering online transcribed indexes to GRO records.

UK GDL (ukgdl.org.uk): 'Genealogical Directories and Lists on the Internet', providing links to all kinds of online databases, indexes and finding aids.

Ultimus haeres: A term in Scottish law for when a person dies inestate, and with no blood relative, meaning their estate can be claimed by the Crown.

Uniformity, Act of: The Act of Uniformity of 1559 set the English Book of Common Prayer at the heart of church services and made it a requirement that everyone had to go to church once a week or face a fine. This followed the previous year's Act of Supremacy. Together these Acts re-established the Church of England's independence from Rome.

Unitarians: This Nonconformist denomination's name comes from the central belief that God is a single entity, rejecting the traditional Christian doctrine of the Trinity. The Essex Street Chapel or Essex Church was the first Unitarian place of worship established in England in 1774. Via BMD Registers (bmdregisters.co.uk) you can access birth, baptism, marriage, death and burial data taken from non-parish sources for all kinds of Nonconformists including Unitarians. The material is also available via subscription with TheGenealogist and there are indexes free of charge at FamilySearch.

United Kingdom: The 1707 Acts of Union unified England and Scotland as the Kingdom of Great Britain. The Acts of Union 1800 formed the United Kingdom of Great Britain and Ireland, which became the United Kingdom of Great Britain and Northern Ireland (Wales, Scotland, Northern Ireland and England) after southern Ireland's independence in 1922.

UNITED STATES:

Federation of Genealogical Societies (www.fgs.org)

International Society for British Genealogy & FH (www.isbgfh.org)

Library of Congress (www.loc.gov)

List of State Archives (www.archives.gov/research/alic/reference/state-archives.html)

National Archives (www.archives.gov)

Vital Records (www.archives.gov/research/vital-records/)

University archives: These are some examples of the kinds of online archives you can find, often offering free access to registers of staff or undergraduates.

The University of Glasgow (universitystory.gla.ac.uk) is the second oldest of Scotland's four ancient universities, founded in 1451 (the University of St Andrews was founded in 1413). Via the University People pages you can explore biographies of alumni, read about student life before the twentieth century, and, most usefully, explore records of nearly 20,000 graduates between 1451 and 1914. There are also thousands of images, rolls of honour and details of those who served.

Cambridge University Archives (www.lib.cam.ac.uk/deptserv/manu scripts/universityarchives.html) looks after internal and administrative records of the University of Cambridge from 1266 to the present. The archives are available for consultation in the Manuscripts Reading Room, but remember that records of the constituent Colleges of the University are not held here – they are normally held by the individual colleges themselves. Similarly, Oxford University Archives (www.oua.ox.ac.uk) is based in the Bodleian Library, in the Tower of the Five Orders. While it preserves administrative records of the University and its departments, the records of the constituent Colleges of the University are also with individual colleges.

Ancestry also has Oxford (1500–1886) and Cambridge (1261–1900) university alumni.

Other examples include University of Huddersfield (heritagequay. org) and University of Nottingham Archives (nottingham.ac.uk/ manuscriptsandspecialcollections/collectionsindepth/university/ introduction.aspx).

US Immigrant Ancestors Project (immigrants.byu.edu): Sponsored by the Center for Family History and Genealogy at Brigham Young University. It uses emigration registers to locate information about the birthplaces of immigrants in their native countries. (*See also* 'UNITED STATES' and 'Emigration'.)

Useless Parliament: The first English Parliament of England during the reign of King Charles I. It adjoined on 1 August 1625, and was dissolved twelve days later having achieved nothing.

V

Vaccination: Widespread vaccination against diseases such as smallpox began in the 1830s (when the first Vaccination Act was passed). Programmes of vaccination were organised by Poor Law unions. Once the system became compulsory (in 1853), vaccination registers were kept which often survive in local record office collections. Indeed, vaccination registers can function as a record of all births that took place within a particular registration district and are found within records of Poor Law unions. Bath Record Office, for example, holds vaccination registers covering the period 1871–1928, while the Highland Archive Centre has a 'Register of Postponed Vaccinations for the parish of Dores', dating from the 1890s.

Vagabond: Another word for any itinerant beggar or rogue.

Valuation records: In Ireland tax and specifically valuation surveys are often the only large-scale national survey available to genealogists. The most famous and useful of these is the Griffith's Valuation of Ireland (askaboutireland.ie/griffith-valuation/index.xml), a detailed survey of every taxable piece of agricultural or built property between the years 1847 and 1864. The valuation books recorded the names of occupiers and landowners, and the amount and value of the property held.

In the UK the Valuation Office oversaw a land survey between 1910 and 1915 and this is useful for researching the use or ownership of property. According to TNA's guide: 'The two main types of Valuation Office survey record are plans (maps) and field books. Generally, you need to consult a plan first to help you find the relevant field book.' Valuation Office records are at TNA and are very hard to use.

An important source for Scottish researchers are the Valuation Rolls available via ScotlandsPeople. Following an Act of 1854 these were compiled listing every house or piece of ground in Scotland, along with the names/designations of proprietor, tenant and occupier.

Verso: If this entry ends up on the left-hand page of the book, it could be said to be 'verso' (abbreviated as v). If it ends up on the right-hand page, then it's 'recto'. If you'd like to know more I strongly recommend John Carter's *ABC for Book Collectors* (Rupert Hart-Davis, 1952).

Vestry: A room in parish churches where vestments are kept. It was also the room where the governing body of the parish would meet – a committee made up of churchwardens, parishioners and the minister. According to the Durham County Record Office information page on the subject: 'The vestry appointed the Constable and the Overseers of the Poor, and the Surveyor of the Highways, subject to the approval of the Justices of the Peace. Vestry meetings were held weekly or fortnightly and the vestry made all the important decisions about the parish, including those about paupers and money.

Vestries could be open, when most parishioners attended, or closed, where a small group of men including the parish officers and usually the incumbent attended. Closed or 'select' vestries were extremely common in the North-East and are often referred to as the 'four and twenty' or the 'twelve'.

Vestry minutes: Usually filed under 'parish chest records', vestry minutes are a fascinating (and underused) resource and certainly offer researchers an insight into the community. Vestry minutes are essentially the minutes of the parish council, and will include lots of names of individuals and references to appointments, as well as agreements of care and lists of parishioners such as men eligible for parish duties and details of illegitimate children. These records were usually kept in the parish chest and have been transferred to local record offices. (*See also* 'Parish chest'.)

Veterans Affairs Canada (veterans.gc.ca): Includes the Virtual Memorial to more than 118,000 Canadians and Newfoundlanders who gave their lives in the First World War. There's also the Maple Leaf Legacy Project at mapleleaflegacy.ca.

Vexillology: The study of symbolism and use of flags. To find out more try the Flag Institute (flaginstitute.org).

Vicar: The Church of England incumbent of a parish. Parish priests were divided into vicars, rectors and perpetual curates. And the parish church was supported by tithes. The rector directly received both the greater and lesser tithes of his parish while a vicar received only the lesser tithes.

Vicar's Index to Prerogative Wills: An important tool for Irish probate research. You can find more detail via NAI research guides (nationalarchives.ie).

Victoria County History: The Victoria History of the Counties of England (usually just Victoria County History/VCH) is an ongoing history project which began in 1899 and is still expanding today – although there was quite a lapse in the mid-twentieth century. It is, as it sounds, a county by county history of the country, covering natural history, topography, industry, agriculture and more. An 'encyclopaedic record of England's places and people from earliest times to the present day'. The first to appear in print was Hampshire, Volume I, published in 1900. The website (victoriacountyhistory.ac.uk) has a parish index of the 3,500 parishes currently covered within the 225-plus published volumes. Lots of volumes can be consulted at British History Online (www.british-history.ac.uk).

Victoria Cross: The highest award for bravery in the field, which may be awarded to a person of any military rank in any service. The first awards were presented by Queen Victoria in 1857. Although civilians under military command can also win the award, no civilian has since 1879. The London jewellers Hancocks has been responsible for the production of every VC awarded since its inception. The website victoriacross. org.uk includes an index of VC holders, along with details of the location of graves, and there's also the website of the Victoria Cross Society (victoriacrosssociety.com), and you can find biographies of VC winners on Wikipedia. The George Cross, the equivalent award for civilians and military personnel showing conspicuous bravery not in the face of the enemy, was instituted on 24 September 1940 by King George VI.

Victorian Military History Society (victorianmilitarysociety.org.uk): The website has many interesting articles on subjects ranging from 'Anti-piracy operations in the Straits of Malacca,1835–1840' to 'A 17th Lancer in the American Civil War'.

Victorian Wars Forum (victorianwars.com): Bustling forum dedicated to British military campaigns from 1837–1902. There are sections focusing on individual conflicts (the most active being the Boer War), while the most popular discussion area is Uniforms, Insignia, Equipment & Medals. There's also the Researching Individual Soldiers & Sailors area, where you can post any genealogical queries.

HMS *Victory* (hms-victory.com): Official website for Nelson's flagship which gives background detail about the lives of members of the Georgian navy.

Victualler: A person who is licensed to sell alcohol. Licensing records will often survive at your local record office. Warwickshire County

Record Office, for example, has an online database of licensed victuallers in the county between 1801 and 1828, searchable by parish, victualler, pub name, year or bondsman's surname (apps.warwickshire.gov.uk/Victuallersdb/victuallers/indexes). Yorkshire records are available via Findmypast.

Villein: A feudal term for a peasant or tenant farmer who was legally tied to a lord of the manor – the ag lab equivalent of a bound apprentice.

Virgate: An archaic unit of land – typically around 30 acres.

Viscount: A rank in the peerage. The first was John Beaumont, who was created Viscount Beaumont by King Henry VI.

Vision of Britain (visionofbritain.org.uk): Useful site where you can explore maps, statistics, census reports and travel writing relating to an area or postcode.

W

Wagner Pedigrees: Important collection of research materials focusing on around 1,000 Huguenot families looked after by the Huguenot Library (www.ucl.ac.uk/library/special-collections/huguenot).

Waifs and Strays' Society: Founded in 1881 by civil servant Edward de Montjoie Rudolf. Today known as the Children's Society, its archive of case papers and institutional records are housed at the society's own Records and Archive Centre. You can find out more via hiddenlives.org.uk.

Waits: These were musicians and minstrels employed by town councils to play at civic celebrations and other public occasions. You can find out more via the official website of the International Guild of Town Pipers at townwaits.org.uk.

WALES:
The tradition of patronymic naming presents family historians with some unique problems. Under this ancient system the child would be given the father's first name as a surname – meaning the family name could change with every generation.

The traces of this system can be still be found in modern surnames. The Welsh word for son is 'mab' – which survives in the contracted prefix 'ap'. So the surname Prichard, for example, essentially comes from 'Son of Richard'.

Although gradually replaced by the modern system of fixed surnames, it does mean that if you're lucky enough to have a Welsh line back to the seventeenth, sixteenth or fifteenth century, the more likely it is that your progress will be halted by the custom of patronymic naming.

More recent research is also made difficult thanks to the relatively small pool of Welsh surnames – making it harder for researchers to be sure that one individual with the name David Thomas, for example, is their David Thomas.

Once you've grappled with these difficulties, however, you'll soon discover that there are also a number of very useful resources aimed at family historians with Welsh interests.

NLW (llgc.org.uk) is the most important Welsh repository. It has some 950,000 photographs, 1,500,000 maps, 5,000,000 digital images and e-resources and 15km of archives. It holds the Church in Wales Archive – preserving registers of baptisms, marriages and burials, bishops' transcripts, wills and marriage bonds.

Library online projects and finding aids include:

Wills
The probate database (www.llgc.org.uk/discover/nlw-resources/wills/) provides access to digital images of pre-1858 wills proved in Welsh ecclesiastical courts (before the system of civil probate was introduced). Wills proved after 1858 can be searched through the Calendar of Grants of Probate on microfiche and original volumes in the Reading Rooms. Remember that if an individual held land in more than one diocese in Wales, the will would be proven in the PCC.

Newspapers
Welsh Newspapers Online (welshnewspapers.llgc.org.uk) grants free access to a huge range of Welsh and English-language titles which you can narrow by family notices and announcements.

Tithes
Cynefin crowdsourcing project (cynefin.archiveswales.org.uk) gives access to tithe maps covering about 95 per cent of the country, and the accompanying apportionment documents have been transcribed by volunteers.

First World War
The Library also led the CYMRU 1914 Centenary project (cymru1914. org), the mass digitisation of sources relating to the First World War from libraries, special collections and archives across Wales.

And the most useful multi-archive resource is Archives Wales (archiveswales.org.uk) – a catalogue that holds information from more than 7,000 collections across 21 archives in Wales.

An important commercially available resource is Findmypast's Wales Collections, produced with NLW and the Welsh County Archivists Group. The result is several million parish records covering Anglesey, Brecknockshire, Caernarfonshire, Cardiganshire, Carmarthenshire, Denbighshire, Flintshire, Glamorganshire, Merionethshire, Monmouthshire, Montgomeryshire, Pembrokeshire and Radnorshire.

Finally Genuki (genuki.org.uk/big/wal/) has this county by county guide to resources, societies, archives and possible pitfalls caused by shifting boundaries and the Welsh naming system.

Useful websites
Anglesey Records & Archives (www.anglesey.gov.uk/leisure/records-and-archives/)

Association of Family History Societies of Wales (fhswales.org.uk)

Cardiganshire FHS (cgnfhs.org.uk)

Carmarthenshire Archives Service (www.carmarthenshire.gov.uk/ english/leisure/archives/pages/archivesrecords.aspx)

Ceredigion Archives (archifdy-ceredigion.org.uk)

Clwyd FHS (clwydfhs.org.uk)

Denbighshire Archives (www.denbighshire.gov.uk/en/resident/libraries-and-archives/denbighshire-archives/denbighshire-archives.aspx)

Digging up the Past (diggingupthepast.org.uk)

Dyfed FHS (dyfedfhs.org.uk)

Flintshire Record Office (flintshire.gov.uk/en/LeisureAndTourism/ Records-and-Archives/Home.aspx)

Glamorgan Archives (glamarchives.gov.uk)

Glamorgan FHS (glamfhs.org.uk)

Gwent Archives (gwentarchives.gov.uk)

Gwent FHS (gwentfhs.info)

Gwynedd Archives Service (gwynedd.gov.uk/archives)

Gwynedd FHS (gwyneddfhs.org)

Montgomeryshire Genealogical Society (montgomeryshiregs.org.uk)

North Wales BMD (northwalesbmd.org.uk)

Pembrokeshire Archives (www.pembrokeshire.gov.uk/content.asp?nav=107,1447)

People's Collection Wales (peoplescollectionwales.co.uk)

Powys County Archives (powys.gov.uk/en/archives/find-archives-local-records/)

Powys FHS (powysfhs.org.uk)

Wales Gen Web Project (www.walesgenweb.com)

Wales Remembers 1914–1918 (walesremembers.org)

Welsh Family History Archive (jlb2011.co.uk/wales/)

West Glamorgan Archive Service (swansea.gov.uk/westglamorgan archives)

Walloon: A person from southern Belgium who speaks a French dialect.

Wapentake: An archaic land division – the Danelaw equivalent of the hundred. Other regional and archaic land divisions just waiting to trip you up include the Kentish 'lathe' and the Sussex 'rape'.

War of 1812: A two-year Anglo-American conflict, in which the US protected its independence.

War diaries: First World War war diaries kept by British Army units (not to be confused with personal diaries) are preserved at TNA in WO 95. They tend to record losses, positions and include daily reports on operations. Although the diaries vary in detail, they do contain information about particular people or notable actions. It is rare for anybody but an officer to be named, but it does happen. The diary for 1/Honourable Artillery Company for 11 October 1916 recorded that 'Pte Freeman A.D. was killed […] his kitten which he carried as a mascot was asleep on his chest, unhurt, when he was found'.

You can explore First World War diaries via the crowdsourcing project Operation War Diary (operationwardiary.org), seeking to 'unlock the hidden stories contained within 1,500,000 million pages of First World

War unit war diaries'. First World War diaries can also be downloaded direct from TNA's website.

War Graves Photographic Project (twgpp.org): Project to build a photographic database of every single war grave, memorial and MoD grave from the First World War to the present day.

War of the Roses (1455–85): Series of wars between noble houses who wished to overthrow King Henry VI, namely the forces of York (under the white rose emblem) and the forces of Lancaster (red rose). Henry Tudor of the House of Lancaster became king Henry VII and married a York – Elizabeth, the daughter of Edward IV.

War Office: Government department responsible for the running of the British Army until 1964, when five departments (Admiralty, Air Ministry, Ministry of Aviation, MoD and the War Office) merged to become the new MoD.

Ward: There are various meanings to this word that might be relevant to family historians. It is the name of a division of land in various northern counties of England and southern counties of Scotland. It also used for electoral districts in the UK. There are also ward records – membership records of members of the LDS Church kept at the ward level. And in law a ward is someone placed under the protection of a legal guardian or court.

Warrant officers: RN warrant officers (as opposed to RN commissioned officers) include gunners, boatswains, carpenters, ropemakers, chaplains, surgeons and engineers. RN officers' service records, 1756–1931 are online and include records for commissioned officers joining the navy up to 1917 and warrant officers joining up to 1931. You can search for free via Discovery and download for a fee.

WARWICKSHIRE:
Warwickshire County Record Office (heritage.warwickshire.gov.uk/warwickshire-county-record-office/)

One underused source is the Proceedings of Warwickshire Quarter Sessions, a calendared series of publications largely covering the Order Books (report of administrative and other records of the session) and the Indictments (the formal accusation and statement or presentment laid before the court). They include cases involving habitation for the poor, apprenticeship disputes, recusancy and common crimes such as theft, assault and fraud.

Warwickshire's Past Unlocked (archivesunlocked.warwickshire.gov.uk/calmview/)

Windows on Warwickshire (www.windowsonwarwickshire.org.uk)

Birmingham & Midland Society for Genealogy & Heraldry (bmsgh.org)

Coventry FHS (covfhs.org.uk)

Nuneaton & North Warwickshire FHS (nnwfhs.org.uk)

Rugby FHG (rugbyfhg.co.uk)

Water-power: Although first introduced by John Lombe (at a Derby silk mill in 1719), it was Preston-born inventor and entrepreneur Richard Arkwright who used water to power his mills in the 1770s.

Waterloo Medal: This was the first true campaign medal in that it was given to all, regardless of rank, and was won by some 39,000 veterans recorded in service at either the Battles of Ligny, Quatre Bras or Waterloo. It was also the first medal issued to families of those killed – with the name of the soldier engraved around the edge.

The medal did cause unrest as some regiments (such as the 43rd Light Infantry which had seen service in America) arrived too late to take part in the battle. They were therefore angered that raw recruits at Waterloo should receive a medal when scarred and battered veterans of the entire Peninsular War should be overlooked.

Watermen: Water-borne porters.

Wayback Machine: *See* 'Internet Archive'.

Webster Signature Database (historydb.adlerplanetarium.org/signatures/): 'A repository for information about people who made and signed scientific instruments preserved in collections worldwide.'

Wellcome Library: The official repository of the Wellcome Trust. To begin delving into the vast Wellcome Library collections online go to wellcomelibrary.org, where there are various online catalogues and digital highlights, such as sections relating to the RAMC. For a general introduction to genealogical research click Collections and scroll down to Biography and Family History. This leads to more detailed research guides broken down into general resources, researching doctors, physicians, surgeons and apothecaries.

The Library's parent, the Wellcome Trust (wellcome.ac.uk), is an independent research-funding charity established through legacies of the pharmaceutical magnate Sir Henry Wellcome in 1936. Its website also provides advice pages aimed at researching doctors, physicians, surgeons, apothecaries, nurses, midwives and dentists. It is currently teaming up with a number of archives across the UK to digitise records of psychiatric hospitals dating back to the eighteenth century. Wellcome Images (wellcomeimages.org) is the Wellcome Trust's online image library. There's also London's Pulse (wellcomelibrary.org/moh/) where you can explore Medical Officer Health Reports from the city between 1848 and 1972.

Welsh Coal Mines (welshcoalmines.co.uk): Catalogues mines situated within Welsh coalfields, with histories, photographs, poems and stories from the once-dominant industry. There's also a list of mining disasters and accidents.

Welsh Experience of the First World War (cymru1914.org): The pick of the First World War commemoration project, here you can see digitised material from libraries and archives across Wales, and browse the collection by keyword or type of record – from newspapers to photographs to sound files.

Welsh Mariners (welshmariners.org.uk): Online index of around 23,500 Welsh merchant mariners active between 1800 and 1945.

Welsh Newspapers Online (newspapers.library.wales): At time of writing this expanding free resource boasted 15 million articles from newspapers preserved at NLW. You can search by categories such as family notices and advertisements, browse by exact date, date range or by region/title.

Wessex: A southern Anglo-Saxon kingdom. Cerdic became the first king of Wessex in 519.

WEST LOTHIAN:
West Lothian Council Archives & Records Centre (www.westlothian. gov.uk/article/2052/Archives)
Lothians FHS (lothiansfhs.org)

West Riding Registry of Deeds (www.archives.wyjs.org.uk/archives-wrrd.asp): If your ancestors owned or leased land in the West Riding, it is possible that they will appear in the Deeds Registry, which holds indexes to 14 million deeds registered between 1704 and 1970. The registered copies are summaries of the full original deed and will tell you the names of all the parties and the location of the land involved.

West Yorkshire Tithe Maps Project (tracksintime.wyjs.org.uk): Access tithe maps and search apportionment data for individuals.

Western Front Association (westernfrontassociation.com): A thriving First World War historical group founded in 1980. The website is full of useful and interesting content, with sections focusing on different theatres of war, as well as specific battles, incidents and a growing day by day diary of the conflict.

Whalers: While records of individual fisherman and whalers don't always survive, it is normally possible to find out more about the wider fishing or whaling community within which they lived and worked. Scotland's East coast was a centre of the herring and whaling trade, and the dated Scotland's East Coast Fisheries site (historyshelf.org/secf/), for example, features all kinds of digitised photographs and documents relating to the trade, drawn from East coast archives and the Scottish Fisheries Museum (scotfishmuseum.org).

Another useful resource is the Friends of Dundee City Archives website (www.fdca.org.uk/Whaling_Industry.html), which looks at the city's whaling trade between 1756 and 1920, with stories of expeditions, whaling statistics and lost whaling vessels.

'Whaling was a very important industry to Dundee, for jobs, for trade, for the manufacture of Jute products, the shipbuilding industry, for Polar exploration and many other aspects of Dundee life. It was a tough and demanding life, it needed rugged hard-muscled men ...'

The site also describes some of the jobs aboard a typical whaling ship that sailed from Camperdown dock on 20 February 1877: 'First mate was James Fairweather. There was a crew member, Alex Donaldson called the "Spectioneer", a sort of 3rd mate, who had charge of all the fishing guns, lines, harpoons, flensing and other gear. Another crewmember was called the "schieman". These names "spectioneer", "harpooner" and "schieman" were names adopted from the early Dutch whalers. There were two engineers, two firemen, boatswain and his mate, the Carpenter and his mate, a blacksmith, a cooper and a sailmaker, all having their respective "mates" these mates were picked after sailing. Five line managers, who pulled stroke oar and looked after the boats gear, four harpooners, mates and "spectioneer" were also harpooners, also there were six boat stearers.'

Another interesting website is Old Weather (oldweather.org) – a crowdsourcing project to chart historic weather patterns recorded in captains' log books, including those from whaling vessels.

Whey cutter: Cheese worker.

Whigs: Political party that contested power with the Tories from the late seventeenth to the mid-nineteenth centuries. The Whig *raison d'être* was to limit the power and influence of the monarchy.

Whipping: Traditional punishment for minor criminals and beggars, officially abolished in 1948. There's also a clear legal distinction between whipping and flogging with a cat-o'-nine-tails.

Who Do You Think You Are?: Popular BBC programme in which every episode takes a celebrity on a journey of self discovery as they unlock the secrets of their family history. The programme launched in 2004 with Bill Oddie. There's also the market-leading *Who Do You Think You Are? Magazine* (whodoyouthinkyouaremagazine.com) and the *Who Do You Think You Are? Live* show in April (whodoyouthinkyouarelive.com).

Who's Who/Who Was Who (www.ukwhoswho.com): Online subscriber's edition of *Who's Who* and *Who Was Who*, an archive going back to 1897.

Wife selling: There was no legal grounding for this custom, it was simply a method by which marriages could be brought to an agreed end. The wife would be led to a public place and auctioned to the highest bidder. Divorce, which before the mid-nineteenth century could only be by a private Act of Parliament, was only open to the wealthy. It's worth remembering too that until the Marriage Act of 1753, a formal ceremony of marriage was not a legal requirement. At the start of Thomas Hardy's *The Mayor of Casterbridge*, Michael Henchard sells his wife and baby daughter after a drunken argument. You may occasionally find references to wife selling in newspapers.

WIGTOWNSHIRE:
Dumfries & Galloway Libraries & Archives (www.dumgal.gov.uk/lia)
Dumfries & Galloway FHS (dgfhs.org.uk)

Wiki: According to Wikipedia, a wiki is 'a website that provides collaborative modification of its content and structure directly from the web browser'. Its name comes from the Hawaiian word for 'quick', and the most famous and widely used is Wikipedia. Today many websites, from FamilySearch (familysearch.org/wiki/en) to the Families In British India Society (fibiwiki.org), have their own dedicated wikis. Always approach wikis with healthy scepticism and follow the sources – the notes, references, further reading and external links at the end of most wiki articles will often lead to valuable digital and printed resources.

Wildcard searches: The * and ? wildcard searches can help search for spelling variants and misspelled names within digital sources. Search by the name 'Sm?th', for example, and the results should include Smith, Smythe and other variants. You can also use multiple wildcard asterisks to include more complex variations for longer surnames. Alternatively, you can employ double quotation marks around names or groups of words and this will make sure searches do not include variants, or only when an exact phrase or group of words occurs – which can be handy for finding references to an individual if you know their middle name.

Wills: Wills potentially provide the name, abode and status or occupation of the testator, their burial instructions, their bequests to named family members, friends and servants, and the names of the appointed executors. They can provide you with a wealth of information about family relationships. A testator may mention a whole array of relatives in his will, including his/her parents, siblings, children, grandchildren, in-laws, nephews and nieces, although these terms cannot always be taken literally – the term cousin, for example, was often used for any blood relation beyond the immediate family. If there's an associate inventory, this can give a detailed list of possessions. And as it was often the practice to work through the house in a methodical way, the inventories may even provide you with a virtual room by room tour of the house and belongings.

Before a will can take effect a grant of probate must be made by a court. And if someone dies without a will, the court can grant letters of administration for the disposal of the estate.

Probate material stretches back to long before the census or civil registration. The further back, the more fragmentary and difficult to read and interpret the documents becomes. They can be full of archaic legal terms, Latin passages and far from obvious abbreviations.

Before the introduction of a civil probate system in 1858, all wills were proved at Church courts. You can search Discovery for records of PCC wills in series PROB 11 (1384–1858) and download them from TNA's website. These are all registered copies of the original probates written into volumes by clerks at the Church courts. Other TNA guides/collections include Wills of RN and Royal Marines personnel (1786–1882) and country court death duty registers and famous wills (1552–1854).

The government probate search engine (probatesearch.service.gov. uk/#wills) can be used to find wills from January 1858 onwards that were proved in the Principal Probate Registry – a network of civil courts that replaced the ecclesiastical courts in England and Wales. Name and year of death is required to find wills, which should be ready for download within ten days of order (costing £10).

There are several important regional websites where you can find pre-1858 material. One example is the NLW. You can search Welsh wills (pre-1858) proved in the Welsh Ecclesiastical courts online at www.llgc.org.uk/discover/nlw-resources/wills/. And wills proven in Wales between 1837 and 1941 are also available at the Library. Similarly, the Durham University Library (familyrecords.dur.ac.uk) has a catalogue to 150,000-plus probate records (1527–1857) from the Diocese of Durham.

TNA's website has a useful guide to wills between 1384 and 1858 which describes what information they may contain, and includes useful sample documents from the fourteenth to the nineteenth centuries. Finally, don't forget that before 1750 heirs often did not prove wills in order to avoid court costs – and some archives do maintain collections of unproved wills.

WILTSHIRE:

Wiltshire & Swindon History Centre (wshc.eu)

Wiltshire and Swindon History Centre has parish registers dating back to 1538. The county is famous for the textile industry and the Centre holds records of many cloth manufacturers in Trowbridge and Westbury, such as Salters or Lavertons. There are also records of Unigate milk manufacturers and the Great Western Railway collection. The Centre's Salisbury Diocesan probate collection includes wills for the whole of the diocese – Berkshire and parts of Dorset, and the parish of Uffculme in Devon.

Wiltshire Wills Project (history.wiltshire.gov.uk/heritage/)

Catalogue to wills and probate records of the diocese of Salisbury (1540–1858) – covering Wiltshire, Berkshire and parts of Dorset and Devon. Search by name, place, occupation and date. You can pay to view digital images of some documents.

Wiltshire FHS (wiltshirefhs.co.uk)

Window tax: A form of property tax that was calculated by the number of windows in a house – famously leading to many properties from the period having bricked-up windows. In England and Wales it was introduced in 1696 and repealed in 1851. In Scotland it was introduced in 1748 and repealed in 1851.

At launch every occupier was charged a flat rate of 2*s*. per year (although those who couldn't pay poor and church rates were exempt). Those with between ten and twenty windows paid 4*s*., and those with more than twenty windows paid 8*s*. The tax was increased and adjusted during its lifespan. From 1709, for example, those with more than thirty windows had to pay 20*s*.

Via scotlandsplaces.gov.uk you can explore the window tax rolls for Scotland, listing the householders and the number of windows in their properties (which survive for the period 1748–98) among the records of the Exchequer in NRS. The rolls are arranged by county and royal burgh. No rolls for England are known to have survived.

Windrush: The arrival of the *Empire Windrush* is a watershed moment in the history of migration to Britain. The vessel set off from Kingston, Jamaica on Empire Day 1948, arriving at Tilbury Docks in June 1948. The majority aboard paid £28 to travel to Great Britain, responding to job advertisements that had appeared in local newspapers. Britain was suffering from major post-war labour shortages, and the passenger lists from that first arrival record an array of occupations – welder, carpenter, mechanic, painter, tailor, bookkeeper, farmer and fitter. To begin with some of the new arrivals were housed in the deep air raid shelter in Clapham Common, many eventually settling in nearby Brixton as this was the location of the nearest labour exchange.

Windster: A winder of silk.

Witchcraft Act: In 1542 Parliament passed this Act which made witchcraft a crime punishable by death. It was repealed five years later, but restored by a new Act in 1562. According to parliament.uk: 'A further law was passed in 1604 during the reign of James I who took a keen interest in demonology and even published a book on it. The 1562 and 1604 Acts transferred the trial of witches from the Church to the ordinary courts. Formal accusations against witches – who were usually poor, elderly women – reached a peak in the late 16th century, particularly in south-east England. 513 witches were put on trial there between 1560 and 1700, though only 112 were executed. The last known execution took place in

Devon in 1685. The last trials were held in Leicester in 1717. Overall, some 500 people in England are believed to have been executed for witchcraft.'

Woad: One of the three staples of the medieval dyeing industry, used to make blue/purple and black cloth. Others were weld (yellow) and madder (red).

Women's Army Auxiliary Corps: The Women's Army Auxiliary Corps was formally instituted in July 1917. It became the Queen Mary's Army Auxiliary Corps in April 1918 and was disbanded in September 1921. It is estimated that by the end of the war more than 50,000 women had joined the Women's Army Auxiliary Corps. Remember that when the RAF was created in 1918 a number of Women's Army Auxiliary Corps volunteers entered the WRAF. TNA has service records of more than 7,000 women who joined the WAAC between 1917 and 1920. Phoebe Chapple was an Australian doctor who sailed to England at her own expense in February 1917 with the intention of joining the Scottish Medical Women's Corps, becoming an honorary Captain in the Women's Army Auxiliary Corps. She was awarded a Military Medal for 'gallantry and devotion to duty', attending to the needs of the wounded regardless of her own safety during an enemy air raid in 1918.

Women's Royal Air Force: The WRAF was formed in 1918 and disbanded two years later, then revived again in 1949. TNA has service records of around 30,000 airwomen who served with WRAF, and these include volunteers from the Women's Army Auxiliary Corps, Women's Legion drivers and the Women's Civilian Subordinates.

Women's Royal Naval Service: Similar to the WRAF, the Women's Royal Naval Service, known as Wrens, was formed in 1917, disbanded soon after the First World War and then revived in 1939. It was integrated into the RN in 1993. Sources include TNA's registers of Wren officers (1917–19) which include appointments, promotions and resignations.

First World War service records for officers and ratings can be downloaded from TNA's website. Those for the Second World War are still with the MoD.

Woodingdean Well: This little known Brighton well is in fact the deepest hand-dug well in the world. At 1,285ft, it is as deep as the Empire State Building is tall. It was green-lit by the local Board of Guardians in 1858 to provide water for a new workhouse and industrial school.

Woollen billy piecer: Pieced together broken yarns in the mill.

Woolworths Museum (woolworthsmuseum.co.uk): Find out more about the history of the retail chain, which began life in 1879 in Utica, New York.

WORCESTERSHIRE:

Worcestershire Archive & Archaeology Service (worcestershire.gov.uk/info/20019/archives_and_research)

There are various useful indexes created by staff and volunteers which have gone online, such as Absent Voters, Apprenticeships, Calendar of prisoners (1839–49), Marriage licences (1853–1916) and Worcester City freemen.

Birmingham & Midland Society for Genealogy & Heraldry (bmsgh.org)

Malvern FHS (mfhs.org.uk)

Birmingham Archives & Heritage (www.libraryofbirmingham.com/archives)

Holds Anglican and Nonconformist registers, court/coroner's records and the Warwickshire Photographic Survey of approximately 10,000 prints. Important industrial collections held here are known collectively as the Archives of Soho, which comprise the Boulton & Watt archive.

Word on the Street (digital.nls.uk/broadsides/): NLS's online collection of nearly 1,800 broadsides.

The Workhouse (workhouses.org.uk): Encyclopedic guide to the workhouse system from expert Peter Higginbotham, with histories and images of individual workhouses, all searchable by Poor Law location.

Workhouses: After the passing of the New Poor Law in 1834, the system of parish-level poor relief was replaced by a system of Poor Law unions run by an elected board of guardians which administered workhouses. (Although many parishes had workhouses before 1834 – indeed the first was at Exeter in 1694.) Records of individual Poor Law unions normally survive at county record offices. Some useful sources include the *Poor Law Unions' Gazette* (available via the British Newspaper Archive), and via TNA's Discovery you can search and download (for a fee) records from more than twenty Poor Law unions from between 1837 and 1871. The Surrey History Centre site (exploringsurreyspast.org.uk/indexes/) has various online indexes including the Chertsey Poor Law Union admission and discharge books and Godstone Poor Law Union application and report books. Meanwhile, via Genuki you can explore a 10 per cent sample of adult paupers in England and Wales, as originally recorded in a House of Commons Parliamentary paper in 1861 (genuki. org.uk/big/eng/Paupers/).

George Sims, the journalist, balladist, playwright and creator of the Sims cure for baldness (which earned a fortune for others but not for him), wrote the familiar ballad about life in the Workhouse:

> 'Christmas Day'
> It is Christmas Day in the Workhouse,
> And the cold bare walls are bright
> With garlands of green and holly,
> And the place is a pleasant sight:
> For with clean-washed hands and faces,
> In a long and hungry line
> The paupers sit at the tables,
> For this is the hour they dine

Useful websites

Dundee Poorhouse Records (fdca.org.uk/Dundee_Poorhouses.html)

Foundling Museum (foundlingmuseum.org.uk)

London Lives: Crime, Poverty & Social Policy in the Metropolis (london lives.org)

Ragged School Museum (raggedschoolmuseum.org.uk)

West Sussex Poor Law Database (sussexrecordsociety.org)

Workhouse Museum, Ripon (ripon.co.uk/museums/)

Working Class Movement Library (www.wcml.org.uk): Salford-based Library which documents the 'labour movement, its allies and its enemies' since the eighteenth century. Archival material includes records of trade unions, individuals and organisations.

Writ: A written court command, ordering or forbidding an act.

Y

Yad Vashem (www.yadvashem.org/yv/en/remembrance/names/index. asp): Organisation working to recover the names of the 6 million Jews who perished in the Holocaust, and adding them to the Central Database of Holocaust victims.

Yardland: Also known as a yard of land or virgate, this was a unit of land used in tax assessments. It was not a fixed unit, but would roughly equate to about 30 acres. In Danelaw counties you also come across 'oxgangs' – which are about half the size.

Year of the Sheep: A wave of mass emigration from the highlands of Scotland that took place in 1792, and part of the Highland Clearances.

Yeoman: The meaning and usage of this term has changed over time, but in general will refer to a prosperous land-owning farmer – as opposed to a mere tenant farmer.

Yeomanry: A volunteer cavalry force – distinct from the militia who were foot soldiers. They were first raised in the 1790s, in response to increased threat of invasion from France following the French Revolution.

YORKSHIRE:

Thanks to an agreement between Findmypast and six Yorkshire archives, lots more parish material is being made available online. At launch some 2,700 parish registers from over 250 parishes in the dioceses of York, Bradford, and Ripon and Leeds were being digitised.

East Riding of Yorkshire Archives, Family & Local History (www2. eastriding.gov.uk/leisure/archives-family-and-local-history/)

North Yorkshire Record Office (northyorks.gov.uk/article/23584)

West Yorkshire Archives Service (archives.wyjs.org.uk)

Home to the important West Riding Registry of Deeds. The Service runs offices in Wakefield, Bradford, Calderdale (Halifax), Kirklees (Huddersfield) and Leeds. The Leeds collections include archives of the Tetley Brewery and Burtons, Hainsworth cloth manufacturers.

Borthwick Institute for Archives, University of York (york.ac.uk/ borthwick/)

Holds the Cause Papers database (hrionline.ac.uk/causepapers/), in which you can explore Church court records between 1300 and 1858.

Local & Family History Library, Leeds (www.leeds.gov.uk/leisure/ Pages/Local-and-family-history-service.aspx)

Leeds Photographic Library (www.leodis.net)

Sheffield Archives & Local Studies (sheffield.gov.uk/libraries/archives-and-local-studies.html)

Picture Sheffield (picturesheffield.com)

Sheffield Indexers (sheffieldindexers.com)

York Libraries & Archives (exploreyork.org.uk)

Hull History Centre (hullhistorycentre.org.uk)
Has important maritime material including 25,000 crew lists.

Teesside Archives (middlesbrough.gov.uk/teessidearchives)

University of Huddersfield Heritage Quay (heritagequay.org)

Barnsley FHS (barnsleyfhs.co.uk)

Bradford FHS (bradfordfhs.org.uk)

Calderdale FHS (cfhsweb.com)

City of York & District FHS (yorkfamilyhistory.org.uk)

Cleveland, North Yorkshire & South Durham FHS (clevelandfhs.org.uk)

Doncaster & District FHS (doncasterfhs.co.uk)

East Yorkshire FHS (eyfhs.org.uk)

Harrogate & District FHS (hadfhs.co.uk)

Huddersfield & District FHS (hdfhs.org.uk)

Keighley & District FHS (kdfhs.org.uk)

Pontefract & District FHS (pontefractfhs.org.uk)

Ripon Historical Society & FHG (riponhistoricalsociety.org.uk)

Rotherham FHS (rotherhamfhs.co.uk)

Ryedale FHG (ryedalefamilyhistory.org)

Selby & District FHG (selbydistrictfamilyhistory.btck.co.uk)

Sheffield & District FHS (sheffieldfhs.org.uk)

Wakefield & District FHS (wdfhs.co.uk)

Wharfedale FHG (wharfedalefhg.org.uk)

Yorkshire Film Archive: yorkshirefilmarchive.com

Yorkshire Quaker Heritage Project: www.hull.ac.uk/oldlib/archives/quaker/

Your Old Books & Maps (youroldbooksandmaps.co.uk): Republishes rare books and maps on disc and/or download, including many county directories.

Z

Zeppelin attacks: On 19 January 1915 two German Zeppelin airships, the L3 and L4, were en route to attack the Humber, but bad weather meant they ended up attacking coastal Norfolk. Samuel Alfred Smith was the first British civilian to be killed by an enemy aerial bombardment after bombs from Zeppelin L3 were dropped on Great Yarmouth. Martha Taylor was also killed by attacks from Zeppelin L3. Raid reports are at TNA in series AIR 1.